INSCRIBING SOLIDARITY

Many governments, large institutions, and collective actors rely on the principle of solidarity to embed social policies on firm normative and legal grounds. In this original volume, a multidisciplinary roster of scholars come together to examine the contributions – and challenges – implicit in relying on the idea of solidarity to "inscribe" this principle in social policies. Chapters explore how the dependence on the solidarity principle, and especially on inclusive understandings of solidarity, can strengthen or weaken institutions and movements. The volume's contributors cover developments across decades with a multilevel approach exploring dynamic interactions between local, national, and supranational arenas in pursuing and adjudicating the solidarity principle. Unique and innovative, *Inscribing Solidarity* examines the implications and dynamics of solidarity across a variety of terrains to illuminate its concrete limitations and specific advantages. This title is also available via Open Access on Cambridge Core.

JULIA LÓPEZ LÓPEZ is Professor of Labor Law and Social Security Law at the Universitat Pompeu Fabra, Barcelona and a leading researcher of greDTiSS (UPF Research Group in Labor Law and Social Security). She has published books in Spanish and English on labor law and social security issues, most recently, *Labour Agency and Governance in the 21st Century?* (Hart, 2019) – as well as has numerous contributions in journals and edited books.

Inscribing Solidarity

DEBATES IN LABOR LAW AND BEYOND

Edited by

JULIA LÓPEZ LÓPEZ

Pompeu Fabra University

CAMBRIDGE
UNIVERSITY PRESS

CAMBRIDGE
UNIVERSITY PRESS

Shaftesbury Road, Cambridge CB2 8EA, United Kingdom

One Liberty Plaza, 20th Floor, New York, NY 10006, USA

477 Williamstown Road, Port Melbourne, VIC 3207, Australia

314–321, 3rd Floor, Plot 3, Splendor Forum, Jasola District Centre, New Delhi – 110025, India

103 Penang Road, #05–06/07, Visioncrest Commercial, Singapore 238467

Cambridge University Press is part of Cambridge University Press & Assessment, a department of the University of Cambridge.

We share the University's mission to contribute to society through the pursuit of education, learning and research at the highest international levels of excellence.

www.cambridge.org
Information on this title: www.cambridge.org/9781009170277

DOI: 10.1017/9781009170260

First published 2023

A catalogue record for this publication is available from the British Library.

ISBN 978-1-009-17027-7 Hardback

Contents

Tables

Contributors

Gian Guido Balandi Professor Emeritus, Labor Law Ferrara University

Rui Branco, Associate Professor NOVA University of Lisbon

Stefania Buoso, Researcher in Labour Law Ferrara University

Daniel Cardoso, Assistant Professor Autonomous University of Lisbon

Alexandre de le Court, Serra Hùnter Fellow in Labor Law and Social Security University of Barcelona

Scott L. Cummings, Professor of Law UCLA School of Law

K. D. Ewing, Professor of Public Law King's College London

Julia López López, Full Professor Labor Law Pompeu Fabra University

Tonia Novitz, Professor of Labour Law University of Bristol Law School

Reignard Zimmer, Professor of Labor Law Berlin School of Economics and Law

Acknowledgements

We gratefully acknowledge a grant from Spain's Ministry of Science and Innovation, Project number PGC2018-097404-B-I00, which provided crucial support for the work published here.

1

Inscribing Solidarity in Labor Law

Promise and Limitations

Julia López López

1.1 OVERVIEW: INSCRIBING SOLIDARITY IN THE DEBATES ON LABOR LAW

What solidarity means and the impact this principle exerts in lived experiences (Borgmann-Prebil and Ross 2010) have long been themes of inquiry – and debate – not only for academics but also for public institutions and social actors. The last decade has been a time of fundamental transformation in societies due to a chain of economic and social crises that have brought about repeated humanitarian challenges and systemic difficulties along with an increase in inequality in many contexts.[1] Actors and institutions have often relied on the solidarity principle in their response to these new challenges but that reliance poses as many new questions as it answers. Some of these questions are related to the fact that invocations of the solidarity principle have thus far largely failed to effectively reverse the tendency toward growing inequality. However, many important regulations and policies have been elaborated under the rubric of the pursuit of solidarity. Exactly how this principle can be put to use or "inscribed" in concrete regulatory approaches and forms of action is the central question underlying this book.

Among the perspectives analyzed in these pages is an examination of how the use of a given "label" for concerns and principles underlying new regulatory objectives or arrangements in effect signifies the very consequential choice by the subjects of a paradigm for their endeavors transforming or implementing concrete policies and behaviors (Collins, Lester, & Mantouvalou 2018: 7). The reliance of actors on the solidarity principle has broad and complex implications that include overarching directions of evolution within democracy itself, conditioning how actors respond to the crisis of democratic capitalism (Wolgand 2011). In such endeavors, this principle

[1] See Salverda et al. 2016.

has served to support efforts to guarantee that dignity and human rights form central parts of contemporary democracy (Rodotà 2018: 149–150).

As we show, however, the reliance on this paradigm has also introduced certain significant challenges for the proponents of progressive and socially inclusive outcomes. Much of our work in this volume concerns ways in which the adoption of the solidarity label has shaped efforts to pursue equality, examining the implications of the solidarity–equality nexus for debates in labor law.

In the context of the neoliberal era, the use of the label of solidarity as a principle underpinning policies intended to address the needs and problems of groups and individuals in need has posed the challenge of how this principle can be "inscribed" in new programmatic formulations by the European Union (EU) and other transnational entities. The commitment to solidarity holds humanitarian advantages in its ability to focus attention on a wide array of vulnerable groups and also some political advantages in its capacity to elicit support from actors outside the social democratic core of the historic proponents of worker interests. However, it is with some difficulty that the solidarity principle is translated into very concrete policies, laws, and institutions – the process labeled here as that of *inscription*. Those actors that have been engaged in the agenda of forging – and interpreting – new directions in labor law have often needed to search out ways to formalize the implications of solidarity in new elaborations of global, transnational, and national regulatory systems.

An understanding of the solidarity principle and its implications is of vital importance for a fully adequate understanding of recent debates and developments in labor law, particularly with regard to sources of regulation and, crucially, enforceability. Both hard-law and soft-law regulations have often been framed as ways to formalize this principle, in effect inscribing solidarity in new regulatory outcomes. A central factor in the role played by solidarity is the increasing use of difficult-to-enforce soft-law instruments in regulatory systems. And even when the principle is rendered in various hard-law inscriptions, these have often suffered from legal deficits in their enforceability. The challenge of enforceability is a major theme in our work.

The growing importance of the solidarity principle as a label underscores the great significance of the relationship between this principle and the fundamental right of equality and nondiscrimination, particularly in the construction of an inclusive solidarity. In pioneering work on this issue, Catherine Barnard argues that solidarity is part of the process of implementing equality but goes beyond that (Barnard 2004: 14). In his broad examination of equality and discrimination, Bob Hepple has defined equality through a distinction between four types: formal equality or consistency, substantive equality understood as equality of results, equality of opportunity, and equality of human dignity.[2] All of these understandings of equality are of potential relevance for the solidarity principle.

[2] Hepple 2001: 6–12.

A broad focus on inscriptions of solidarity thus leads us into a new and important terrain that explores the interactions – in application – between the principles of solidarity and equality, underscoring the usefulness of efforts to build synergies between those two legal framings or "labels" for initiatives designed to protect vulnerable sectors of the population, constructing an inclusive solidarity. In practice, actors have faced choices about how to frame policies that address crucial social needs. For example, the treatment of conciliation between life and work in the Charter of Fundamental Rights of the EU is undertaken in the Chapter on Solidarity, not in the elements of the Charter devoted to the right of equality and non discrimination.

The volume's contributions cover developments over the last couple of decades with a multilevel approach that explores dynamic interactions in pursuing and adjudicating the solidarity principle in complex models of regulation in which national dynamics are connected with global (Blackett & Trebilcock 2015) and transnational (Bogg, Costello, & Davies 2016) arrangements and outcomes. The guiding conceptualization of the volume's scholarship is multilevel, as is reflected not only in the focus on interactions between regulatory systems as such but also in the study of dynamics involving actors and institutions that operate locally, nationally, and in supranational arenas (Craig & Lynk 2006). Our analysis of inscriptions of solidarity examines hard- and soft-law instruments at the transnational level – for example in the International Labor Organization (ILO) and EU – and within national cases. The inscription of solidarity is also studied through its relation to the application of recognized freedoms and rights including, among others, the freedom of circulation; equality and nondiscrimination; freedom of association; the welfare state and dignity (Hepple 2015).

Our focus in *inscribing solidarity* looks well beyond the response to crisis and efforts to scale back labor rights. In examining "inscriptions" of the solidarity principle, and the challenges encountered in attempts to render this important principle as law, policy, or practice, we turn to a broad set of concrete questions and dynamics that bring to light the opportunities and difficulties posed by framing progressive initiatives as an application of the solidarity principle. I now turn to an elaboration of several key issues and challenges in the inscription of solidarity as a way to elucidate the central analytical challenges to be addressed in studying how reliance on the solidarity principle conditions various elements of the broader effort to address the concerns and needs of socially vulnerable groups.

1.2 SOLIDARITY AS LABEL: FORMALIZING CONTENTS OF THE PRINCIPLE

The intellectual foundations for what we do in this volume involve a long and distinguished tradition of thought. Solidarity was classically defined by Bourgeois[3] as a concept without precision and scope, but that can be summarized as the "mutual

[3] Bourgeois 2018.

responsibility between two or more people." Among the most influential scholarly formulations of the concept, Durkheim wrote that it constitutes "a bond of unity between individuals, united around a common goal or against a common enemy, such as the unifying principle that defines the labor movement."[4] He connects this with forms of justice, elaborating the distinct notions of "mechanical" and "organic" solidarity. Simmel constructed the notion of sociology of conflict in close connection with the study of within-group and cross-group forms of solidarity in modern societies (Simmel 1908).

The study of solidarity has been an interdisciplinary field in the European intellectual tradition[5] and in legal studies. In the analysis of legal forms and expressions of solidarity, a pioneering contribution has been offered by Rodotà on the constitutionalization of the principle and its enforcement in the EU's Charter of Fundamental Rights. In his perspective, the connection between solidarity and democracy holds important implications for the future,[6] offering an avenue to the construction of a livelier democracy (Rodotà 2018). Supiot takes the strength of solidarity as a fundamental principle for legal order, with connections to the principles of freedom, equality, and justice in the EU legal order. The relation between the supranational legal order and the national level has been studied as integral to analyses of the frame of principles and rights that regulate labor relations (Prassl: 42) with special emphasis in the Charter of Fundamental Rights (O'Cinneide 2016: 191). Barnard emphasizes the connection of solidarity and legitimacy,[7] while Freedland and Countoris have studied the elaboration of solidarity in policies – in essence what I call here the inscribing of solidarity – as an essential requirement for the re-mutualization of social risk in the European context of economic crisis. Sciarra has studied the reaction of courts against austerity and cutbacks of fundamental social rights as an approach to solidarity. Scholarly work on the construction of solidarity from below by de Sousa Santos and Rodriguez-Garavito (de Sousa Santos and Rodriguez-Garavito 2005: 1–27), on actors working together transnationally (Estlund 2015: 260), or on "voices at work" (Bogg & Novitz 2014), offer significant examples of research on the construction of solidarity from popular actors. The importance of the solidarity principle is both deep and broad, thereby underscoring the importance of our effort in this volume to delineate and analyze how this principle is actually inscribed in concrete policies, legislation, and arrangements,

I identify below the significance of solidarity in the debates on labor law of recent decades. Those debates have dealt with a wide array of issues and dynamics including globalization – with a focus on multinationals and the challenges of freedom of

4 Durkheim 1933. See Schoenfeld & Meštrović 1989.

5 Stgerno 2011.

6 Rodotà 2016.

7 Barnard 2017.

circulation – climate change and its implications for labor; the technology-induced transition to a new paradigm of labor organization; new forms of organization of the working class; and crucially the increasing prevalence at the transnational level of soft-law regulations in contrast with hard-law ones. The shifting regulatory terrain that these debates seek to understand has been constituted by the outcome of political conflicts over the redefinition, or in some cases the reduction, of existing understandings of social rights. In a very overarching sense, economic and social crises have conditioned such efforts to either redefine or reduce fundamental rights as a consequence of the marketization of society. Whether this process will lead to robust new guarantees and rights for the socially vulnerable or only to an evisceration of pre-existing forms of protection is obviously a matter of broad significance. This is the scenario in which the "inscription" of the principle of solidarity needs to be studied and understood.

A major and very concrete challenge for labor law in this context involves ways of dealing with growing differences or distinctions within the working class that challenge the legal boundaries of work regulation (Fudge, McCrystal, & Sankaran 2006) and the frontiers of labor law (Davidov & Langille 2006). In actual practice, labor law has been immersed in a long and continuous process of segmentation and flexibilization,[8] creating a complex universe of employment relations, in which the application of a long-standing principle that has served worker interests greatly – the right of equality and nondiscrimination – has become increasingly difficult because of the challenges posed by delineating the parameters of comparison between workers in defense of the fundamental right to equal treatment for equal or similar work. The difficulties in applying antidiscrimination policies in a flexible and segmented context also hold consequences for pro-equality policies. It is precisely for this reason that it has become very important to reconstruct the universe of the fundamental right of equality and nondiscrimination with a basis in the fundamental principle of solidarity. Efforts to elaborate very concrete applications of the solidarity principle face the task of finding ways to offer guarantees or forms of protection that can cover what seem to be the waning abilities of the equality and nondiscrimination principles to "do the work" they have done in the past. This is one of the central challenges posed by efforts to inscribe solidarity "rethinking workplace regulation."[9]

Although inscriptions of solidarity offer new opportunities for the elaboration of social guarantees in the legal and institutional orders, our analysis and earlier work also serve to underscore the value of the fundamental right of equality and nondiscrimination as pillars of a social democratic understanding of rights that has long provided for integrative policies that have in effect provided bases for solidarity. Analytically, the two approaches should be differentiated from one another but in

8 The increasing trend to formalize the segmentation of workers' rights: López López 2015.

9 Stone & Arthurs 2013.

actual practice they are often woven together in ways that have been highly useful. Solidarity as a programmatic principle has offered important value to social democracy, especially in order to achieve labor rights, but as our study of solidarity inscriptions demonstrates, if this principle is articulated without an explicit linkage to equality as such, it presents important deficits. These deficits include the lack of accountability and enforceability of many assertions of solidarity, thereby limiting the contribution offered to progress in the implementations of labor rights. Yet despite the existence of such potential deficits, the principle that we study is of potential relevance for a wide range of socioeconomic outcomes that encompass broad patterns in the organization of the economy. In the important literature on *varieties of capitalism*, the impact of solidarity has been studied in analyses of industrial relations, vocational educational, and training and labor institutions (Thelen 2014). Research on such connections offers an interesting approach to study the inscriptions of solidarity.

1.3 THE *SOLIDARITY ECONOMY* AS AN ILO INSCRIPTION: SOFT LAW, SUBSIDIARITY, AND DECENTRALIZATION OF POLICIES

The evolution of the international legal order has as a central feature the move from a hard regulation model to a hybrid one with strong components of soft law. The new generation of ILO Conventions has placed a decreasing emphasis on hard-law guarantees of labor rights, instead turning toward broader soft-law instruments with important consequences in terms of accountability and enforceability. The inscription of solidarity in ILO instruments has contributed to the elaboration of new soft-law instruments but these instruments have lacked certain points of strength of earlier hard-law conventions. The increasing influence of multinationals as powerful actors that put in place transnational arrangements and outcomes has created growing challenges for effectively elaborating an inclusive solidarity in contemporary democracy (López López 2021). It is in the light of this challenge introduced by globalization that the practice of transnational or supranational entities such as the ILO gains special significance.

In the initiatives of the ILO, one of the most important inscriptions of solidarity is the effort to construct what this entity has labeled a *solidarity economy*. Among the main components of this ILO goal are cooperatives emblematic of the approach elaborated in broad but "soft" instruments such as the ILO Declaration of Social Justice for a Fair Globalization, and the ILO 2030 Agenda: A Plan of Action for People, Planet and Prosperity. This last ILO instrument seeks to reinforce the role of cooperatives in a "revitalized Global Partnership for Sustainable Development, based on a spirit of strengthened global solidarity, focused in particular on the needs of the poorest and most vulnerable and with the participation of all countries, all stakeholders and all people."

Such soft-law regulations, understood here as inscriptions of solidarity, reinforce ILO Recommendation 193 about the Promotion of Cooperatives (2002). The ILO's framing of the significance of cooperatives is quite explicit in underscoring their linkage to the principle of solidarity, specifying that cooperatives offer "the fullest participation in the economic and social development of all people," and defining cooperatives as "stronger forms of human solidarity at national and international levels [that] are required to facilitate a more equitable distribution of the benefits of globalization." This emphasis on cooperatives is intended to promote at least two main concerns of this entity: the spirit embodied in the Declaration of Philadelphia that "labor is not a commodity," and the realization of decent work for workers everywhere as a primary objective of the ILO. In this understanding, cooperatives organize production systems in ways that humanize the workplace (Restakis 2010) and question the concentration of powers by multinationals challenging democratic institutions (Leonard 2019). This framing of the solidarity economy in ways that identify its connection with democracy and equality underscores how the ILO is strongly oriented toward the advancement of solidarity inscriptions. More concretely, the ILO agenda on cooperatives is also intended to foster a form of organization for firms that provides the strongest possible participation of members and the defense of both equality and nondiscrimination for members and workers within these firms. In this and other cases, the promotion of solidarity is understood as a way of assuring quite tangible results in the conditions enjoyed by workers within firms – and in the broader polity.

One important point of the ILO's support for an economic model that enhances the role of cooperatives concerns the value of these organizations for encouraging the modernization of production under new technologies and as a source of decent work. The quality of the work process is among the concerns that the ILO assumes are likely to be addressed in a spirit of solidarity in cooperative enterprises. Thus, for a variety of reasons, the ILO Recommendation encourages governments, worker's associations, and employers' associations to promote cooperatives within the solidarity economy. However, it should be underscored that this broad support for cooperatives is in essence a soft-law recommendation, not a hard-law and enforceable set of requirements for the practices of enterprises.

A separate but crucial theme concerns a key pillar of EU practice: the subsidiarity principle. This principle has been formulated as the orienting framework to regulate the relations between supranational and national level decision-making in the EU. I will turn later to this theme, but for now it is important to note that in effect the subsidiarity approach involves the formulation of soft-law objectives at the EU level and their translation into hard-law instruments that achieve – or in some cases may fail to achieve – those objectives at the national level. Solidarity-centered initiatives at the supranational and international level have tended to follow this dynamic, thereby widely extending the principle of solidarity but limiting the extent to which it serves as a hard guarantee for affected persons and collectivities at the country level.

Thus, ILO and EU initiatives articulated around the principle of solidarity present their most difficult challenge in the translation from soft-law regulation at the transnational level to hard law within the national geographies. The inscription of solidarity in terms of hard regulation and enforceability typically moves from the international level to the national one. In one example of the dynamic at the country level, Spain has enacted not only a law at the national level but also initiatives within some comunidades autónomas such as pro-cooperatives legislation in the Basque Country, the home of one of the most successful cooperatives anywhere, the Mondragón Group (Flecha & Ngai 2014) .

The solidarity economy as a label for a very broad and important objective initially takes the direct form of soft law, which is then implemented through the subsidiarity principle and hard-law regulation at the national level. The solidarity economy formulation is intended to combine efficiency with the promotion of democratic workplace organization and in this sense offers an alternative at the enterprise level to the tendencies that some authors have named new neo-feudalism.[10]

1.4 SOLIDARITY AS HARD-LAW INSCRIPTIONS: COLLECTIVE LABOR RIGHTS

The significance of solidarity for labor law and for the welfare of workers and other citizens is, of course, not limited to the forging of legal and regulatory instruments. The evolution of workers' representation and of collective rights is closely linked to processes of organized solidarity by social actors such as the labor movement (Hyman 2001) with implications often for the emergence of democracy itself (Fishman 1990). Unions have suffered the impact of an often hostile external environment in many national contexts and in the world economy in the neoliberal era, but they continue to hold great importance for the themes that we study here. Despite the external and internal crisis of unions and workers' representation structures, collective rights have permitted social actors to achieve some spaces of social progress, countervailing the most untamed forms of capitalism (López López 2015). The trilogy of collective rights such as freedom of association, collective bargaining, and collective protests – including strikes – has constructed a foundation for solidarity in various forms to reinforce the collective interests of workers in the face of the neoliberal era's increasing promotion of individualism (López López 2019). However, along with unions and other forms of collective action, legal structures hold great importance in the attainment of objectives expressive of the solidarity principle. The process that Rodotà has called "the devaluation of

[10] See Stone & Kuttner 2020. The private capture of entire legal systems by corporate America goes far beyond neoliberalism. It evokes the fiefdoms of the Middle Ages.

constitutions" makes it more important than ever to revitalize structures that guarantee the right of equality (Rodotà 2011: 85) as is the case of collective rights.

In this context, a main piece in the construction of inscriptions of solidarity is the EU's Charter of Fundamental Rights under Article 2 and Article 6 of the EU Treaty. The Charter is understood to form part of the EU's primary law through the application of Articles 6 and 52 of the Treaty. This crucially implies both accountability and enforceability for the Charter when the courts of member states apply EU law. In substantive terms, the Charter's structure recognizes in Title I Dignity, in Title II Freedoms, in Title III Equality, and in Title IV Solidarity from Article 27 to Article 38. Paragraph 7 of the Charter's Article 5/1 specifies that the text constitutes a valid aid both for EU judges and for those of the member states. As CH Amalfitano has argued, "the Charter thus substantially reproduces in a written catalogue the general principles of law set forth by the ECJ in its jurisprudence, developed over the years. It is only their inclusion in the Charter that determines their final consecration as binding 'principles' or 'rights' in the EU legal system."

The Chapter of Solidarity, in other words, Title IV of the Charter, includes broad *inscriptions* of both individual and collective content. Articles 27 to 34 bear directly on employment and industrial relations: workers' right to information and consultation (Article 27). The rights to collective bargaining and action (Article 28) are recognized as part of the solidarity principle.

A fundamental feature of the Charter's approach is that it divides its treatment of equality and solidarity into separate Chapters. Crucially, some matters that had previously been treated under the label of equality are now elaborated under the heading of solidarity. To put this somewhat differently, some of the Charter's important inscriptions of the principle of solidarity were previously treated as inscriptions of the principle of equality. I will examine later the significance and implications of this shift in the underlying principle that is used to frame the specific and tangible discussion of rights and outcomes, that is to say "inscriptions."

An important element of the new formulation is the inscription of solidarity in the provision of collective rights such as labor organization and collective action. Participation, information, freedom of association, and collective action are all now found in the Chapter of Solidarity. This conception of democratic solidarity offers a strong constitutional base for these fundamental rights. Solidarity in the Charter of Fundamental Rights is understood to function through two overarching and interrelated instruments: the subsidiarity principle and (as a result) the diversity of national regulations.[11]

Inscriptions of collective rights at the transnational level are to be found in various provisions. The ILO has defined freedom of association as a fundamental right, as a

[11] Article 152. The Union recognizes and promotes the role of the social partners at its level, taking into account the diversity of national systems. It shall facilitate dialogue between the social partners, respecting their autonomy.

pillar of labor rights. The ILO has developed its treatment of collective rights within two important Conventions, Freedom of Association and Protection of the Right to Organize Convention, 1948 (No. 87) and Right to Organize and Collective Bargaining Convention, 1949 (No. 98). At the transnational level, the inscription of underlying principles in the elaboration of collective rights takes two forms: the hard international regulation provided by these ILO Conventions and more recently by the Chapter of Solidarity with its invitation to national level elaborations. Collective rights have been enacted as a fundamental right or freedom at the national level by member states, in some cases in their constitutions or laws of development. Through the twin approaches of subsidiarity and national-level diversity, the regulation of collective rights is handled in a fundamentally multilevel fashion that provides for some elements of commonality along with a good deal of difference between national cases. This complex process suggests that we can usefully think of much that goes on inscribing solidarity as the elaboration of collective rights within the legal order – albeit in ways that vary in their enforceability.

Understanding solidarity as collective rights enacted by the legal order makes it possible to understand the tendency toward a layered multilevel form of enforceability and accountability of the principle. From this perspective, it is crucial to construct an inclusive solidarity because of the spillover that such an understanding of solidarity generates with regard to collective rights. The layering, with its articulation of transnational and national instruments and institutions, does enable many important inscriptions but it also limits their uniformity and opens the door to possible shortfalls or deficits in some national contexts. Those deficits are especially evident with regard to the enforceability of very general principles provided by soft-law instruments.

1.5 INSCRIPTIONS OF SOLIDARITY AS FAIR LABOR CONDITIONS: SUBSIDIARITY AND HYBRID MECHANISMS OF WORKERS' PROTECTION

Solidarity as fair labor conditions and protection against unfair dismissal is inscribed in a variety of soft and hard regulatory instruments. Among the most important examples are the construction of the notion of decent work in the ILO Agenda and Article 151 of the Treaty on the EU with its commitment to improve working conditions.[12] Also of great significance is the Charter of Fundamental Rights in

[12] "The Union and the Member States, having in mind fundamental social rights such as those set out in the European Social Charter signed at Turin on 18 October 1961 and in the 1989 Community Charter of the Fundamental Social Rights of Workers, shall have as their objectives the promotion of employment, improved living and working conditions, so as to make possible their harmonization while the improvement is being maintained, proper social

the Chapter of Solidarity.[13] The first of these is a soft-law instrument and the second is an example of hard law.

However, the inscription of solidarity in these ways has taken place in the context of – and sometimes in response to – strong counter-currents. The evolution of labor law during recent decades marked by cutbacks in labor rights has challenged the development of inscriptions of solidarity as fair labor conditions. In this setting an especially important debate concerns protections against unfair dismissal, defined in the Charter of Fundamental Rights as a matter of solidarity. This theme has been extensively covered in EU legislation and policies through discussions of the "flexi-security" model.

Applications of the flexi-security model have promoted liberalization of the regulation of dismissal in various ways, including: defining the period of causes, the pre-notice period, procedural requirements, and conceptualizing effects of unlawful dismissal as an economic cost. National law within the EU is not uniform on such matters; the regulation of a wide array of questions – including causes, procedural requirements such as probationary period, pre-notice, severance payments, and the legal treatment of consequences of unfair dismissal – differs among member states.

This national-level diversity in protections against unfair dismissal is one of the clearest examples of the use of the subsidiarity principle. Unfair dismissal is defined in legal terms at the national level. The EU considers protection against unfair dismissal as part of the solidarity principle, but the enforceability and accountability of what that really mean in concrete terms differs among the member states. Maximum protection against unfair dismissal is offered when there is held to be a violation of fundamental rights, but after the legal reforms of labor market regulations (in many instances under pressure from the EU), the protection is weaker when dismissals are held to be caused by economic reasons. The protection against unfair dismissal is, then, understood as an inscription of the principle of solidarity but its concrete manifestation in hard law suffers from the problem of diversity in the definition of this content because of the subsidiarity principle. The indirect and varied connection between the general principle and concrete legal expressions of it tends to produce an imbalance of power between workers and employers in bringing cases to the courts.

protection, dialogue between management and labour, the development of human resources with a view to lasting high employment and the combating of exclusion."

[13] The Solidarity Chapter of the Charter of Fundamental Rights, includes: Right of access to placement services (Article 29), Protection in the event of unjustified dismissal (Article 30), Fair and just working conditions (Article 31), Prohibition of child labor and protection of young people at work (Article 32), Family and professional life (Article 33), and Social security and social assistance (Article 34). The four remaining articles in the Solidarity Chapter are: Healthcare (Article 35), Access to services of general economic interest (Article 36), Environmental protection (Article 37), and Consumer protection (Article 38).

The debates on protection against unfair dismissal take place in a complex legal and sociopolitical setting. Disagreements over how to handle precarious work and temporary contracts form part of broader debates on the pathway to protecting the principle of solidarity in the context of instability in the definition of work contracts. Among the themes subject to debate is the relation between national regulation and the Charter of Fundamental Rights (Barnard 2014: 303).

In terms of solidarity as a precept held to offer protection against unfair dismissal, inscriptions of this principle should fortify the right of stability of the contractual nexus in those cases where there is no legal reason to terminate the labor relation. However, concrete elaborations of that general guideline are extremely varied and provide many avenues to an effective reduction of hard-law protections for workers.

Under the heading of solidarity, protection against dismissal is recognized by the ILO Conventions, the EU Charter of Fundamental Rights, the EU Treaty, and EU Directives setting requirements for collective redundancies, information and consultation, and fixed-term and temporary work. These Directives provide a common minimum level of protection for workers in all member states. Thus, there is an underlying grid of worker protection linked to the principle of solidarity.

All these previous references on protection against termination reveal the complexity of the protection against unfair dismissal as inscriptions of solidarity. However, even though the very general solidarity-based shared elements of protection have proved to be compatible with very large-scale reductions in such protections within some national cases and with major differences *between* national cases, there is some advantage even in soft-law commitments to worker protection. The common commitment to the spirit of protection against unfair dismissal has helped underpin the crafting of more complete legal references to obtain better worker protection and to countervail the national-level differences imposed by the subsidiarity principle.

One more point should be added. solidarity is written into transnational labor law through primarily soft-law promises of protection against unfair dismissal, attributing this protection to the principle that we are examining. However, this labeling – and the related soft-law treatment – of unfair dismissal fails to produce real guarantees at the transnational level. This shortfall exists precisely because of the use of the subsidiarity principle in application of the transnational promise and, relatedly, the soft-law character of many EU and ILO formulations.

The deficits in protection against unfair dismissal are pointed out by Collins,[14] who argues that there are three ways in which the legal regulation of unfair dismissal is inconsistent with the principles of the European Convention on Human Rights: the narrow personal scope of protection, the lax standard of review applied by the tribunals, and the inadequate remedies available to claimants.

[14] Collins 2018. See also Collins 2021.

There is a second important theme introduced in Article 32 of the Charter of Fundamental Rights, in the Solidarity Chapter, with regard to fair labor conditions and the rights of young workers. The text includes a reference to the prohibition of child labor and the protection of young people at work as objectives linked to the principle of solidarity. Young people admitted to work must have working conditions appropriate to their age and must be protected against economic exploitation as well as any work likely to harm their safety, health, or physical, mental, moral, or social development or to interfere with their education. Crucially from my perspective, there is a connection between the inscriptions of solidarity in legislation on unfair dismissal and in protections for the youngest from exploitation, because in both cases an approach that is limited to a general affirmation of the solidarity principle lacks specificity and enforceability. This deficit is clearly evident in the failure to provide tangible forms of protection for workers. I argue that a crucial pathway to generate more enforceable guarantees for young workers is to link the elaboration of the solidarity principle to the EU's policies on equality and nondiscrimination by age. Thus, I suggest that a labeling of social guarantees that focuses exclusively on the solidarity principle – without making explicit and elaborating the long linkage to the equality principle – tends to suffer from certain characteristic deficits.

An important example of the results produced by the existing approach is to be found in the treatment of problems faced by young workers. In the context of the EU an important initiative is the recommendation of March 15, 2018 on a European Framework for Quality and Effective Apprenticeships.[15] This soft law helps to construct the conceptualization of exploitation by "precarization" and instability that young workers suffer in the labor markets. The Recommendation cited stipulates that quality apprenticeships "lead to a combination of job-related skills, work-based experience and learning, and key competences [that] facilitate young people's entry in the labor market, as well as adults' career progression and transition into employment" and calls upon member states to implement "criteria for quality and effective apprenticeships." The EU calls on member states to develop this agenda, in an application of the subsidiarity principle. The results have varied considerably among countries especially in the regulation of rights.[16] As a consequence, despite the concerns and objectives expressed in the EU soft law, young workers are potentially subject to both unpaid and precarious work.

I argue that despite the EU's positive framing of apprenticeships, creating and normalizing legal opportunities for unpaid traineeships and poorly paid apprenticeships has created a dynamic of cheap labor that predominantly affects young people in the workforce. For many young workers, this crystallizes in a series of precarious post-traineeship contracts, which has significant and concerning consequences for

[15] [2018] OJ C153/1.
[16] See Stewart et al. 2018.

young people's professional careers and social security rights. Together, these consequences amount to a pattern of increasingly entrenched systemic age discrimination that affects the growing numbers of young people who are struggling to enter the labor market. In practical terms, despite the invocation of the solidarity principle in the soft-law treatment of this matter, young workers are left in circumstances that generate consequences that provide unequal results essentially on the basis of age.

Thus, there is at present a vicious circle of informal employment and precarious work that effectively creates a dynamic of systemic discrimination for young workers. In recent decades, the development and implementation of policies that are directly or indirectly linked to the pressure to liberalize labor regulation have increased the prevalence of systemic age discrimination.[17] Systemic discrimination is a pattern, practice, or policy of discrimination that has a broad impact on a class or category of persons within an industry, profession, company, or geographic area. If the inscription of solidarity in policies oriented toward young workers is explicitly tied to guarantees against systemic discrimination – in effect connecting solidarity to the principle of equality and nondiscrimination – the effect is to produce stronger protections of fair labor conditions for young workers. A clear conclusion is that a regulatory approach that addresses the problem of systemic discrimination, building on the principles of *both* solidarity and equality, is required if the rights of young workers are to be fully protected.

1.6 THE LABEL OF SOLIDARITY FOR POLICIES OF CONCILIATION BETWEEN FAMILY AND WORK: PROMOTING EQUALITY AND NONDISCRIMINATION POLICES BY GENDER

As a general matter I argue that some of the deficits identified here are addressable by linking solidarity to the principle of equality; when that is done each principle can ultimately serve to reinforce the other. Solidarity can contribute an agenda or map of vulnerable groups requiring attention under the equality principle. In turn the principle of equality can provide crucial enforceability support to the inscriptions of solidarity. This linkage is in some instances already to be found in existing practice. An important example concerns the use of the labels in the Charter of Fundamental Rights. As already noted, the Charter clearly opts for placing policies of conciliation of family and work within the Chapter on Solidarity, in effect labeling such policies as an inscription of the solidarity principle and leaving them outside the separate treatment of equality and nondiscrimination in a different Chapter of the Charter. Nonetheless, in practice, the development of family–work conciliation policies has been closely linked to law on equality and

[17] On age as a factor of discrimination, see Numhauser-Henning, Julén Votinius, & Zbyszewska 2017; López López 2017; López López 2019.

nondiscrimination that has proved to be crucial for underpinning the binding character of work–family guarantees in the legal order. This clearly suggests that formally understanding and labeling this thematic area as exclusively a matter of solidarity is insufficient and could at worst undermine the basis for treating family–work conciliation rights as binding. From this perspective the linkage of solidarity to the principle of equality is underscored in actual EU practice in this area. I argue that this linkage should be extended to other areas, thereby strengthening inscriptions of solidarity, enhancing their enforceability.

The different inscriptions of solidarity studied in this introductory chapter include efforts to build a solidarity-based economy (for example, through cooperatives), the elaboration of collective rights relating to forms of joint action or representation, the conciliation of family and work, and protections against unfair dismissal. These matters are taken up at the transnational level through soft-law instruments that tend to promote the process of policy decentralization, displacing crucial decisions to member states or lower-level entities. However, many of these matters – understood to form points of central relevance in constructing an inclusive solidarity – are potentially also subject to treatment by the legal order through the use of the principle of equality and nondiscrimination. This alternative legal approach has often been deployed at the transnational level in ways that make use of hard-law instruments such as EU Directives and ILO Conventions. The equality approach has also been relied upon within sovereign states in Constitutions and national law. This hard-law approach generates binding effects and enforceability with regard to concrete policies, advantages that have often been missing in inscriptions of the solidarity principle. However, the solidarity principle has proved very useful as a way to ground and broaden measures intended to address the problems of vulnerable sectors. Emphasizing this connection builds on the basis provided by important scholarly work. Barnard's contribution is especially relevant with regard to how hard-law instruments have been developed by their interface with soft law and the decisions of the ECJ, all of this building the relation between the pursuit of solidarity and equality (Barnard 2010: 214). There is a strong foundation to argue for the usefulness of synergies between these two principles, thus underscoring the importance of this volume's extensive analysis of solidarity inscriptions.

As I have argued, this is very much evident in the area of family-work conciliation policies. Concretely, several soft and hard instruments in both transnational and national regulation declare the right to conciliate family and work, placing this right within the overarching right to equality and nondiscrimination. The explicit prohibition of direct and indirect sex discrimination creates an array of follow-on guarantees, some of which apply to statutory social security schemes (Directive 79/7/EEC) and to self-employment (Directive 2010/41/EU). Sex discrimination is also prohibited in access to and the supply of goods and services (Directive 2004/113/EC). In addition, some directives apply to specific groups, such as the Pregnancy Directive (92/85/EEC), the Parental Leave Directive (2010/18/EU), or the Part-time

Work Directive (97/81/EC). The great majority of part-time workers in the EU being women, the requirement of equal treatment of part-timers and full-timers is also relevant for them.

In another area of relevance, the Racial Equality Directive (2000/43/EC) prohibits discrimination on the ground of racial or ethnic origin in a broad range of fields, including employment, social protection and social advantages, education, and goods and services available to the public, including housing. The Employment Equality Directive (2000/78/EC), however, is limited to the field of employment and occupation but covers the grounds of religion or belief, disability, age, and sexual orientation. This wide range shows the broad coverage of effects provided by the right to equal treatment and nondiscrimination and the binding, hard-law character of those effects. It is this broad and binding character that is much needed if the frequent enforceability deficit of many inscriptions of solidarity is to be overcome.

With regard to another major area of discrimination, the EU Gender Equality Strategy presents policy objectives and actions to make significant progress by 2025 towards a gender-equal Europe. According to this Strategy, the goals are ending gender-based violence; challenging gender stereotypes; closing gender gaps in the labor market; achieving equal participation across different sectors of the economy; addressing the gender pay and pension gaps; closing the gender-care gap; and achieving gender balance in decision-making and in politics. The Strategy is based on a gender mainstreaming approach and the notion of intersectionality serves as a basic supporting principle. The Strategy also integrates the policy on pay transparency, which is very important to reduce the gender salary gap and discrimination in retribution by gender.

In the ILO framework, equality and nondiscrimination stand as fundamental rights. Several ILO Conventions protect against discrimination, for example the Discrimination in Employment and Occupation Convention no. 11 and the Equal Remuneration Convention no. 100. In the 1998 ILO Declaration of Fundamental Principles and Rights at Work, member states are called on to promote and realize within their territories the right to be free from discriminatory employment practices. The objective of conciliation between family and work has been inserted in the EU level and in the domestic member-state level as part of the treatment of equality and nondiscrimination legislation. Nonetheless, as noted above, the EU Charter of Fundamental Rights labels this policy an inscription of solidarity rather than equality. However, this new labeling does not modify the underlying significance of the equality guarantee for the foundational basis of hard-law regulation on the conciliation between family and work. However, the labeling of conciliation between work and life as a matter of solidarity does reinforce the need for public policies through which the state provides the resources needed to attain this objective with its significance for the broad principles of solidarity, equality, and nondiscrimination. Moreover, the pursuit of a genuinely inclusive solidarity in the area of conciliation requires the incorporation of guarantees against discrimination not only on the basis of gender but also by age and country of origin.

1.7 INSCRIPTIONS IN PURSUIT OF INCLUSIVE SOLIDARITY AS GOAL

Due to the COVID pandemic, the EU has faced strong economic and social challenges that have been met in part by articulating responses through reference to the principle of solidarity. This opens up a new angle on the study of solidarity inscriptions, examining new possibilities – or limitations – linked to the framing of policies through this approach. This new scenario also provides us with a fresh and important opportunity to examine the connection between solidarity and equality as either alternative or complementary frameworks for underpinning policies that address human needs and rights.

A major point of departure in the EU's analysis of the pandemic crisis suggests that people will need time to overcome the current situation and that inequality may increase in the period of recovery. In the formulation of the Commission's Work Program for 2020, it is maintained that "Europe showed that it can act fast when it needs, show real solidarity when it must and collectively change things when it wants fair and inclusive recovery." This "real solidarity" means for the Commission ensuring that all workers in the EU earn a decent living, closure of the gender pay gap, and the provision of reinforced youth employment support that will help young people get into work, training, or education.[18]

Building on the analysis of the past but looking toward the future, several points deserve emphasis. As suggested above, the COVID crisis holds great significance for this examination of solidarity inscriptions. The pandemic has opened a new scenario for labor rights within the frame of the EU Charter of Fundamental Rights. The economic crisis caused by this malady was of such magnitude that the EU was pushed to enact measures to rescue not only financial institutions but also ordinary people – in very large numbers. This offers a way to achieve not only a real solidarity but also an inclusive solidarity. One arena that will be of great significance in the next years will be the construction of more fair labor conditions for all. The global scenario created by the pandemic-related crisis is an opportunity to think in solidarity terms about the regulatory framework for employment, and this demands new rules on decent work based not only on programmatic declarations but also on hard-law regulations that establish mechanisms of accountability and enforcement of the elaborated rights. Solidarity is a principle that can potentially help to achieve agency and rights for the most vulnerable members of society. Such inscriptions in specific

[18] Brussels, 30.9.2020, COM(2020) 580 final, Communication from the Commission to the European Parliament, the Council, The European Economic and Social Committee and the Committee of the Regions (2020), Rule of Law Report.

policies and practices can help to build stronger democracies that are rooted in a demos characterized by solidarity.

Finally, the two principles discussed here – solidarity and equality – are both of potential usefulness, offering synergies in the construction of what Stone, Sweet, and Ryan (2018) call a "cosmopolitan legal order" in which labor law plays an important role in the enforceability of human rights as fundamental social rights. The processes and challenges that we examine also hold importance for the depth of democracy and for the ability of the political system to successfully address a wide range of citizen concerns (Robert 2021). How broad principles such as solidarity are mobilized or drawn upon in the elaboration of policies and regulatory arrangements is a matter that has a technical legal side and a broadly political one. The resulting inscriptions are intended to achieve better societies with stronger links among community members engaged in the reconstruction of the conditions to recover "the democratic dialectic"[19] in contexts conditioned by new developments such as artificial intelligence.[20]

1.8 PLAN OF THE BOOK

The volume's contributors analyze the inscriptions of solidarity with a range of substantive emphases. This chapter, the volume's Introduction, by Julia López López, formulates central analytical and practical challenges posed by efforts to inscribe solidarity in concrete policies or regulatory arrangements. This introductory chapter identifies both promises and limitations of reliance on the solidarity label and offers analytical perspectives on useful ways to think about and study both advantages and potential disadvantages of that reliance. To that end, a number of substantive themes are taken up and examined. Many of the arguments offered in the Introduction also serve to identify common threads discussed in the contributing chapters. Those common threads include the relation between hard- and soft-law instruments as well as decentralization of regulatory regimes and the multilevel dynamics of solidarity inscriptions, both of these being themes that shed light on the important matter of enforceability. The introductory chapter also argues for the usefulness of synergies between the principles of solidarity and equality to construct inclusive solidarity.

Chapter 2, authored by Tonia Novitz, is entitled "Sustainability as Solidarity Unbound: Labor Rights and Collective Voice in the United Nations Sustainable Development Goals and the European Union." This chapter argues that solidarity should be understood as being "unbound" by geographical or temporal borders. The chapter examines the United Nations Sustainable Development Goals adopted in 2015, identifying their recognition of inclusive solidarity in the context of decent

[19] See Rodotà 2011: 90–91.

[20] Bales & Stone 2020: 41.

work and their potential limitations. Her analysis of unbound solidarity examines both intra- and intergenerational dimensions as well as hard- and soft-law manifestations. The substantive themes taken up include solidarity from below, sustainability links with fair labor conditions, and both United Nations and EU programs on equality and nondiscrimination.

Reingard Zimmer is the author of Chapter 3, "Solidarity as a Central Aim of Collective Labor Law?" This chapter takes as its starting point the fact that solidarity is one of the rights that the Charter of Fundamental Rights of the EU mentions as a central value in its preamble and is the title of chapter IV. The elaboration in the chapter concludes that inclusive as well as exclusive solidarity may be detected in the work of trade unions and (European) works councils and is an important characteristic of their endeavors. The argument suggests that the architecture of collective labor law, both in Europe and more specifically in Germany, contains solidarity as a central element of its structure. This chapter links solidarity, defined in the Charter at the EU-transnational level, with the definition at the national level of freedom of association as right or freedom and with the role of social actors in pursuing equality and nondiscrimination.

Gian Guido Balandi and Stefania Buoso author Chapter 4, "Solidarity: Different Issues in a Community Perspective." This chapter argues that community is the space of expression of solidarity, the key word that connects the inscriptions of solidarity in different issue terrains: in social security, in the transnational perspective of the EU, in the gig economy era, in the labor law of the pandemic. Solidarity may provide for the transfer of money or services, with their cost being borne, entirely or partially, by others who are not the users of the services themselves. In their analysis, the fragmentation of employment imposes on us the need to articulate the answer to the need for protection. It is important to widen the dimension of solidarity towards universalism; the perspective they defend is a system of general taxation in which solidarity should remain the point of reference, adapting this principle to new realities, also in the pandemic era.

K. D. Ewing addresses a new challenge for the principle of solidarity in Chapter 5, entitled "Solidarity, Covid-19 and a New Social Contract." This chapter explores the concept of solidarity in the context of Covid-19, with a view to examining its role as we pass through the pandemic and as we rebuild afterwards. The focus is on the social dimension, social rights and workers' rights in the context of EU law, and the EU response in particular. The text seeks to (i) explore the meaning of solidarity; (ii) understand its multiple constitutional dimensions under EU treaties; (iii) examine its role as a conceptual underpinning of a new social contract as proposed by the ETUC and others; and (iv) consider the problems of its development as revealed by the social pillar and the proposed Minimum Wage Directive. The chapter examines multilevel dynamics and insists on both the soft- and hard-law dimensions of solidarity. The text also examines multiple actors – including unions – and discusses a new social contract that connects solidarity with the fight against poverty and inequality.

Scott L. Cummings in Chapter 6, "Solidarity in the City," draws on a study of the labor movement's challenge to inequality in Los Angeles from 1992 to 2008. The chapter presents a critical analysis of the city as a site of solidarity. It shows how, in order to build local labor law, the labor movement must promote solidarity not just among workers but among different progressive movements, which become interlinked around campaigns to reshape low-wage work, while also promoting related goals including immigrant inclusion, expanding affordable housing, and promoting environmental justice. Building decentralized power as a way to rebuild labor law, this chapter suggests, requires conceptualizing solidarity as a local, city-wide project, with two related components: inter-movement solidarity between labor and allied movements; and intra-movement solidarity, which is located within movements among workers fighting together for better lives. The chapter argues that while both visions of solidarity are necessary to build local labor reform, there are tensions between the two that must always be managed.

Alexandre de le Court in Chapter 7 addresses "Regulation of the Access of Undocumented Migrants to Social Protection: Exploring the Boundaries of Solidarity." This contribution takes the case of undocumented migrants as an opportunity to ask important questions about solidarity toward especially vulnerable groups. Based on the concepts of inclusive and exclusive solidarity, the chapter centers on the regulation of the access of undocumented migrants to different aspects of social protection (social insurance, insurance against accidents at work, social assistance, and healthcare) in continental welfare states. Drawing on the different rationales behind solidarity on which those different aspects of social protection are built – primarily reciprocity, the guarantee of dignity, and the commitment to protection of vulnerable persons – it analyses critically the logic of exclusion manifested by the subordination of social protection to immigration policy and argues that there are legal arguments in favor of more inclusive systems of social protection.

Rui Branco and Daniel Cardoso are co-authors of Chapter 8, "Solidarity in Hard Times: The Politics of Labor Market and Social Protection Reform in Portugal (2010–2020)." How did Portuguese domestic politics and institutions matter in shaping employment and social protection statuses – crucial bases for solidarity towards the vulnerable – in the decade spanning the Great Recession and the COVID-19 pandemic? Their chapter examines how cooperation between government, opposition parties, and social partners, and the Portuguese Constitutional Court, worked to moderate external pressures to liberalize labor market regulation and social protection regimes during the Great Recession. After the crisis, the "Geringonça" Socialist government and its left partisan and trade union allies enacted inclusive and solidaristic policies that de-segmented atypical and independent work, bettered the work–family balance, and improved outcomes for the working poor, unemployed youth, and elderly. In a context shaped by the aftereffects of crisis, the role played by the law enacting solidarity as an inclusive agenda for the "Geringonça" with special impact on equality and nondiscrimination objectives led to very concrete policies on protection against poverty, conciliation between family and work, and protection of the elderly.

The substantive and focused analysis presented in these chapters provides strong evidence of both the promise and the challenges of reliance on the solidarity label as a platform for the defense of socially vulnerable sectors. As the work brought together in this volume shows, it is only by studying the actual inscriptions of the solidarity principle that we can genuinely understand the implications of growing reliance on this principle. In a world that continues to suffer from a wide range of social needs and problems, the insights to be learned from our study of solidarity inscriptions hold wide significance for both analytical and practical purposes.

REFERENCES

Bales, R. A. & Stone, K. V. W. (2020) The invisible web at work: Artificial intelligence and electronic surveillance in the workplace. *Berkeley Journal of Employment and Labor Law* 1. UCLA School of Law, Public Law Research Paper Nos. 19–18, available at https://ssrn.com/abstract=3410655.

Barnard, C. (2014) Equality, solidarity and the Charter of Fundamental Rights in times of crisis: A case study in dismissal. In Silveira, A., Canotilho, M., & Froufe, P. M. (eds.), *Citizenship and solidarity in the European Union: From the Charter of Fundamental Rights to the crisis, the state of art*. Brusells: Peter Lang, 303–326.

(2017) Solidarity and legitimacy. In Vandenbroucke, F., Barnard, C., & De Baere, G. (eds.), *A European social union after the crisis*. Cambridge: Cambridge University Press, xxxvii–xl.

(2010) Solidarity and the Commission Renewed Agenda. In Ross, M. G. & Borgmann-Prebil, Y. (eds.), *Promoting solidarity in the European Union*. Oxford: Oxford University Press, 260–273.

Blackett, A. & Trebilcock, A. (eds.), *Research handbook on transnational labour law*. Cheltenham: Edward Elgar.

Bogg, A. & Novitz, T. (2014) *Voices at work: Continuity and change in the common law world*. Oxford: Oxford University Press.

Bogg, A., Costello, C., & Davies, A. C. (eds.) (2016) *Research handbook on EU labour law*. Cheltenham: Edward Elgar.

Bourgeois, L. (2018) *Solidarité*. Classic Reprint Series. London: Forgotten Books.

Collins, H. (2021) An emerging human rights protection against unjustified dismissal. *Industrial Law Journal* 50 no. 1 (March): 36–69.

(2018) The inadequate protection of human rights in unfair dismissal. *Industrial Law Journal* 47 no. 4 (December): 504–530.

Collins, H., Lester, G., & Mantouvalou, V. (eds.). (2018) *Philosophical foundations of labour law*. Oxford: Oxford University Press.

Craig, D. R. & Lynk, S. (2006) *Globalization and the future of labour law*. Cambridge: Cambridge University Press.

Davidov, G. & Langille, B. (eds.). (2006) *Boundaries and frontiers of labour law*. Oxford: Hart.

De Sousa Santos, B. & Rodríguez-Garavito, C. (eds.) (2005) Law and globalization from below: Towards a cosmopolitan legality. Cambridge: Cambridge University Press.

Durkheim, E. (1933) *On the division of labor in society*. Trans. Simpson, G. New York: The MacMillan Company.

Estlund, C. (2015) Working together transnationally. In Blackett, A. & Trebilcock, A. (eds.), *Research handbook on transnational labour law*. Cheltenham: Edward Elgar, 260–273.

Fishman, R. (2019) *Democratic practice: Origins of the Iberian divide in political inclusion*. Oxford: Oxford University Press.

(1990) *Working-class organization and the return to democracy in Spain*. New York: Cornell University Press.

Flecha R. & Ngai, P. (2014) The challenge for Mondragon: Searching for the cooperative values in times of internationalization. *Organization* 21 no. 5: 666–682. doi:10.1177/1350508414537625.

Fudge, J., McCrystal, S., & Sankaran, K. (eds.) (2006) *Challenging the legal boundaries of work regulation*. Oxford: Hart.

Hepple, B. (2001) Equality and empowerment of decent work. *International Labour Review* 140 no. 1: 6–12.

(2005) *Labour laws and global trade*. Oxford: Hart.

Hyman, R. (2001) *Understanding European trade unionism: Between market, class and society*. London: Sage.

Leonard, C., (2019) *Kochland: The secret history of Koch industries and corporate power in America*. New York: Simon & Schuster.

López López, J. (2017) A note on the Deconstruction of Protection against Age Discrimination: Spanish Jurisprudence from the Constitutional Court. In Rönnmar, M. & Julén Votinius, J. (eds), *Festskrift till Ann Numhauser-Henning*. Lund: Juristförlaget i Lund, pp. 439–446.

(2015) Anti-austerity activism strategies: Combining protest and litigation in Spain. In Blackett, A. & Trebilcock, A. (eds.), *Research handbook on transnational labour law*. Cheltenham: Edward Elgar, 164–181.

(2021) Pursuing democratic depth in the age of multilevel power and soft labour law: The case of platform workers protest. In Cornell, A. & Barenberg, M. (eds.), *Handbook on labor and democracy*. Cambridge: Cambridge University Press, 307–318.

(2013) Solidarity and the re-socialization of risk: Analysing ETUC strategies to face the crisis. In Contouris, N. & Freedland, M. (eds.), *Resocialising Europe in a time of crisis*. Cambridge: Cambridge University Press, 353–372.

(2019) Systemic discrimination y políticas de igualdad efectiva de género. *Revista del Ministerio de Empleo y Seguridad Social* 133.

(2015) Tensions among regulatory levels. In López López, J. (ed.), *Segmentation and labor rights: Monographic Issue of the Comparative Labor Law and Policy Journal* 36 no. 2, 281–292.

López López, J. (ed.) (2019) *Collective bargaining and collective action: Labour agency and governance in the 21st century?* Oxford: Hart.

Numhauser-Henning, A., Julén Votinius, J., & Zbyszewska, A. (2017) Equal treatment and age discrimination: Inside and outside working life. In Numhauser-Henning, A. (ed.), *Elder law: Evolving European perspectives*. Cheltenham: Elgar.

O'Cinneide, C. (2016) The European Social Charter and the EU labour law. In Bogg, A., Costello, C., & Davies, A. C. (eds.), *Research handbook of EU labour law*. Cheltenham: Edward Elgar, 191–217.

Pauga, S. (2007) *Repenser la solidarité. L'apport des sciences sociales*. Paris: Presses Universitaires de France.
Prassl, J. (2016) The interaction of EU law and national level: Between myth and reality. In Bogg, A., Costello, C., & Davies, A. C. (eds.), *Research handbook of EU labour law*. Cheltenham: Edward Elgar, 191–217.
Restakis, J. (2010) *Humanizing the economy: Co-operatives in the age of capital*. Gabriola Island, BC: New Society Publishers.
Robert, K. (2021) Labor and democracy: Constructing, deepening and defending citizenships rights. In Cornell, A. & Barenberg, M. (eds.), *Handbook on labor and democracy*. Cambridge: Cambridge University Press, 36–49.
Rodotà, S. (2011) *Elogio del moralism*. Roma: Editori Laterza.
(2016) *Solidarietà: Un utopia necessaria*. Roma: Economica Laterza.
(2018) *Vivere la democracia*. Roma: Editori Laterza.
Ross, M. & Borgmann-Prebil, Y. (2010) *Promoting solidarity in the European Union*. Oxford: Oxford University Press.
Salverda, W., Nola, B., Checchi, D., Marx, I., McKnight, A., Tóth, I. G., & van de Werfhorst, A. (eds.) (2016) *Changing inequalities in rich countries: Analytical and comparative perspectives*. Oxford University Press, 2016.
Schoenfeld, E. & Meštrović, S. G. (1989) Durkheim's concept of justice and its relationship to social solidarity. Thematic issue, *Durkheimian Miscellany* 50 no. 2 (Summer, 1989).
Simmel, G. (1908) *Individuality and social forms*. Heritage of Sociology Series. Chicago: University of Chicago Press.
Stewart, A. et al. (2018) The regulation of internships: A comparative study. Employment Policy Department Working Paper No. 240, International Labour Office.
Stgerno, S. (2011) The idea of solidarity in Europe. *European Journal of Social Law* 3 (September).
Stone, K. V. (2013) The decline in the standard employment contract: A review of the evidence. In Stone, K. V. & Arthurs, H. (eds.), *Rethinking workplace regulation: Beyond the standard labor contract of employment*. New York: Russell Sage Foundation Press, 42–58.
(2019) New social policies to address new forms of work. In Bales, R. A. & Garden, C. (eds.), *The Cambridge handbook of U.S. labor law: Reviving American labor for a 21st century economy*. Cambridge: Cambridge University Press, 154–157.
Stone, K. V. & Bales R. A. (2020) The Invisible Web at work: Artificial intelligence and electronic surveillance in the workplace. *Berkeley Journal of Employment & Labor Law* 41: 1.
Stone, K. V. & Kuttner, R. (2020) The rise of neo-feudalism. *The American Prospect*. April 8.
Stone, K. V. M. & Arthurs, H. (eds.) (2013) *Rethinking workplace regulation: Beyond the standard contract of employment*. New York: Rusell Sage Foundation.
Streeck, W. (2011) The crisis of democratic capitalism. *New Left Review* 71: 5–29.
Supiot, A. (2005) *Homo juridicus, Homo juridicus. Essai sur la fonction anthropologique du Droit*. Paris: Editions du Seuil, Essais, 314–316.
Stjernø, S (2011) The idea of solidarity in Europe. *European Journal of Social Law* 3, September.
Sweet, A. S. & Ryan, C. (2018) *A cosmopolitan legal order: Kant, constitutional justice and the European Convention of Human Rights*. Oxford: Oxford University Press.
Thelen, K. (2014) *Varieties of liberalization and the new politics of social solidarity*. Cambridge: Cambridge University Press.

2

Sustainability as Solidarity Unbound

Labour Rights and Collective Voice in the United Nations Sustainable Development Goals and the European Union

Tonia Novitz

2.1 INTRODUCTION

This chapter begins by considering the concept of 'solidarity', which I argue can and should be promoted in a way that is 'unbound' in terms of both geography and temporality. I offer an inclusive understanding of its dimensions, including acting for and with others, involving empathy rather than merely shared identity. I also explain how operationalising solidarity can require political and social action, including collective worker representation and voice. In this context, I detect connections between solidarity and sustainability, observing that realisation of the latter entails cross-border intra- and inter-generational commitments as well as activity by civil society, including trade unions. The chapter then goes on to examine the United Nations General Assembly (UNGA) Resolution on the 2030 Agenda and the seventeen Sustainable Development Goals (SDGs) adopted in 2015,[1] scrutinising evidence of engagement with solidarity but also recognising the limitations of UN texts in this respect. The chapter continues by itemising how the European Pillar of Social Rights 2017 shares many of the aspirations set out in the 2030 Agenda, but also displays comparable tensions between economic and social objectives. This part considers how the Pillar (and indirectly the SDGs) is being translated into the European Commission's new policy agenda for sustainability. It emerges that there is potential for unbounded solidarity between those at work to be actualised through both soft and hard EU law, and that this initiative is gaining momentum.

2.2 UNBOUNDED SOLIDARITY AND SUSTAINABILITY: CONCEPTUALISATIONS AND CONNECTIONS

Here I briefly explore the different ways in which two controversial ideas have been conceptualised: 'solidarity' and 'sustainability'. I reject an exclusive or 'bounded'

[1] Transforming Our World: The 2030 Agenda for Sustainable Development, UNGA Res. 70/1.

vision of 'solidarity', arguing for its inclusivity and indeed recognition of its transnational dimensions. I argue that this approach can be connected to a holistic understanding of 'sustainability', which suggests that it is legitimate to be concerned with an inclusive distributional justice that entails solidarity within a generously defined 'world of work', but also the broader community, economy and environment in which work is carried out. The intersections between economic, environmental and social pillars of sustainability can in this way be acknowledged, alongside the ways in which they extend beyond the borders of any given country. A sustainability approach also prompts attention to concerns beyond our contemporary situation, prompting us to look to the future effects (of what happens now) on people in a later time and even another place. In this context, I identify the potential significance of civil society and trade unions here as political actors. In so doing, I seek to explain why it is imperative that there be respect for labour standards, including protection and promotion of collective worker voice beyond national boundaries, thereby enabling a response to both present and future concerns at local, national, regional and international levels. This would be solidarity 'unbound'.

2.2.1 *Conceptualising Solidarity as 'Unbound'*

Solidarity can be understood in a variety of ways. An inclusive idea of solidarity does not merely cover a particular community or those who share a particular identity of ethnicity within a region, nation or federation. It can be understood in terms of empathy with others and action for them as much as for one's personal gain. The alternative is to protect as solidarity (or fraternity) merely 'clubs' oriented towards self-interest. I realise that I am pushing at the boundaries of this idea, since most writing on even 'inclusionary' and redistributive solidarity examines how this operates at the level of the nation state (Banting and Kymlicka 2017) or a federation (Stepan 1978), or even within a regional organisation such as the European Union (EU) (Bauböck 2017; Sciarra 2018). For example, Veronica Federico (2020) talks about how solidarity has a 'perimeter', ostensibly at the EU border.

Banting and Kymlicka (2017: 6, 13), in their introduction to an impressive edited collection on *The Strains of Commitment: The Political Sources of Solidarity in Diverse Societies*, insist on the 'bounded nature of solidarity', which is 'societal in scope'. They insist that solidarity is 'inextricably linked to an ethic of shared social membership, and in the contemporary world of nation-states, nationhood is the default boundary of social membership' (Banting and Kymlicka 2017: 23).

However, our ideas of 'social membership' no longer only operate at the level of the nation state or even of regional entities such as the EU. Society may be geographically and temporally more extensive than this. We live in a global world in which much of what is done by a government or a corporate entity in one country can affect another (Sjåfjell et al. 2020). This is evidenced by current problems of climate change (Grear 2014), but also global supply or 'value' chains that can promote problematic conditions of work throughout the globe (Novitz 2019). Marx and Engels (1848) once exhorted workers of the world to 'unite!'. While this might be hard to achieve, the ability to act in solidarity to achieve common goals, whether in one country or another, or whether formally recognised as a 'worker' or not, has become a matter of pressing concern (De Stefano 2017).

Solidarity unbounded need not be mere 'humanitarianism', as suggested by Banting and Kymlicka (2017: 6), but can be viewed instead as a collective insistence on human rights and other basic values (such as those regarding social sustainability outlined below) that have traction across national borders. Moreover, it may be inappropriate to think of society as merely temporally limited to a particular generation. What has happened to past generations shapes the society of the present, just as the decisions made now regarding work, its conditions and remuneration affect future generations. A broader view of society as less time-bound also enables a reconceptualisation of solidarity.

Leaving to one side their insistence on geographical (and temporal) borders, Banting and Kymlicka (2017: 33) do provide helpful observations regarding the role of political actors and action: 'Political agents are necessary both to carry the idea of solidarity into politics and to press for its subsequent institutionalization.' This is not a passive but an active process. They conceive of solidarity as a political mission to represent an entire group, not rooted in class or national identity, which is also indicative of this idea's deep connection with empathy for others who engage in a common project. My point of departure is that this empathy can be greater than Banting and Kymlicka conceive in what is a global society.

Solidarity is inherently a collective and dynamic enterprise, which means that it requires more than individual self-interest, a reason that the very idea is in disfavour among libertarians who think that 'we *can't have it* and *shouldn't want it*' (Levy 2017: 111; emphasis added). My concern also lies with addressing how markets and current transnational and national legal market structures (intertwined) require forms of collective action. Roberto Frega (2019: 4) considers that solidarity demands 'collective intentionality' and 'social involvement'. He is concerned more with 'acting with' others as a social practice than 'acting for' but recognises the two as intertwined (Frega 2019: 18). This makes sense insofar as acting collectively involves empathetic connections, in which we seek to understand the concerns and needs of others, just as we jointly seek to pursue our own interests.

2.2.2 *Connecting Sustainability to Solidarity*

'Sustainable development' emerged as a global concern in the 1970s (Pieraccini and Novitz 2020). In this context, environmental and economic dimensions have tended to dominate, but the social aspect has now also been widely and increasingly recognised as a third 'pillar' of sustainability. The idea is to promote all three facets of sustainable policymaking in durable ways that moderate the temptations of short-term capitalism (Clark et al. 2018; Grießler and Littig 2005). Further, each facet of sustainability (economic, environmental and social) is interrelated and co-dependent, rather than neatly severable, which also reflects workers' relational attachments not only to their social community but also to the markets in which they participate and their ecological environment (Seck 2019: 158).

For some time now, there has been recognition that action on sustainability is a legitimate subject of transnational political action, whether in the EU or through UN structures, such as the UN 1972 Stockholm Declaration of Principles for the Preservation and Enhancement of the Human Environment[2] or the 1992 Rio Declaration on Environment and Development.[3] If solidarity is only a nationally bounded concept, then it would seem to be unlinked to sustainability, but that exclusion seems both problematic and unnecessary.

Sustainability inherently involves fraternity, empathy and collective action across spatial and temporal borders. This is because policies based on sustainability aim to meet 'the needs' of present and future generations.[4] Present generations are to be protected through application of agreed precepts of intra-generational redistributive justice, while inter-generational justice for future generations is to be achieved through durable environmental, economic and social policies that preserve the planet and all the sustenance of life that it can provide. From this source comes the language of 'planetary boundaries' (French and Kotzé 2021; Raworth 2012, 2017). The discourse of (and evidence base for) sustainable policymaking regards the actions of actors all over the world (whether economic, environmental or social) as interconnected, having impacts across state or other territorial borders.

There are potent sustainability concerns that connect to work in terms of both intra- and inter-generational justice. The economic harms that occur when labour is paid an insufficient amount to meet the basic costs of living are obvious. For example, exclusion from the basic coverage of employment law, providing minimum wages and protection from dismissal, can have devastating personal effects on the persons concerned (which impact on human rights to food, water, housing, health and so on). This is the experience of a growing number of precarious workers (Kenner et al. 2019; McCann and Fudge 2017). Further, low wages and poor working conditions have been linked to systemic poverty and social forms of deprivation, as well as societal breakdown (Carr et al. 2018; Sissons et al. 2017).

Collective bargaining has the potential to deliver distributional justice in terms of wage levels for current workers, enabling the satisfaction of certain essential needs, such as food, housing and other aspects of social welfare and socio-economic rights.

2 Declaration of the United Nations Conference on the Human Environment, UN Doc. A/Conf.48/14.

3 Rio Declaration on Environment and Development, UN Doc. A/Conf.151/26.

4 Report of the World Commission on Environment and Development; Item 83(e) of the Provisional Agenda, UN General Assembly, 42nd Session, A/42/427. New York, 1986.

Also, terms included in collective agreements can prevent long working hours or poor health and safety standards, affecting the ability to provide reproductive labour outside the workplace, which ensures the well-being of the elderly and children – our present and future generations (Zbyszewska 2018). A lack of active collective voice to challenge employer practices can mean that those who sell their labour, who are also often residents in the locality in which they work, lack the ability to challenge poor environmental practices, which then may go on unabated with profound consequences to them in their homes and nearby (Novitz 2020).

Trade unions are known for promoting gradual 'just transition' to reconcile economic, environmental and social concerns when they might seem to conflict, offering negotiated pathways to effective and durable change (Doorey 2017). They have prompted state and employer funding to assist workers affected by changes to the structure of production and delivery of services, which respond to environmental or other needs. Indeed, 'the imperatives of a just transition of the workforce and the creation of decent work' were acknowledged in the preamble to the 2015 Paris Agreement.[5] On a broader scale, just transition also requires careful consideration of distribution of investment and influence between actors in the global North and the global South, including collaboration between trade unions in these locations (Stevis and Felli 2015). Notably, the International Labour Organization (ILO) has produced its own 'Guidelines for a Just Transition', which makes particular provision for social dialogue and collective bargaining in processes of adjustment.[6] Moreover, in the context of global inequalities and the need for global solidarity, which has been powerfully exposed by the COVID-19 pandemic, the International Labour Office (the ILO secretariat) has stressed the importance in the longer term of promoting labour standards, including access to collective worker voice in the 'world of work'.[7] Notably, this is a term that has been devised to offer far-reaching protections potentially including 'persons working irrespective of their contractual status', and coverage of 'all sectors, whether private or public, in both the formal and informal economy, and whether in urban or rural areas'. An example of this broader extension of solidarity can be found in Article 2 of the ILO Convention No. 190 on Violence and Harassment recently adopted in 2019, which also envisages collective bargaining for these persons.

Sustainability then seems an important emergent species of international dynamic political solidarity amongst those called (and those who labour but are not called) 'workers' for the greater social, environmental and economic benefit of all. Intra-generational justice is called for, which entails not only empathy beyond

[5] For the text of the UN Paris Agreement, see https://unfccc.int/sites/default/files/english_paris_agreement.pdf.

[6] ILO, *Guidelines for a Just Transition towards Environmentally Sustainable Economies and Societies for All* (Geneva: ILO, 2015), available at: www.ilo.org/wcmsp5/groups/public/—ed_emp/—emp_ent/documents/publication/wcms_432859.pdf.

[7] See www.ilo.org/global/topics/coronavirus/lang–en/index.htm.

those working at the national level but recognition of the ways that different labour markets globally interconnect. A sustainability perspective also prompts concern with the experiences of all those in a broader 'world of work'. Inter-generational justice encourages attention to be paid to the future implications of contemporary working practices, whether social, economic or environmental, or most probably, a combination of all three. Moreover, collective action in the sense of enabling representative worker voice and collaboration across national borders (given the transnational activities of employers and their global effects) becomes vital in this dynamic vision of sustainability. The connections between sustainability and 'solidarity unbound' are readily apparent.

2.3 UN SDGS AND THE CALL FOR SOLIDARITY

A call for broader solidarity emerges from the UN 2030 Agenda, being evident in the preamble and the seventeen SDGs but also the accompanying targets and indicators. The preamble makes clear that the economic, environmental and social pillars are to be regarded as 'integrated and indivisible' and that 'no one will be left behind', thereby stressing simultaneously the importance of a holistic approach to sustainability and the necessity of inclusivity. The preamble commits to 'respect, protect and promote' universal human rights established under international law,[8] with particular reference to gender equality and the treatment of migrants.[9] It is harder to detect a strong commitment to collective worker representation and action, but certainly the notion of a 'global partnership' encourages solidarity that is not to be limited by national borders. The difficulty may be that the emphasis placed by Agenda 2030 on economic growth may limit the potential efficacy of such solidarity.

2.3.1 *Evidence of an Unbounded Solidarity Approach in the SDGs*

Reference is made repeatedly throughout the 2030 Agenda to 'just and inclusive societies', the concept of inclusion being repeated throughout. The aim seems to be the broad welfare of 'people' globally. For example, SDG 1 is to 'end poverty in all its forms *everywhere*' (my emphasis). Although this does not include in the target or indicators reference to people's working lives, as was the case in the amended First Millennium Development Goal, SDG 1 speaks of a need for redistributive justice across the world, including that of work. This is reflected in the fact that the ILO plays a key role in assessing SDG indicators 1.3.1 and 1.a.2 (Frey & Naughton 2016: 5–6).

Also promising in terms of inclusivity is SDG 5, which seeks to 'achieve gender equality and empower all women and girls', SDG target 8.5 addresses discrimination

8 UN 2030 Agenda n. 1, for example, paras 8 and 19.

9 Ibid., paras 20 and 29.

and target 8.7 seeks to prevent forced and child labour. SDG target 8.8 makes provision for protection of the most vulnerable workers ('all workers'), including migrant, female migrant and precarious workers. The vulnerability of young workers is recognised in target 8.6. More broadly, SDG 8 can be linked to ILO norms regarding foundational aspects of 'decent work', as is reflected in its title.[10]

Target 8.10 envisages strengthening 'the capacity of domestic financial institutions', while target 8.a envisages aid for trade and technical assistance for trade for developing (especially the least developed) countries. In broader global redistributive terms (aiming at intra-generational justice), SDG 10 addresses reduction of inequality within and between countries and refers to social and economic inclusion and outcomes, including wages in target 10.4 and labour share of GDP in the attached indicator. These ambitions can also be linked to other social objectives, such as the need to end hunger (SDG 2), promote health (SDG 3) and provide education (SDG 4).

Notable environment objectives include protection of the 'planet' by goals and targets set concerning agriculture (SDG 2), water (SDG 6), energy (SDG 7), climate change (SDG 13), oceans and seas (SDG 14), as well as ecosystems and biodiversity on land (SDG 15). 'Prosperity' can also be sought through economic growth and employment (also under SDG 8), industry, innovation and infrastructure (SDG 9); as well as working towards sustainable cities and communities (SDG 11), and responsible consumption and production (SDG 12).

A universal right to access to justice is highlighted in SDG 16, which is supplemented by targets concerned with representation and participation in institutions. SDG target 16.6 aims to '[d]evelop effective, accountable and transparent institutions at all levels', while target 16.7 seeks to '[e]nsure responsive, inclusive, participatory and representative decision-making at all levels'. SDG 16.10 requires protection of fundamental rights.

This chimes with SDG 17, which seeks to promote a 'Global Partnership for Development' and 'Policy Coherence'. All countries have a role to play at a national level in implementing the SDGs and to assist each other. There is an expectation that this will entail collaborative efforts by states, such that they will be aided by international organisations (like the ILO) and regional institutions (like the EU) to ensure policy coordination, with particular attention to the needs of developing countries.[11] Further, SDG targets 17.16 and 17.17 recognise that various private

[10] ILO Declaration on Social Justice for a Fair Globalization, International Labour Conference, 97th Session, Geneva, 2008.

[11] For example, altogether the ILO is custodian for 14 SDG indicators; see https://ilostat.ilo.org/topics/sdg/#:~:text=%20As%20custodian%20for%2014%20SDG%20indicators%2C%20the,producing%20high-quality%20data%20on%20SDG%20labour...%20More%20. See also ILO Centenary Declaration 2019, Article IV(F). For the EU current strategy, see Commission Staff Working Document, *Delivering on the UN's Sustainable Development Goals – A Comprehensive Approach*, Brussels, 18 November 2020, SWD (2020) 400 final.

'stakeholders' can and should act as partners in this process, including civil society, such as the representatives of those at work, presumably including non-governmental organisations (NGOs) and trade unions (as recognised in 16.10.1). This is again an inclusive approach, which speaks of the potential for global solidarity and action of various kinds, around work and other issues.

2.3.2 *Challenges to Inclusive Solidarity in the Sphere of Labour Rights*

Nevertheless, the capacity of the SDGs to promote inclusivity of the kind advocated here is limited in various respects. For example, SDG 8 places considerable emphasis on growth and innovation, while omitting any express endorsement of collective worker representation or action that might constrain employers' profitability. This may reflect the dominance of business interests in procedures established for drafting and adoption of the SDGs (Pingeot 2014).

SDG 8 begins by seeking to 'promote sustained, inclusive and sustainable economic growth' and only after that, 'full and productive employment' and finally 'decent work for all'. The all-encompassing aspect of the final aspect of the goal (being 'for all') is encouraging, but the priority given to concerns other than 'decent work' may be a matter for concern.

Economic objectives are emphasised in target SDG 8.1: 'sustain per capita economic growth in accordance with national circumstances and, in particular, at least 7 per cent gross domestic product growth per annum in the least developed countries'. Target 8.2 seeks to achieve 'higher levels of economic productivity through diversification, technological upgrading and innovation, including through a focus on high-value added and labour-intensive sectors'. The accompanying indicator SDG 8.2.1 attempts measurement of the '[a]nnual growth rate of real GDP per employed person', which looks suspiciously like the commodification of labour,[12] placing an implicit constraint on collective action that might constrain employer profits. Notably, the problematic aspects of this kind of target for economic growth was flagged in the *UN Sustainable Development Outlook 2019*,[13] which observed that 'highly unequal societies tend to have lower union density and coverage and former employment protections ... which could be linked to the argument that the high concentration of political power allows the rich to impose their public policy preference on the rest of society'. Recovery from the pandemic and the pressing need to attend to environmental objectives might also call the feasibility of a 7 per cent growth rate into question (Wells et al. 2020: 33–34 citing Kallis 2011).

[12] The first ILO Constitution to be found in Part XIII of the Treaty of Versailles 1919 stated in Section II (Article 427) that 'labour should not be regarded merely as a commodity or article of commerce'; repeated in Article I(a) of the ILO Declaration of Philadelphia 1944.

[13] UN Department of Economic and Social Affairs, *Sustainable Development Outlook 2019: Gathering Storms and Silver Linings* (Geneva, UN: 2019) at 25.

The other matter for concern may be that there is no explicit mention of a right to strike in any of the SDGs or accompanying targets. There is only reference to trade unions and collective bargaining in indicators, adopted subsequently.[14] The UN Special Rapporteur Report in 2018 was adamant that a right to strike as a facet of freedom of association must be understood to be included in 'fundamental freedoms' referred to in SDG 16.10.[15] That would certainly be consistent with a recent statement of the UN Human Rights Committee and the Committee on Economic, Social and Cultural Rights, which states that the right to strike is 'corollary to the effective exercise of the right to form and join trade unions'.[16] This raises questions as to whether the SDGs envisage (as part of any global partnership) effective cross-border collective bargaining. Such bargaining should also entail a right to engage in solidarity strikes, which have been advocated as vital to regulation of the current global market economy (Bogg and Ewing 2014; De Stefano 2017: 202–205).

2.4 SUSTAINABILITY AND SOLIDARITY IN THE EU: THE PILLAR, LEGISLATIVE CHOICES AND POLICY PLANS

Subsequently, an intertwined sustainability and unbound solidarity agenda, evident in part in the SDGs, has seemingly shaped the content of the European Pillar of Social Rights, as well as subsequent Commission policy-making and legislative initiatives. It is suggested here that EU developments indicate some acceptance of 'action for' the vulnerable as well as 'action with' others to secure inter- and intra-generational justice. However, these initiatives reveal a conflicted approach, which is still subject to the market pressures evident in SDG 8. Nevertheless, recent steps taken to promote solidarity as sustainability indicate a possible shift from a soft-law to a hard-law paradigm in the EU context, despite the challenges that this may present.

2.4.1 *The European Pillar of Social Rights: Encouraging Inclusive Solidarity and Collective Voice?*

The preamble to the Interinstitutional Proclamation of the European Pillar of Social Rights[17] refers in its first paragraph to Art. 3 of the Treaty on the European Union (TEU), which states that 'the aims of the Union are inter alia to promote the

[14] See indicators SDG 8.8.2 and SDG 16.10.1 adopted in 2017.

[15] *Report of the Special Rapporteur on the Rights to Freedom of Peaceful Assembly and of Association*. Item 74(b) of the provisional agenda, General Assembly, 73rd Session, A/73/279. New York, paras 6 and 58, and see also paras 87–89.

[16] 'Freedom of Association, Including the Right to Form and Join Trade Unions', Joint Statement by the Committee on Economic, Social and Cultural Rights and the Human Rights Committee, 23 October 2019, E/C.12/2019/3-CCPR/C/2019/1.

[17] Interinstitutional Proclamation on the European Pillar of Social Rights 2017/C 428/09, 13.12.2017, https://eur-lex.europa.eu/legal-content/EN/TXT/PDF/?uri=CELEX:32017C1213(01)&from=EN.

well-being of its peoples and to work for the sustainable development of Europe based on balanced economic growth and price stability, a highly competitive social market economy, aiming at full employment and social progress, and a high level of protection and improvement of the quality of the environment' (in other words, all three pillars recognised as key facets of sustainability, discussed above). The term 'sustainable' is repeated again in paragraphs 7 and 11 of the preamble, with the latter setting out the ambition to 'build a more inclusive and *sustainable* growth model by improving Europe's competitiveness' (my emphasis).

So, the rhetoric of sustainability is present in the Pillar, but is this conceived in terms of solidarity that is 'bounded' or 'unbounded'? One promising sign is paragraph 15 of the preamble, which indicates an inclusive approach to the scope of coverage of employment law. This states that, 'Where a principle refers to workers, it concerns all persons in employment, regardless of their employment status, modality and duration.' Similarly, Chapter 1 of the Pillar, engaging with 'Equal opportunities and access to the labour market', reflects concerns with gender and racial equality evident in SDGs 5 and 8. In Chapter 2 concerning 'Fair working conditions', Principle 5 states that, 'Regardless of the type and duration of the employment relationship, workers have the right to fair and equal treatment regarding working conditions, access to social protection and training.' There is still arguably here a requirement to be a 'worker', not necessarily a more wide-ranging inclusion of protection for all those in the 'world of work', as envisaged in ILO Convention No. 190 on Violence and Harassment.[18] However, this phrasing is suggestive at least of the extension of protection to a wider range of different forms of 'work' and 'employment'.

Also evident in the text of the Pillar is the importance of collective voice and action, which as we have seen above is not as prominent in the UN 2030 Agenda. For example, paragraph 20 of the preamble states that 'social partners at all levels have a crucial role to play in pursuing and implementing the European Pillar of Social Rights, in accordance with their autonomy in negotiating and concluding agreements and the right to collective bargaining and collective action. Principle 8 of the Pillar likewise recognises 'social dialogue and involvement of workers', seeking to promote access to information and consultation of collective representatives at the European and national levels, as well as collective bargaining and collective action.

However, just as there are potential conflicts evident from SDG 8 between decent work objectives and those relating to economic growth, so too there are statements in Principle 5 that detract from inclusive protection of workers and mechanisms for voice otherwise acknowledged in the Pillar. For example, flexibility is protected in paragraph (b) to enable 'employers to adapt swiftly to changes in the economic

[18] Available at www.ilo.org/dyn/normlex/en/f?p=NORMLEXPUB:12100:0::NO::P12100_ILO_CODE:C190.

context' and under paragraph (c), '[e]ntrepreneurship and self-employment shall be encouraged'. This does not seem likely to tame the explosion of use of precarious work (Kenner et al. 2019), which has further expanded in the pandemic (Adams-Prassl et al. 2020).

However, while the Pillar was initially intended as a vehicle for managing social policy for those EU Member States who have adopted the Euro (Garben 2019: 110), it has become a key reference point more generally, gaining what could be regarded as traction in hard law. Various commentators have linked its terms and its influence to promotion of a broader social sustainability agenda in the EU (Bednarowicz 2019: 623; Polomarkakis 2019). An example was the adoption of the 2019 Directive on Transparent and Predicable Working Conditions,[19] the Commission in its initial Proposal for the Directive having relied explicitly on Principles 5 and 7 of the Pillar.[20] In this sense, the Pillar has gone beyond a mere soft-law statement to the instantiation of sustainability (and solidarity) objectives in hard law. However, those initiatives have, so far, been limited in their scale and scope.

For example, despite a more ambitious ambit stated in recital (8) of the preamble, Article 1(2) of the 2019 Transparency Directive limits its application to the situation where there is 'an employment contract or employment relationship as defined by the law, collective agreements or practice in force in each Member State with consideration to the case-law of the Court of Justice'. In other words, the Directive does not cover all those 'in the world of work', such that those who are the most vulnerable may remain outliers unprotected in the EU labour market (Bednarowicz 2019; Novitz 2021).

2.4.2 *A New Explicit Sustainable Policy Strategy in 2020?*

On appointment as President of the European Commission, Ursula von der Leyen made clear her commitment to a multifaceted sustainability agenda, setting out her stall for a 'just transition to a "future-ready economy"' (von der Leyen 2019: 5). The Commission proposal for 'The European Green Deal', published in December 2019, makes reference to 'social dialogue' (but not collective bargaining and action) as a means to facilitate such changes. This is arguably partially but not wholly compliant with the ILO 2015 Guidelines on Just Transitions,[21] as observed by Sebastian Sabato and Boris Fronteddu at the European Trade Union Institute (2020). That statement of intent from the Commission was followed in January 2020 by a Commission Communication on 'A Strong Social Europe for Just

[19] Directive 2019/1152/EU on transparent and predictable working conditions in the European Union OJ L 186/105.

[20] COM (2017) 797, 2.

[21] Commission Communication, 'The European Green Deal' COM (2019) 640 final 11.12.19, 16 and 23.

Transitions',[22] an interesting choice of language which conjures up visions of past collective worker voice engagement with environmental and other sustainability objectives.

However, the Communication's content is more restrictive than its title might suggest. It begins with recognition of the UN SDGs and a commitment to their integration in the EU social model and social policy.[23] However, Europe is still to be 'a vibrant hub of innovation and competitive entrepreneurship'. In other words, economic growth remains a priority, as was envisaged under SDG8 and Principle 5 of the Pillar. The motivations for 'just transitions' are not only said to be environmental (although climate is understandably a key factor) and may be triggered by digitalisation and demographic change.[24] The Commission does recognise that sustainability is not only economic and environmental but is also social and important for the world of work. With an emphasis on inclusive labour markets, support is planned for: (1) training; (2) professional mobility and 'economic reconversion'; (3) job creation; (4) fostering equality as part of a Sustainable Europe Investment Plan for Green New Deal; (5) fair working conditions; and (6) social protection.

This is neither a straightforward ILO 'decent work' plan, nor does it easily fit with the more inclusive and bold aspects of the UN SDGs. Migration is avoided as an issue, for instance, and so this policy proposal suffers with reference to SDG targets 8.7 and 8.8. Moreover, social dialogue and collective bargaining only receive a brief and late mention under 'fair working conditions'.[25] This is curious, given the long tradition of an active role for trade unions in just transition negotiations around green adjustments and their recognition in the ILO 'Just Transition' Guidelines.[26] This Communication has arguably become more notable on the subject of proposals it envisaged for digital workers and minimum wage standard-setting than a touchstone for sustainability and solidarity.[27] Nevertheless, it is interesting that these initiatives are still pursued, as anticipated in the Communication, despite the effects of COVID on the EU economy and working conditions.[28]

At the end of June 2020 consultation was launched in respect of collective bargaining for the self-employed in the platform economy, as part of the wider Digital Services Act Package.[29] On 9 December 2021, the Commission published a *Proposal for a Directive on improving working conditions in platform work*,[30] together

[22] Commission Communication, 'A Strong Social Europe for Just Transitions' COM (2020) 14 final 14.1.20.
[23] Ibid., 3.
[24] Ibid., 2.
[25] Ibid., 9.
[26] See n. 6 above.
[27] Commission Communication nn. 22, 8–9.
[28] Cf. Commission Communication, 'Coordinated Economic Response to the COVID-19 Outbreak' COM (2020) 112 final, 13.3.20.
[29] See https://ec.europa.eu/commission/presscorner/detail/en/ip_20_1237.
[30] COM(2021) 762 final, 9 December 2021.

with 'Guidelines on the application of EU competition law to collective agreements regarding the working conditions of self-employed persons'. Those Guidelines may enable collective bargaining for those who are 'solo-self-employed', including platform workers, although certain definitional issues and thresholds still have to be addressed.

Also promising may be the more concrete and controversial Commission proposal for a Directive on adequate minimum wages published in October 2020.[31] This proposal seems to have been formulated in response to opposition to EU intervention on this issue by Scandinavian and Nordic unions that see statutory regulation as problematic, when collective bargaining is their way of ensuring adequate wage-setting.[32] The Commission has sought to be sensitive to competence constraints in Art. 153(5) of the TFEU, which excludes from social policy competence, 'pay, the right of association, the right to strike or the right to impose lock-outs'. The proposal is based on Art. 153(1) of the TFEU on 'working conditions' ('within the boundaries of subsidiarity and proportionality').[33] The idea is that, as the proposed directive does not set pay and only promotes collective bargaining, competence issues are evaded. There is a positive duty on member states to promote collective bargaining in what would be Article 4, although this is limited to wage-setting.

The proposed Directive looks to promote capacity (including collective capabilities) and to encourage 'constructive, meaningful and informed negotiations'. Where collective bargaining coverage is less than 70 per cent, the member state is to establish an 'action plan' to encourage collective bargaining (either by law after consultation with the social partners or by agreement with them). Public procurement could be based on compliance with wages set out in collective agreements for the relevant sector and geographical area under Article 9, bypassing what were the apparent limitations of *RegioPost*,[34] as discussed by contributors to Albert Sanchez-Graells' edited collection (2018).

Reporting obligations would also arise under the proposed Article 10, for example on the rate of collective bargaining coverage. Moreover, implementation may be undertaken by the social partners under Article 13. This proposed instrument is not stuck in a consultative 'social dialogue' frame, which was all that seemed to be envisaged on a bare reading of the Commission Communication on 'A Strong

[31] Commission Proposal for a Directive of the European Parliament and of the Council on adequate minimum wages in the European Union COM (2020) 682 final, 28.10.20.

[32] Although it should be noted that they remain unconvinced by the terms of the proposal, as is evident in their joint statement 23.11.2020, EU minimum wage directive undercuts Scandinavian model (euobserver.com).

[33] See n. 31, 6.

[34] Case C-115/14 *RegioPost GmbH & Co. KG* v. *Stadt Landau in der Pfalz (RegioPost)*, judgment of 17 November 2015.

Social Europe for Just Transitions', but arguably reverts to the stronger norms set out in Principle 8 of the European Pillar of Social Rights.

The proposal might also be applauded for acknowledging the benefits of having wage-agreements tailored to 'the needs and conditions of particular sectors and occupations'.[35] Also, as Torsten Muller and Thorsten Schulten have observed, this is a model where strong collective bargaining is 'no longer viewed as impediments to "flexibility" and competitiveness'.[36] This is certainly an improvement on the Commission Communication on the 'New Industrial Strategy for Europe', which failed to mention social dialogue, collective bargaining or trade unions.[37]

However, what is missing in the proposed Directive is any reference to the prospect of lawful industrial action, which should be present for meaningful negotiations (as opposed to 'collective begging'). Collective bargaining across national borders, and related solidarity action, is not contemplated at all in the Commission proposal. This seems out of touch with the ways in which European business works, both across EU Member State national boundaries and globally. In that sense, the profitability of EU commerce is still implicitly prioritised (cf. Sjåfjell et al. 2020). Nevertheless, the Council has now endorsed the key aspects of this Proposal,[38] and shows no sign of a desire to address this omission.

In November 2020, a Commission Staff Working Document has set out in a more detailed way how the EU intends to deliver on the SDGs, offering 'a comprehensive approach'.[39] This is interesting insofar as it makes an explicit direct link between the Pillar and a sustainability agenda, stating for example that: 'the European Pillar of Social Rights is the EU's social strategy to make sure that the transitions to climate-neutrality, digitalisation and demographic change are socially fair and just'; and that '[t]he objectives set by the SDGs . . . are being pursued through the implementation of the Pillar'.[40] It is evident that reports on SDGs are to be incorporated into country reports in the European Semester and that they will also be linked to the targets of EU funding programmes both within the EU and externally.[41] There is also recognition in this document of the need for 'a holistic and cross-sector policy approach',[42] with the Commission appreciating that it also has a global role in promoting sustainability objectives in international organisations and through its

35 https://uklabourlawblog.com/2020/11/12/the-eu-minimum-wage-directive-a-missed-opportunity-by-zoe-adams/.

36 www.socialeurope.eu/minimum-wage-directive-yes-but.

37 Commission Communication, 'A New Industrial Strategy for Europe' COM (2020) 102 final, 10.3.2020.

38 Employment, Social Policy, Health and Consumer Affairs Council, 6–7 December 2021: Main results, www.consilium.europa.eu/en/meetings/epsco/2021/12/06-07/.

39 Commission Staff Working Document, 'Delivering on the UN's Sustainable Development Goals – A Comprehensive Approach' SWD (2020) 400 final 18.11.2020.

40 Ibid., 6 and 7.

41 Ibid., 7–9.

42 Ibid., 11.

trade and aid connections.[43] In this, the Communication builds on the Commission's earlier EU Action Plan on Human Rights and Democracy, which had also seized on the UN SDGs as an opportunity, seeing 'the commitment to leave no one behind' as 'a call to enhance the human rights of all, without discrimination on any grounds' as vital for EU internal market and external relations policies.[44] Moreover, '[i]mplementation of SDGs is not only a matter for public authorities but requires the full participation of civil society', and the 2020 Working Document makes clear that this involves the 'social partners', namely employers and trade unions.[45]

2.4.3 *The 2021 Action Plan and 'Porto Social Commitment'*

The aspirations set out in Commission Communications during 2020 have now been incorporated, albeit in a modest way, into the European Pillar of Social Rights Action Plan issued on 4 March 2021. The Plan begins by stating the Commission's commitment to sustainability and implementation of the UN SDGs, which are to be reflected in various social measures and their funding.[46] The Plan further contains sparse but arguably still significant commitments to promote collective bargaining, both from the EU (in relation to the proposed Directive on an adequate minimum wage) and from Member States and social partners.[47] In particular, an initiative to consider collective bargaining for 'self-employed workers' planned for the final quarter of 2021 is a potentially important innovation in terms of the inclusive expansion of solidarity.[48]

In the process of recovery from the economic and social crisis presented by the pandemic, it is said that 'dialogue between social partners is of essence to foster socially responsible restructuring',[49] offering appreciation of the role that can be played by collective worker voice, but again it is difficult to know how this commitment will be operationalised. What is evident from the Action Plan is that social dialogue is regarded as appropriate both at the national and European levels to navigate change, as is bargaining at the national level in order to secure EU-level collective agreements.[50] An initiative for social dialogue was planned for 2022, and it has since emerged that this may concern reform of sectoral dialogue and project

43 Ibid., 12–17.

44 Commission Joint Communication, 'EU Action Plan on Human Rights and Democracy 2020–2024', JOIN (2020) 5 final, 25.3.20, 3.

45 See n. 38 above, 18; although trade unions are not specifically mentioned at any point in the Working Document.

46 European Commission Employment and Social Affairs DG, 'European Pillar of Social Rights Action Plan', 4 March 2021, 5–10.

47 Ibid., 19 and 36–37.

48 Ibid., 42.

49 Ibid., 16.

50 Ibid., 36–37.

funding to encourage information and consultation, participation and support for social dialogue.[51] There is no mention in the main body of the Action Plan of 'collective action' or a right to strike, although this is to be respected under 'The Pillar Principles Proclaimed at the 2017 Gothenburg Summit', which are appended to the document.[52] In this way, it does seem that there is a trajectory towards taking the social dimension of sustainability at work much more seriously, enabling something that looks more like solidarity 'unbound'.

That assessment is perhaps given further (at least rhetorical) force by the Porto Social Commitment. That Commitment is significant as a declaration of intent made, not just by EU institutions (in particular, the Commission and the Parliament), but also the social partners and the NGO Platform.[53] It sets out their 'shared ambition for a transition towards a green, socially just and digital economy', while appreciating the far-reaching changes that COVID-19 has wrought. In this context, the Commitment is made to intra-generational justice, addressing 'inequalities' and integrating the vulnerable in the labour market. The Pillar is to be regarded as 'a compass to guide us towards a strong, sustainable, inclusive recovery and towards upward economic and social convergence', and the Action Plan made two months' earlier welcomed. Notably reference is made to the broader 'world of work', as well as the circumstances of those 'with a migration background' and who otherwise suffer disadvantage and exclusion. Social dialogue is to be promoted at 'the European, national, regional, sectoral and company levels, with special attention on ensuring an enabling framework for collective bargaining'. Once again, there is no specific mention of collective action or a right to strike, but the statements in the Porto Commitment seem ever closer to a generous unbounded notion of solidarity. It is, however, a Commitment made only in respect of what goes on inside Europe, as opposed to the EU's role as a global actor. While some will suspect that these assertions amount merely to rhetorical flourish, they arguably give some flavour of the extent to which sustainability and the inclusiveness it prompts could become an entrenched and effective aspect of EU social policy. This could yet be the EU direction of travel.

2.5 CONCLUSION

Recognition of social sustainability in international and EU instruments has the potential to enhance inclusive employment law protections for a wider range of

[51] Ibid., 42.

[52] Ibid., 44–45. Plans regarding sectoral dialogue are set out at https://ec.europa.eu/social/main.jsp?langId=en&catId=89&newsId=10123&furtherNews=yes; and regarding calls for proposals on information, consultation and participation and support for social dialogue, see https://ec.europa.eu/social/main.jsp?catId=629.

[53] Porto Social Summit, Porto Social Commitment, 7 May 2021 available at www.2021portugal.eu/en/porto-social-summit/porto-social-commitment/.

people in 'the world of work', as well as collective voice and action regionally and globally. However, it is difficult to detect full political commitment to this transformative vision in the UN SDGs, which suggests an uneasy journey of compromise between economic growth and environmental and social justice objectives. We seem likely to witness further battles ahead regarding distribution of income within and between countries and those who work within them, given the failure in Agenda 2030 to explicitly recognise the need for solidarity between workers hired in diverse ways and across borders and the legitimacy of their collective action.

While harder EU legislative proposals are being devised and presented to the political institutions, it is the softer policy documentation, political commitments and Commission practices that chime with a bolder sustainability agenda. There now seems to be at least some appreciation of the economic, environmental and social consequences of the regulation of work in documents like the Porto Social Commitment and the Commission's own Working Document on how to deliver the SDGs. They offer a vision of a more inclusive and participatory approach to improving working and broader social conditions, which will have implications for environmental and other transitions expected in the years to come. The trajectory is encouraging, but what may now be needed is a more tangible appreciation of the interconnectedness of labour markets across the borders of different countries and the importance of a collective voice that traverses these.

Building on UN and EU policy initiatives to date, transformative change may be possible, and the direction of travel is promising. More may still be achieved with reference to the underlying principles on which the ideals of sustainability are based, namely intra- and inter-generational justice, which prompt inclusive solidarity across national and temporal boundaries – that is to say, 'solidarity unbound'.

REFERENCES

Adams-Prassl, Abi et al. 2020. 'Inequality in the Impact of the Coronavirus Shock: Evidence from Real Time Surveys', *Journal of Public Economics* 189: 104245–104277.

Banting, Keith and Kymlicka, Will. 2017. 'The Political Sources of Solidarity in Diverse Societies', in Keith Banting and Will Kymlicka, eds, *The Strains of Commitment: The Political Sources of Solidarity in Diverse Societies*. Oxford: Oxford University Press, pp. 1–58.

Bauböck, Rainer. 2017. 'Citizenship and Collective Identities as Political Sources of Solidarity in the European Union', in Keith Banting and Will Kymlicka, eds, *The Strains of Commitment: The Political Sources of Solidarity in Diverse Societies*. Oxford: Oxford University Press, pp. 80–103.

Bednarowicz, Bartlomiej. 2019. 'Delivering on the European Pillar of Social Rights', *Industrial Law Journal* 48, 4: 604–623.

Bogg, Alan and Ewing, K. D. 2014. 'The Implications of the RMT Case', *Industrial Law Journal* 43: 221–252.

Carr, Stuart Colin et al. 2018. 'How Can Wages Sustain a Living? By Getting Ahead of the Curve', *Sustainability Science* 13, 4: 901–917.

Clark, Brett, Auerbach, Daniel and Longo, Stefano B. 2018. 'The Bottom Line: Capital's Production of Social Inequalities and Environmental Degradation', *Journal of Environmental Studies and Sciences* 8, 4: 562–569.

De Stefano, Valerio. 2017. 'Non-Standard Work and Limits on Freedom of Association: A Human Rights-Based Approach', *Industrial Law Journal* 46, 2: 185–207.

Doorey, David. 2017. 'Just Transitions Law: Putting Labour Law to Work on Climate Change', *Journal of Environmental Law and Practice* 30, 2: 201–239.

Federico, Veronica. 2020. 'Talking about Solidarity . . . It Sounds Like a Whisper: Solidarity in Law and Public Policies', in Christian Lahusen, ed., *Citizens' Solidarity in Europe: Civic Engagement and Public Discourse in Times of Crises*. Cheltenham: Edward Elgar, pp. 101–119.

Frega, Roberto. 2021. 'Solidarity as Social Involvement', *Moral Philosophy and Politics* 8, 2: 179–208.

French, Duncan and Kotzé, Louis J. eds. 2021. *Research Handbook on Law, Governance and Planetary Boundaries*. Cheltenham: Edward Elgar.

Frey, Diane F. and MacNaughton, Gillian. 2016. 'A Human Rights Lens on Full Employment and Decent Work in the 2030 Sustainable Development Agenda', *Journal of Workplace Rights* 6, 2: 1–13.

Garben, Sacha. 2019. 'The European Pillar of Social Rights: An Assessment of Its Meaning and Significance', *Cambridge Yearbook of European Legal Studies* 21: 101–127.

Grear, Anna. 2014. 'Towards "Climate Justice"? A Critical Reflection on Legal Subjectivity and Climate Injustice: Warning Signals, Patterned Hierarchies, Directions for Future Law and Policy', *Journal of Human Rights and the Environment* 5: 103–133.

Grießler, Erich and Littig, Beate. 2005. 'Social Sustainability: A Catchword between Political Pragmatism and Social Theory', *International Journal of Sustainable Development* 8, 1–2: 65–79.

Kenner, Jeff, Florczak, Izabela and Otto, Marta, eds. 2019. *Precarious Work: The Challenge for Labour Law in Europe*. Cheltenham: Edward Elgar.

Levy, Jacob T. 2017. 'Against Fraternity: Democracy without Solidarity', in Keith Banting and Will Kymlicka, eds, *The Strains of Commitment: The Political Sources of Solidarity in Diverse Societies*. Oxford: Oxford University Press, pp. 107–123.

Marx, Karl and Engels, Frederich. 1848. *The Communist Manifesto*. London: Vintage Books.

McCann, Deirdre and Fudge, Judy. 2017. 'Unacceptable Forms of Work: A Multidimensional Model', *International Labour Review* 156, 2: 147–184.

Novitz, Tonia. 2019. 'Supply Chains and Temporary Migrant Labour: The Relevance of Trade and Sustainability Frameworks', in Diamond Ashiagbor, ed., *Re-imagining Labour Law for Development*. Oxford: Hart, pp. 191–211.

2020. 'Engagement with Sustainability at the International Labour Organization and Wider Implications for Collective Worker Voice', *International Labour Review* 159, 4: 463–482.

2022. 'Addressing "Social Dumping" and "Unfair Competition" – An Analysis of EU Pillar Initiatives from a Sustainability Perspective', in A-C Hartzen et al. eds, Law, Solidarity and the Limits of Social Europe: Constitutional Tensions for EU Integration. Cheltenham: Edward Elgar, pp. 2–21.

Pieraccini, Margherita and Novitz, Tonia, eds. 2020. *Legal Perspectives on Sustainability*. Bristol: University of Bristol Press.

Pingeot, Lou. 2014. Corporate Influence in the Post-2015 Process. Working Paper (Jan). Aachen/Berlin/Bonn/New York, Misereor, Brot für die Welt and Global Policy Forum: www.globalpolicy.org/images/pdfs/GPFEurope/Corporate_influ ence_in_the_Post-2015_process_web.pdf.

Polomarkakis, Konstantinos Alexandris. 2019. 'The European Pillar of Social Rights and the Quest for EU Social Sustainability', *Social and Legal Studies* 29, 2: 183–200.

Raworth, Kate. 2012. *A Safe and Just Space for Humanity: Can We Live within the Doughnut?* Oxford: Oxfam Discussion Papers.

2017. *Doughnut Economics: Seven Ways to Think Like a 21st Century Economist*. Harmondsworth: Penguin.

Sabato, Sebastian and Fronteddu, Boris. 2020. *A Socially Just Transition through the European Green Deal?* Brussels: European Trade Union Institute.

Sanchez-Graells, Albert, ed. 2018. *Smart Public Procurement and Labour Standards: Pushing the Discussion after RegioPost*. Oxford: Hart Publishing.

Sciarra, Silvana. 2018. *Solidarity and Conflict. European Social Law in Crisis*. Cambridge: Cambridge University Press.

Seck, Sara. 2019. 'Relational Law and the Reimagining of Tools for Environmental and Climate Justice', *Canadian Journal of Women and Law* 31, 1: 151–177.

Sissons, Paul, Green, Anne E. and Lee, Neil. 2017. 'Linking the Sectoral Employment Structure and Household Poverty in the United Kingdom', *Work, Employment and Society* 32, 6: 1078–1098.

Sjåfjell, Beate et al. 2020. Securing the Future of European Business: SMART Reform Proposals. Oslo: University of Oslo Faculty of Law Research Paper no. 2020-11.

Stepan, Alfred. 1978. *The State and Society: Peru in Comparative Perspective*. Princeton: Princeton University Press.

Stevis, Dimitris and Felli, Romain. 2015. 'Global Labour Unions and Just Transition to a Green Economy', *International Environmental Agreements* 15, 1: 29–43.

von der Leyen, Ursula. 2019. *A Union That Strives for More: My Agenda for Europe Political Guidelines for the Next European Commission 2019–2024*. Brussels: European Commission, available at: https://ec.europa.eu/info/sites/default/files/political-guidelines-next-commission_en_0.pdf.

Wells, Peter, Abouarghoub, Wessam, Pettit, Stephen and Beresford, Anthony. 2020. 'A Socio-technical Transitions Perspective for Assessing Future Sustainability Following the COVID-19 Pandemic', *Sustainability: Science, Practice and Policy* 16, 1: 29–36.

Zbyszewska, Ania. 2018. 'Regulating Work with People and "Nature" in Mind: Feminist Reflections', *Comparative Labor Law and Policy Journal*, 40, 1: 9–28.

3

Solidarity as a Central Aim of Collective Labour Law?

Reingard Zimmer

3.1 INTRODUCTION

Solidarity is one of the rights that the Charter of Fundamental Rights of the EU (CFR) mentions as a central value in its preamble and it is the title of Chapter IV, which contains Art. 27 (workers' right to information and consultation within the undertaking) and Art. 28 (right of collective bargaining and action), central rights of collective labour law. The protection of the weaker party is the central idea, both in individual labour law and in collective labour law. But to which extent does that include the idea of solidarity? If solidarity would be the basic idea of the concept of collective labour law, this would imply a strong social approach. The following elaboration looks for an attempt of a definition and analyses the components of solidarity in collective labour law based upon European and German Labour Law.

3.2 ATTEMPT OF A DEFINITION

3.2.1 *Solidarity in History*

Signs of the concept of solidarity can be found very early in history. Already in Roman Law, which was developed between the middle of the fifth century BCE and the third century CE as a general set of rules carved in stone, there is to be found the principle 'in solidum'.[1] This could be interpreted as an early thought of a community of solidarity. In younger history, 'freedom, equality, fraternity' was the battle cry of the French Revolution and in the post-revolutionary nineteenth century, the category of solidarity moves to the centre of theories of social gratitude, as proclaimed for example by Auguste Comte.[2] In solidarism, solidarity even became the

[1] Which could be translated, 'all for one and one for all'.

[2] Comte, 1891, p. 215.

yardstick for a sociopolitical reform movement.[3] In Germany, the social democrats developed in the meantime an extremely differentiated social-oppositional social-democratic club culture, which proved for their leader, Karl Liebknecht, that the working class would not only be able to take power, but also to culturally form society.[4]

3.2.2 *General Definition of Solidarity*

If we look at current definitions of solidarity, the online dictionary for example uses a wide definition, defining solidarity as 'arising from common responsibilities and interests, as between members of a group or between classes, peoples, etc.',[5] similar to the definition of the most notable German dictionary *Duden*, where solidarity is seen as an absolute (social) cohesion with someone based upon the same opinions and aims.[6] Common identity and common interests are thus defined as starting points for a definition of solidarity.[7] This reminds of Durkheim's 'mechanical solidarity' of older, less structured, segmental societies[8] and might serve as a point of departure, though further elements have to be added. Solidarity implies up to a certain point the abstraction of own interests.[9] An act of solidarity may also be to refrain from doing something to support others or another group. In practising solidarity, a group is acting without being obliged to do so.[10] The idea of mutual support is partly also considered a central issue of solidarity[11] and some authors describe the welfare state as an expression of institutionalized solidarity.[12] Several authors emphasize that solidarity, in addition, has to be differentiated from charity,[13] where there are not necessarily common interests or values with the subject of charity. As Hyman holds, moreover, there must be differentiation between 'solidarity with' and 'solidarity against'.[14] The previous elaborations refer to 'solidarity with others' – the context of a 'solidarity against' something or somebody will be elaborated below.

3 Bude, 2019, p. 29.
4 Liebknecht, 1871, p. 99.
5 Online dictionary, www.dictionary.com/browse/solidarity (13.4.2022).
6 'Unbedingtes Zusammenhalten mit jemandem aufgrund gleicher Anschauungen und Ziele', see www.duden.de/rechtschreibung/Solidaritaet (16.1.2020).
7 Hyman, 2002, p. 2; Lessenich, Reder and Süß, 2020, p. 319 (322).
8 Durkheim, 1988, pp. 200ff.
9 Klindworth and Schröder, 2010, p. 7.
10 Bude, 2019, p. 11; Ludwig, 2019, p. 43.
11 Bertram, 2007, p. 215; Bude, 2019, p. 32; Hyman, 2002, p. 2; Kock and Kutzner, 2020, p. 327; Lessenich, Reder and Süß, 2020, p. 319 (323); Ludwig, 2019, p. 43; Wersig et al., 2006, p. 314.
12 Bude, 2019, p. 45.
13 Bayertz, 1998, p. 49; Bude, 2019, p. 20; Hoffmann, 2004, p. 38; Lange and Thiersch, 2006, pp. 214f.; Zoll, 2000, p. 12; Lessenich, Reder and Süß, 2020, p. 319 (321).
14 Hyman, 2002, p. 2.

3.2.3 *Internal Dimension of Solidarity*

Solidarity is also an expression of a social relation, which includes an element of responsibility.[15] As Durkheim holds with his 'organic solidarity', consensus results from a differentiation of the individual members of the group,[16] who are not similar to one another but are dependent on one another (cohesion through dependencies).[17] Such concepts might be described as an internal dimension of solidarity. Social relations of that kind are more visible in times of crisis, as was the case in the shutdown periods of the COVID-pandemic in 2020 and 2021.

3.2.4 *External Dimension of Solidarity*

Beyond the internal, there's also an external dimension of solidarity, when solidarity is practised in political struggle, being solidary with people (or groups) who stand up and fight for their rights, as some authors emphasize[18] and as is shown impressively by Bertolt Brecht in his song 'Solidarity'. Solidarity is thus seen as a process that is defined by interactions and collective action.[19] As Hyman holds, this might be described as 'solidarity against' the oppressor,[20] which is defined by some authors as transformative solidarity.[21]

Sangiovanni furthermore links solidarity with justice, when he defines 'global or international justice' as the basis of 'social solidarity across borders'.[22] This reminds of the findings of Durkheim, who already considered justice a fundamental element of a production based upon the division of labour.[23] Whereas other authors like Nagel believe that social justice ultimately is only possible among those who are subject to a comprehensive system of societal norms backed by coercion,[24] Sangiovanni opposes this theory with the concept of internationalism,[25] upon which trade unions build their international practice.[26] He defines internationalism as the 'mutual production of collective goods', which is based upon an element of fairness

[15] Bude, 2019, p. 21; Lessenich, Reder and Süß, 2020, p. 319 (322).
[16] In Durkheim's work, he relies upon society.
[17] Durkheim, 1988, pp. 428ff.; for a more recent take see Hondrich and Koch-Arzberger, 1992, p. 13.
[18] Bayertz, 1998, p. 49; similarly, see Sangiovanni, 2013, pp. 118ff. and Lessenich, Reder and Süß, 2020, p. 319 (322).
[19] Ludwig, 2019, p. 44; similarly: Lohmeyer et al., 2018, p. 400 (402); Lessenich, Reder and Süß, 2020, p. 318.
[20] Hyman, 2002, p. 2.
[21] Lessenich, Reder and Süß, 2020, p. 319 (323f.).
[22] Sangiovanni, 2013, pp. 118ff.
[23] Durkheim, 1988, pp. 421ff.
[24] Nagel, 2005, pp. 113ff.; similarly: Schäfer, 2006, p. 355.
[25] Sangiovanni, 2013, p. 119.
[26] Hoffmann, 2004, pp. 34ff.

in global production.[27] A striking description points out that solidarity is a specific form of social practice, which is born in daily discussion of the collective construction of the social.[28] Several authors see solidarity linked to the idea of justice.[29] To counter Nagel, this might be complemented by the idea that solidarity is practised without obligation, as elaborated above and as will be shown by the examples from trade union practice. As will be elaborated below, both the internal and external forms of solidarity are to be detected in the practice of trade unions.

3.2.5 *Inclusive and Exclusive Solidarity*

Two more differentiations of solidarity are elaborated in literature: inclusive and exclusive solidarity. Researchers describe it as inclusive solidarity, when the group concerned has on the one side a common concern, but the actual interest is not homogeneous, nor is the group in itself homogeneous.[30] It is an inclusive project insofar as different interests are included. Partly it is emphasized that inclusive solidarity is practised with others outside the own collective,[31] as is the case in international solidarity described by Giovanni. Exclusive solidarity, on the other hand, is practised for the benefit of a particular group,[32] potentially at the expense of others.[33] The group concerned is composed of rather homogeneous interests and emphasizes the identity of the interests of the solidarity actors, [34] at least insofar as the 'solidarity between equals' of Zoll (and Durkheim) is categorized as external solidarity.[35]

3.3 SOLIDARITY IN THE PRACTICE OF TRADE UNIONS

Solidarity has always been an important topic of social partners, nevertheless this applies to a greater extent to the workers' side. As the weaker party, the support of others is an important element to strengthen trade unions.[36] Although there might be detected certain elements of solidarity also in employer organizations,[37] the companies that are members of the employers' organization ultimately face each other as market competitors. This analysis therefore refers to the concept of solidarity

[27] Sangiovanni, 2013, p. 120.
[28] Lessenich, Reder and Süß, 2020, p. 324.
[29] Bude, 2019, p. 140; Zoll, 2000, p. 105.
[30] Zeuner, 2004, pp. 325f.
[31] Bude, 2019, p. 144; Zeuner, 2004, p. 332.
[32] Bude, 2019, p. 144; Lessenich, Reder and Süß, 2020, p. 319 (322).
[33] Lessenich, Reder and Süß, 2020, p. 319 (322).
[34] Zeuner, 2004, pp. 325f.
[35] Zeuner, 2004, p. 332.
[36] Lohmeyer et al., 2018, p. 401 (403).
[37] Höpner, 2007, p. 329 f; Keller, 2008, pp. 368f., 377.

of trade unions in their general work and in collective bargaining and the legal basis for that.

3.3.1 *Legal Background*

Art. 28 CFR assumes that workers have the right to form their own organizations and guarantees the right to bargain collectively and to make use of the right to strike in defence of the workers' interests. In Germany, freedom of association and collective bargaining are enshrined in Art. 9.3 of the German Basic Constitutional Law. A central aim of these fundamental rights is the autonomy of the collective bargaining partners for the shaping of laws.[38] They define themselves, how they want to organize, to run their organization and which values are the basis of their work. Thus freedom is granted, in which the conflicting interests of workers and employers may be carried out by their own responsibility,[39] which sometimes is also called 'social self-government'.[40] The concept of solidarity therefore is defined first and foremost by the social partners themselves, or more precisely by the members of the social partners whom they are representing.[41] Nevertheless restrictions might exist, as the rules for collective bargaining and for collective action are defined by law, either by statutory law or by jurisdiction,[42] depending on the system of the respective member states. To be acknowledged as trade unions, sometimes linked with the ability to bargain collectively, trade unions have to be representative.[43]

3.3.2 *Solidarity in the Work of Trade Unions: Introduction*

Solidarity has always been a central value of trade unions,[44] as was already declared 1848 by Stephan Born, co-founder of the General German Workers' Fraternization (Allgemeine Deutsche Arbeiterverbrüderung): 'Free competition! Everyone for-himself!' is opposed here by the principle of 'solidarity', 'the fraternization'.[45] In the (German) Weimar Republic, solidarity was an important value for the working class, which could be characterized by communality and mutuality.[46] Today, trade

[38] Linsenmaier, 2020, Art. 9 GG, Rn 51.

[39] BVerfG (Constitutional Court) of 2.3.1993 – 1 BvR 1213/85, BVerfGE 88, 103 (114).

[40] Scholz, Art. 9 GG, Rn 160.

[41] On the representativeness of trade unions: Mundlack, 2020b.

[42] The right to strike is mostly guranteed in the constitution of EU member states, with the exception of Austria, Belgium, Luxembourg, Malta, the Netherlands, Ireland and the UK. In Germany and Finland the right derives from the freedom of association: Warneck, 2007, p. 7; Waas, 2014, pp. 5ff.

[43] Mundlack, 2020a, pp. 86ff.; Mundlack, 2020b.

[44] Hoffmann, 2004, pp. 34ff.

[45] Born, in the journal *'Die Verbrüderung'*: *'Freie Konkurrenz! Jeder für sich!'*, wird hier gegenübergestellt dem Prinzip der *'Solidarität' der 'Verbrüderung'*! Jeder für alle.

[46] Bude, 2019, p. 32.

unions proclaim solidarity as a central value of their self-image,[47] based upon the subjective conviction that only together can something be achieved. This includes the practice of solidarity across borders,[48] as the example of the Accord in Bangladesh after the breakdown of the Rana Plaza factory with the death of more than 1,000 workers impressively showed.[49] Such values are characterized by individual and collective experiences, as well as by social discourses, which is more visible in times of crisis, like in the COVID-19 pandemic. The head of the German Federation of Trade Unions thus declared on the first of May 2020 in his online speech, 'We'll get through the corona crisis together only with solidarity, because you are not alone in solidarity' ('Nur mit Solidarität stehen wir die Corona-Krise gemeinsam durch, denn solidarisch ist man nicht alleine').[50] The crisis indeed strongly visualizes importance, values and the role of trade unions in society, as collectives create security in insecure times.[51]

3.3.3 *Inclusive and Exclusive Solidarity of Trade Unions*

Solidarity in trade unions is practised collectively[52] and trade unions may practise at the same time inclusive and exclusive solidarity. While establishing inclusive solidarity among their membership, they are to a certain extent naturally exclusive organizations,[53] representing primarily the interests of their members. The question of which sector a trade union is open to workers is defined by the statutes of the organization, which thus define implicitly the boundaries of solidarity.[54] Nevertheless a closer look at the different types of trade union is necessary. In Germany, industrial unions[55] organize all kinds of different workers in a sector and due to their heterogenous membership, face tremendous problems with the unification of the differentiating group-specific interests.[56] Their basic organizational efforts may be categorized as inclusive solidarity. Occupational trade unions,

47 See explanations on webpages of (the most important) German trade unions: IG-Metall: www.igmetall-nrw.de/mitglied-werden/solidaritaet-ist-kein-prinzip-von-gestern/?L=0; Ver.di: www.verdi.de/ueber-uns/idee-tradition and the DGB: www.dgb.de/themen/++co++b0c8af80-c5cc-11ea-ad59-001a4a160123 (all 13.4.2022).

48 For further information, see Lohmeyer et al., 2018, pp. 400ff.; Zimmer, 2019, pp. 167ff., both with further references.

49 Smith, 2014, p. 51 (56); Zimmer, 2016.

50 Hoffmann: www.vorwaerts.de/artikel/dgb-chef-hoffmann-nur-solidaritaet-stehen-corona-krise-gemeinsam (13.4.22).

51 Lindemann, 2020, p. 374 (376); Steg, 2020, p. 60.

52 Lindemann, 2020, p. 374.

53 Ludwig, The politics of Solidarity, p. 43.

54 Hyman, 2001, p. 170; Zeuner, 2004, p. 334.

55 The German industrial unions organize all employees within their organizing territory regardless of status, occupational category or profession, qualification, political conception or religion; see Dribbusch and Birke, 2019, p. 7; Keller, 2008, p. 365.

56 Keller, 2016, p. 6; similarly coincerning the difficulties, Zeuner, 2004, p. 334.

in contrast, organize only homogenous, specialized groups of workers of the same kind.[57] As these trade unions exclusively organize specific professional or status groups,[58] they don't have to show consideration for the interests of other groups of workers and therefore practise solidarity exclusively for their clientele. Their daily work thus may be categorized as exclusive solidarity.[59]

Industrial trade unions, however, which are based upon the concept of inclusive solidarity, may practise exclusive solidarity under certain circumstances. In the economic crisis of 2008/2009 for example, German trade unions ensured that only few workers were dismissed. But this only applies to the regular workforce – the use of agency work was terminated[60] and fixed-term employment not prolonged. With this policy, trade unions thus interacted on behalf of their members, which are mostly composed of the regular workforce – and they acted on the back of the non-members. Another example of exclusive solidarity might occur in both types of trade unions, as well in industrial unions, as in occupational unions. As research has shown, racist tendencies may also be detected among the members of trade unions, of which a good many in Germany strongly support the right-wing racist party Alternative für Deutschland (AfD).[61] Even members of an inclusive industrial union thus may exclude minorities when they go for 'Germans first', as well as members of occupational unions.

Furthermore, developments in the working world have to be borne in mind, which makes it more difficult for trade unions to unite people on the basis of solidarity as a central value. In the last century, a soft form of solidarity was somehow the product of socialization in the factory. As Durkheim held, although not being homogenous, due to mutual interdependencies in the working process based upon the division of labour, the workforce acknowledged colleagues and there might be described a solidary community as a collective, although there was always also rivalry among proletarians.[62] Nevertheless, this consciousness was an ideal starting point for the work of trade unions. Currently the end of Fordism with the end of standardized mass production and the change towards more flexible and decentralized forms of production has been sufficiently described.[63] Industrial workers, in addition, are not the majority of the workforce anymore.[64] Most people work in offices, in laboratories or practices and are socialized in the office, not in the factory. Employees, though, tend to be more sceptical of the idea of a collective than workers and separation is

57 E.g. in Germany, the Marbuger Bund organizes only doctors, the Gewerkschaft der Flugsicherung only air traffic controllers, etc. For further information, see: Dribbusch and Birke, 2019, p. 7 or Keller, 2016, pp. 6f.

58 Dribbusch and Birke, 2019, p. 9.

59 Keller, 2008, pp. 368f.

60 Dribbusch and Birke, 2019, p. 22.

61 Dribbusch and Birke, 2019, p. 4.

62 Bude, 2019, pp. 62f.

63 See instead of many: Fichter and Zeuner 2002, p. 13 (15), with further references.

64 Hyman, 2002, p. 3.

growing.[65] This is even more the case with workers in part-time work, freelancers, agency workers or crowd workers, which impedes the work of trade unions. As a consequence, specific trade unions and organizations for precarious workers were founded in some countries, like SEWA in India,[66] GMB-union for Uber-drivers in GB[67] or organizations for domestic workers.[68] But also industry-wide unions seem to have become more open for 'non-traditional' workers. In Germany the trade union Ver.di from the service sector has been open for freelancers since its foundation in 2001[69] and the IG-Metall opened up since a change in its statutes some years ago.[70] The IG-Metall, in addition, was the first union in Germany that made an effort to support crowd workers,[71] with other unions following.[72] As research indicates, trade unions have become more open towards precarious workers and in some countries form specific structures to represent precarious workers,[73] as the German example of IG-Metall and Ver.di shows. This may be described as a stronger approach of inclusive solidarity. Furthermore, alliances of trade unions with NGOs and public agencies can be detected.[74] Another factor for trade unions is the shift from sectorial collective bargaining towards company bargaining, which leads to a higher risk of 'company-egoism' with competition between enterprises, which might easily lead towards a rather exclusive solidarity, focused on the members of the own collective, the workforce of a specific company.[75] Therefore, a closer look at the specifics of solidarity in the current work of trade unions and at the legal background is necessary.

3.3.4 *Solidarity among the Members of the Trade Union*

3.3.4.1 Solidarity concerning Membership Fees

Trade unions act on behalf of their members in order to protect workers' interests and the activity of a trade union therefore is defined by the members.[76] There might be given several examples of how solidarity is practised among these members: as a general principle, members pay a certain percentage of their income as

65 Bude, 2019, pp. 64ff.; Pulignano et al., 2016, p. 39 (40).
66 For further information see www.sewa.org (10.3.2021).
67 For further information see www.gmb.org.uk (10.3.2022).
68 For further information see www.wiego.org/domestic-workers-organizing (10.3.2022).
69 For further information see https://selbststaendige.verdi.de/ (10.3.2022).
70 For further information see www.igmetall.de/service/leistungen/vorteile-einer-mitgliedschaft-fuer-solo-selbststaendige (10.3.2022).
71 For further information see http://faircrowd.work/de/ (10.3.2022).
72 For further information see www.ich-bin-mehr-wert.de/support/cloudworking/ (10.3.2022).
73 Pulignano et al., 2016, p. 39 (41ff.); similarly: Durazzi, 2017, p. 265 (271ff.).
74 Doellgast, Lillie and Pulignano, 2018, p. 1 (8).
75 Kock and Kutzner, 2020, p. 327 (331).
76 Zimmer, 2016, p. 18.

membership fee,[77] but specific groups with very little income do pay less. Students, people who receive the basic income by the state and those who provide voluntary service pay the minimum contribution, which is (in Germany) between €2,05 and €2,50. Other groups that for example receive pensions, unemployment or parental benefit, do pay only 0.5 per cent of their gross income to the union. The economically weakest parts of the membership are thus supported by a lower membership fee – based upon the idea that every single member potentially might get into an economic situation that requires an indirect form of support. Elements of this idea are to be found in all trade unions and can be categorized as inclusive solidarity. Such forms of solidarity within trade unions are based upon the idea of mutual support and have an ethical normative side, as an instrumental side, which distinguishes it from charity. Furthermore, there is no force to make use of such elements of solidarity; the members autonomously choose such a practice when defining the statutes of the organization.

3.3.4.2 Solidarity within the Process of Collective Bargaining

Another example might be given from collective bargaining negotiations of (representative) trade unions,[78] where sometimes the lowest wage groups receive a specific amount of pay rise, which is higher than the percentage rise for the members of all other groups,[79] as was the case for healthcare workers in autumn 2020 in Germany due to the COVID pandemic. Nursing stuff in addition received a pay rise between 8.7 and 10 per cent, whereas the pay rise of other groups was only 3.2 per cent.[80]

The whole group of workers that are subject to the specific collective bargaining agreement (CBA) has on the one side a common interest, the wage increase, but the actual interest is not homogeneous. Qualified workers in general might receive a higher wage rise within an isolated struggle, but support within the process of collective bargaining in industrial unions the less assertive unqualified workers. The balance inside the trade union is always unstable and has to be negotiated before and within the negotiations with the employer side. Such an interrelation may be characterized as solidarity and can be described as inclusive solidarity.[81] A practice of solidarity that is not exclusive tries to expand the distributive discretion and will receive more support if a fair distribution is intended.[82] As already elaborated, the basis of collective bargaining is the autonomy of the bargaining partners. The demands in an industrial dispute therefore are autonomously defined by the

77 In Germany this is 1 per cent of the regular gross income.

78 The trade union has to be representative, see Mundlack, 2020a, pp. 86ff.; Mundlack, 2020b.

79 Further examples are to be found in Wirth, 2021, pp. 1f.

80 See trade union Ver.di: https://gesundheit-soziales.verdi.de/tarifbereiche/oeffentlicher-dienst/++co++9407eb6a-16b5-11eb-8249-001a4a16012a (9.3.2022).

81 Keller, 2008, pp. 368f.

82 Kock and Kutzner, 2020, p. 327 (332).

social partners themselves, and they define the level of solidarity in the bargaining committees of the respective union, where the demands for the negotiations are specified, although in some countries legal limitations might exist.[83]

3.3.4.3 Solidarity through Strike Activities

Another similar example may be detected in the strike activity of industrial trade unions, where often some workers in specific positions are chosen to strike in the industrial conflict, on behalf of themselves, but also on behalf of other workers of the same union within the respective bargaining district, who belong to a different (and weaker) status group. The workers whose work stoppage hits the employer side most effectively are chosen for strike activity of the whole section, for example, garbage collectors or train/bus drivers. This counts at least for industrial unions, which organize all the workers of a company in a specific sector. This is another example of inclusive solidarity. If occupational trade unions, which organize only a specific occupational group, go on strike, they only strike for their own interest – and thus practise an exclusive form of solidarity. Based upon the strike provisions in the different EU member states, the form of solidarity that is practised in a strike could be analysed for the trade union organization (see above) or for the individual striking worker as well, if the strike rule guarantees the right to strike for trade union organizations. This is the case in Belgium, Italy, France and Spain, where the right to strike is granted also to individuals, whereas in Germany, Greece, Poland, the Czech Republic, Slovakia and Sweden only strikes are lawful that were called by trade union organizations.[84]

3.3.4.4 Solidarity Strikes

Solidarity strikes are the clearest practice of the inclusive solidarity of trade unions (and trade union members), as the workers are not striking in their own interests or for their own collective bargaining agreement (CBA) , but supporting others in their primary industrial action.[85] Solidarity strikes are practised in solidarity with the interests of others, often by workers of the same sector, but also from another section of the same or from another company or of the same trade union, or of another sector or even practised by members of other trade unions, partly even in another country. The further away the solidarity strikers are from the initial strikers, the less homogenous the group of striking workers is, which was elaborated as a sign of inclusive solidarity. Nevertheless, if solidarity strikes are not admissible in certain

[83] In Germany restrictions for CB are discussed (controversely) concerning economic decisions and corporate policy. For further information, see Däubler, 2016, pp. 27ff.; Däubler, 2012.

[84] Warneck, 2007, p. 8.

[85] Linsenmaier, 2022, Art. 9 GG, para. 120, 278; Zimmer, 2018, p. 508 (510).

countries (as elaborated below), this form of solidarity is not an option for the respective trade unions.

3.3.4.4.1 PRACTICAL EXAMPLE A classical example of inclusive solidarity comes from the International Transportworkers Federation (ITF), which has used industrial action in the form of boycott activity[86] by ITF-affiliated unions to support pay disputes for many years. There is a variety of possible scenarios. The most common scenario within which ITF affiliates resort to boycott action is the one where the ITF requests the owner of a ship sailing under a flag of convenience[87] to conclude an ITF-CBA. If the shipowner (or the operating company) fails to comply with this request, the competent ITF union will call for a boycott as soon as the ship makes for a port of which the dockworkers are organized in an ITF-affiliated union. The ITF's common practice in such situations is to call on the dockworkers to boycott loading and unloading operations for such a ship, in order to compel the shipowner to conclude an ITF-CBA. Another option would be to have the ITF-affiliated union of another country that is involved in a collective bargaining dispute and call on its foreign sister unions to initiate a boycott in support of its industrial action. Nevertheless, such action is not lawful in all member states and thus may be practised only in some countries.

3.3.4.4.2 LEGAL QUESTIONS Most constitutions of EU member states guarantee the right to strike or it is granted by either ordinary statutory law or by jurisdiction (s. a.). Solidarity strikes, however, are not always considered lawful. Only in some EU member states are solidarity strikes lawful if they support a lawful strike (Austria,[88] Bulgaria,[89] Cyprus,[90] Denmark,[91] Iceland,[92] Italy,[93] Malta,[94] Portugal,[95] Sweden[96]) or lawful even if the primary strike is unlawful (Belgium).[97]

In other legal orders solidarity strikes are only legally admissible if there's some sort of link to the main labour conflict, so that the employer may influence the

86 Such boycott activity of dockers may be characerized as solidarity action (strike); see Zimmer, 2018, p. 508 (510f.).
87 Concerning the FOC-campaign of the ITF, see www.itfseafarers.org/en/focs/about-the-foc-campaign (29.03.2022).
88 In Austria, solidariry strikes are not explictly regulated, and therefore considered lawful: Burger, 2014, p. 121 (126).
89 Warneck, 2007, p. 18.
90 Ibid., p. 21.
91 Ibid., p. 25.
92 Warneck, 2007, p. 38.
93 Pascucci, 2014, p. 331 (341).
94 Warneck, 2007, p. 50.
95 Warneck, 2007, p. 58.
96 Malmberg and Johansson, 2014, p. 525 (526).
97 Warneck, 2007, p. 17.

negotiations and thus the ending of the strike activity (Czech Republic,[98] France,[99] Greece,[100] Spain[101] and Slovakia[102]). Sometimes solidarity strikes are lawful in principle, although subject to specific rules (for example in Croatia,[103] Estonia,[104] Hungary,[105] Finland,[106] Ireland[107] and Romania[108]) or considered lawful only under specific (restricted) conditions, as is the case in Poland.[109] In other countries, like Slovenia, it is still disputed whether solidarity strikes are admissible.[110] Solidarity strikes are classified as illegal in Latvia, if the dispute does not concern a general agreement (sectoral-level CBA),[111] whereas in Lithuania,[112] Luxembourg[113] and the Netherlands,[114] solidarity strikes are considered unlawful.

Although the right to strike falls under national law and as is well known, Art. 153 (5) TFEU bans the EU of legal acts in this area, EU law still has an impact on national law. The CJEU has taken decisions in the 'famous' strike cases of Viking and Laval, where the right to strike was acknowledged as a fundamental right and balanced with the fundamental freedoms (with economic rights prevailing, as is well known).[115] Also Art. 28 EU-CFR guarantees the right 'to take collective action', and due to Art. 52(2) CFR, the rights of the Charter (which correspond to rights of the ECHR) have to be interpreted in line with those of the Convention. According to the explanatory notes on Art. 52 of the Charter, 'the level of protection afforded by the Charter may never be lower than that guaranteed by the ECHR'. The meaning and scope of the CFR therefore are also defined by the jurisprudence of the European Court of Human Rights (ECtHR),[116] which was confirmed by CJEU

[98] Section 16 (3) and 20 (e) Collective Bargaining Act; Hurka, The right to strike: Czech Republic, p. 169 (173); Waas, The right to strike, p. 50; Warneck p. 22.
[99] Kessler, 2014, p. 207 (224f.).
[100] Art. 19(1) of Law No. 1264/1982; Bakirtzi, 2014, p. 259 (276).
[101] Solidarity strikes are admissable, if the professional interests of the strikers are somehow effected: Guastavino, 2014, p. 509 (517).
[102] Warneck, 2007, p. 64.
[103] Warneck, 2007, p. 20.
[104] Art. 18(2), Collective Labour Dispute Resolution Act; Warneck, 2007, p. 26.
[105] Solidarity strikes are the only strikes that have to be organized by a trade union: Kajtár and Kun, 2014, p. 285 (294); Waas, 2014, p. 51.
[106] Lamminen, 2014, p. 193 (195).
[107] Kerr, 2014, p. 303 (310); Warneck, 2007, p. 40.
[108] Warneck, 2007, p. 60.
[109] Grzebyk, 2014, p. 427 (440f.)
[110] Končar, 2014, p. 467 (472f.); Waas, 2014, p. 51.
[111] Such sectoral agreements are rare; ETUI: www.etui.org/covid-social-impact/latvia/strikes-in-latvia-background-summary (30.03.2022).
[112] Petrylaitė, 2014, p. 369 (379); Warneck, 2007, p. 46.
[113] Warneck, 2007, p. 48.
[114] Houwerzijl and Roozendaal, 2014, p. 413 (422); Warneck, 2007, p. 50.
[115] CJEU, C-438/05 Viking (2007), ECR I-10779-10840; CJEU, C-341/05 Laval (2007), ECR I-11767-118904. The court was heavily criticized for the proportionality test of the decision.
[116] Zimmer, 2015, p. 194 (198).

decisions.[117] Art. 11(1) of the ECHR does not explicitly mention the right to strike, nevertheless the famous decision Demir & Baykara[118] marked a change in the interpretation of freedom of association of the Court and one year later the ECtHR also saw also the right to strike encompassed by Art. 11 (1) ECHR.[119] Limitations to this right are only admissible if there's a legal basis and interference is only justified if 'necessary in a democratic society in the interests of national security or public safety, for the prevention of disorder or crime, for the protection of health or morals or for the protection of the rights and freedoms of others' (Art. 11(2) ECHR). Although this test corresponds at first sight to the proportionality test used by the CJEU, the ECtHR makes use of a different standard of judicial review and interprets the right to strike much wider than the CJEU.[120] The ECtHR has reconfirmed with further decisions that the right to strike falls within Art. 11 of the ECHR[121] and in the RMT decision the court has generally acknowledged the right to take solidarity action as part of Art. 11 ECHR, as well.[122] In this case nevertheless, the ECtHR distinguished between direct strikes and so-called 'secondary' strike action, where it has acknowledged a wide margin of appreciation for the state and accepted the argument of the British government that excessive economic damage would result from legal secondary strike action. This formal distinction between direct strike activity of the trade union involved and indirect solidarity activities showed the limitations of the findings of the court, especially concerning solidarity strikes.[123]

As the right to strike is also guaranteed explicitly in Art. 6(4) of the European Social Charter (ESC), both in the 1961 version and in the revised ESC (of 1996), the findings of the European Committee of Social Rights[124] might also influence the interpretation of the right to strike in the member states, although it is disputed to what extend the findings of the committee have to be considered by national courts.[125] The right to strike under the ESC encompasses the right to strike in solidarity, as well.[126] Moreover, the Committee acknowledges the right to strike as fundamental and important and emphasizes, that 'the facilitation of free cross-border movement of services ... cannot be treated, from the point of view of the system of values, principles and fundamental rights embodied in the Charter, as having a greater a priori value than core labour rights, including the right to make use of

[117] See explanations of C-279/09 (DEB Deutsche Energie- und Beratungsgesellschaft, n 50), para. 35 and C-400/10 (PPU McB, n 36), para. 53.
[118] ECtHR 12.11.2008, no. 34503/97 (Demir and Baykara).
[119] ECtHR 21.04.2009, no. 68959/01 (Enerji Yapi Yol Sen).
[120] For further information, see Vogt et al., 2020, pp. 87ff.; Zimmer, 2015, p. 194 (199ff.).
[121] ECtHR 27.11.2014, no. 36701/09 (*Hrvatski liječnički sindikat/Croatia*), para. 49.
[122] ECtHR 8.4.2014, no. 31045/10 (*RMT/UK*), para. 77.
[123] Lörcher, 2014; Vogt et al., 2020, p. 194 (203f.).
[124] ECSR, Digest of the Case Law of the European Committee of Social Rights, 2018, Art. 6(4), pp. 101ff.
[125] Schlachter, 2019, para. 507ff.; Schubert, Arbeitsvölkerrecht, 2017, p. 98.
[126] Conclusions XX-3 (2014), United Kingdom.

collective action'.[127] Nevertheless, member states (of the Council of Europe) are not necessarily bound by Art. 6(4) ESC, as the Charter allows to choose six of nine articles of Part II (Art. 1, 5, 6, 7, 12, 13, 16, 19 and 20, see part III, Art. A, 2 (b) ESC). Moreover, the possibilities in the supervisory system of the ESC in case of violations are limited[128] and might be described as naming and shaming. But still the influence of the ESC should not be underestimated, as the German example shows. The change in German jurisdiction in 2007, with which solidarity strikes were (under certain conditions) acknowledged, was based upon Art. 6(4) ESC.[129]

3.3.5 *Elements of Direct Democracy in the Work of Trade Unions*

Direct democracy means that relevant decisions are taken by the people effected.[130] Although the basic structure of trade unions is based upon the idea of representative democracy,[131] several elements of direct democracy may be found as well in the practice of the organizations. Demands for collective bargaining rounds, for example, are elaborated and discussed in bargaining commissions, composed of delegates of the members. Even though guidelines for the claims of the organization are given by the board of the union, these are in most trade unions only general guidelines, supplemented by info-material of the collective bargaining departments. Central questions are defined by the members, or rather by their delegates, who also have to be consulted before the collective agreement is signed. Elements of direct democracy are thus mixed with those of representative democracy.

Although in most trade unions a strike has to be finally approved by the board, strike-balloting of the members is necessary before a strike can start, and as a rule 75 per cent of the members or more have to vote in favour. Moreover, the statutes of most trade unions provide for a second ballot, which has to be executed to receive an approval for the result of the negotiations by the members, and mostly about 75 per cent (or more) are as well necessary to reject the result.

3.4 (EUROPEAN) WORKS COUNCILS

3.4.1 *Solidarity in the Practice of (European) Works Councils*

Another actor that might practise solidarity in the working world is the European Works Council (EWC), and in a few countries works councils operate at the

[127] ECSR, Digest of the Case Law of the European Committee of Social Rights, 2018, Art. 6(4), p. 104.
[128] Schlachter, 2019, §6 Europarat, para. 507.
[129] BAG 19.6.2007 – 1 ABR 396/06, NZA 2007, 1055; Beer, 2019, §13, para. 47.
[130] See: BP, Das Politiklexikon: Direkte Demokratie, online: www.bpb.de/nachschlagen/lexika/politiklexikon/17361/direkte-demokratie (28.3.2022).
[131] In a representative democracy, the important decisions are taken by the parliament, which is elected by the people, see: BP, Das Politiklexikon: Repräsentative Demokratie, online: www.bpb.de/nachschlagen/lexika/politiklexikon/18137/repraesentative-demokratie (28.13.2022).

national level, as well. EWCs are Europe-wide bodies of workers' representation in a company or group of companies with delegates of workers representatives of each member state, sometimes even with further delegates from outside Europe.[132] As EWCs are set up for the purpose of information and consultation, their defined function is to receive information regarding central management (with further consultation). Some EWCs nevertheless have developed further and created trans-national structures for cooperation. It could be described as an act of inclusive solidarity when EWC delegates from the home country share their usually good resources, as well as their frequently preferential access to information, with representatives from other countries[133] or create network structures across Europe. Some EWCs have even developed into bodies that actively negotiate agreements about topics like non-discrimination, training, data protection or even restructuring (beyond the founding agreements)[134] and actively practise solidarity across Europe.[135] Haipeter and Banyuls examined the work of EWCs in the European subsidiaries of General Motors and concluded that solidarity practised throughout Europe would be comprised of refraining from activities, which would be useful for one plant, but could harm others. Representatives of other plants in turn behave in the same way and solidarity is created in some sort of negotiation process. Actors with whom central management wants to compete throughout Europe, by refraining to do so, finally promote their interests.[136]

In Germany and Austria the main body of workers' representation at the workplace level is the works council (WC). WCs are elected by the employees and formally independent of trade unions.[137] As WCs represent the whole workforce, which often will be composed of different kinds of workers, structurally elements of inclusive solidarity are part of their work. On the other hand, as research has shown, WCs rather represent the typical permanent (male) workforce,[138] with minorities or atypical, precarious workers rarely elected into the body. And what is more, the legal order does not provide WCs with the possibility to solve the main problems of fixed-term contracts or agency workers.[139] Elements of exclusive solidarity thus are structurally also part of the work of WCs, which might differ, based upon the concrete work of the workers' representatives.

[132] EWCs may be founded, if the company/group has at least 1,000 workers in one EU member state and a minimum of 150 workers in two members states.
[133] Platzer and Rüb, 1999, p. 393 (403); Zimmer, 2013, p. 312 (316).
[134] For further information see: Zimmer, 2013, p. 312 (317ff.).
[135] Zimmer, 2003, pp. 620ff.
[136] Haipeter and Banyuls, 2007, pp. 393f.
[137] Dribbusch and Birke, 2019, p. 6.
[138] Däubler, 2019, pp. 1601ff.
[139] Däubler, 2019, p. 1601 (1602ff.).

3.4.2 *Elements of Direct Democracy in the Work of (European) Works Councils*

In Germany, WCs are elected by the workforce every four years (§13.1 BetrVG) and represent the workforce of the company, which may rather be described as a form of representative democracy. Inquiries of the workforce are only voluntary and rarely practised, although 'good' works councils try to get to know the will of the workers and to integrate them into their work. In case of severe misconduct, one quarter of the workers are entitled to vote and may apply at the labour court for the dismissal of the WC, or of individual members (§23.1 BetrVG),[140] which could be seen as an element of action besides and before the next election. But this is rarely practised and hardly ever by the workforce, but rather by the employer or by the respective trade union. There are thus far fewer elements of direct democracy in the operating principle of German works councils. This counts even more for EWCs, as in most EU member states they are nominated by the workers' representatives and only in cases where there are no such representatives, the workforce is involved directly.[141]

3.5 CONCLUSION

As has been elaborated, inclusive as well as exclusive solidarity may be detected in the work of trade unions, EWCs and WCs and is partly characterized by their work. Therefore, the architecture of collective labour law, both in Europe as in Germany, contains solidarity as a central element of its structure. It has to be questioned whether this is reflected enough in current EU law interpretation.

REFERENCES

Bakirtzi, Effosyni, The right to strike: Greece, in: Waas, Bernd (ed.), *The right to strike: A comparative view*. Wolters Kluwer, 2014, pp. 259–283.

Bayertz, Kurt, *Solidarität: Begriff und Problem*. Suhrkamp Verlag, 1998.

Beer, Susanne, §13 Rezeption des Völkerrechts im Rahmen des nationalen Rechts, in: Schlachter, Heuschmid and Ulber, Daniel (eds), *Arbeitsvölkerrecht*. Mohr Siebeck, 2019.

Bertram, Hans, Differenzierung, Pluralisierung, Individualisierung und Netzwerke – Soziale Beziehungen, Solidarität und neue Zeitlichkeit, in: Mückenberger, Ulrich and Timpf, Siegfried (eds), *Zukünfte der europäischen Stadt. Ergebnisse einer Enquete zur Entwicklung und Gestaltung urbaner Zeiten*. VS Verlag für Sozialwissenschaften, 2007, pp. 215–231.

Bude, Heinz, *Solidarität. Zukunft einer großen Idee*. Hanser Verlag, 2019.

[140] This dismissal would be a dismissal of the function; the individual works contract of the person remains in force.

[141] Art. 5.2a directive 2009/38/EG leaves it to the member states to choose whether the delegates to the EWC are nominated or voted for by the workforce.

Bundeszentrale für politische Bildung (BP), Das Politiklexikon: Direkte Demokratie: www.bpb.de/nachschlagen/lexika/politiklexikon/17361/direkte-demokratie (28.3.2022).

Das Politiklexikon: Repräsentative Demokratie: www.bpb.de/nachschlagen/lexika/politiklexikon/18137/repraesentative-demokratie (28.3.2022).

Burger, Florian, The right to strike: Austria, in: Waas, Bernd (ed.), *The right to strike: A comparative view*. Wolters Kluwer, 2014, pp. 121–127.

Comte, Auguste, *Katechismus der positiven Religion*. Nach der 2. Ausgabe des Originals, 1891.

Däubler, Wolfgang, *Die Unternehmerfreiheit im Arbeitsrecht – eine unantastbare Größe?* Bund-Verlag, 2012.

Tarifverträge zur Unternehmenspolitik. *Rechtliche Zulässigkeit und faktische Bedeutung*. Bund-Verlag, 2016.

Der Betriebsrat – Sprecher auch der Randbelegschaften? *Neue Zeitschrift für Arbeitsrecht* (2019), pp. 1601–1606.

Doellgast, Virginia, Lillie, Nathan and Pulignano, Valeria, From dualization to solidarity: Halting the cycle of precarity, in: Doellgast, Virginia, Lillie, Nathan and Pulignano, Valeria (eds), *Reconstructing solidarity: Labour unions, precarious work, and the politics of institutional change in Europe*. Oxford University Press, 2018, pp. 1–41.

Dribbusch, Heiner and Birke, Peter, *Trade unions in Germany: Challenges in a time of transition*. Friedrich–Ebert–Stiftung, 2019.

Durazzi, Niccolo, Inclusive unions in a dualized labour market? The challenge of organizing labour market policy and social protection for labour market outsiders, *Social Policy & Administration*, 51 2 (2017), pp. 265–285.

Durkheim, Émile, *Über die Teilung der sozialen Arbeit. Studien über die Organisation höherer Gesellschaften*. Suhrkamp Verlag, 1988.

European Committe of Social Rights, Digest of the case law of the European Committee of Social Rights, 2019: https://rm.coe.int/digest-2018-parts-i-ii-iii-iv-en/1680939f80 (2.4.2022).

Fichter, Michael and Zeuner, Bodo, Zukunft der Gewerkschaften. Erkenntnisse aus einer Literaturstudie, *Forschungsjournal Neue Soziale Bewegungen* 15 (2002), pp. 13–28.

Grzebyk, Piotr, The right to strike: Poland, in: Waas, Bernd (ed.), *The right to strike: A comparative view*. Wolters Kluwer, 2014, pp. 427–449.

Guastavino, Nogueira, Magdalena, The right to strike: Spain, in: Waas, Bernd (ed.), *The right to strike: A comparative view*. Wolters Kluwer, 2014, pp. 509–524.

Haipeter, Thomas and Banyuls, Josep, Arbeit in der Defensive? Globalisierung und die Beziehungen zwischen Arbeit und Kapital in der Automobilindustrie, *Leviathan* 3 (2007), pp. 373–400.

Hoffmann, Jürgen, Jenseits des Mythos – Internationale Solidarität als Herausforderung der Gewerkschaftspolitik im Zeitalter der Globalisierung und Europäisierung, in: Beerhorst, Joachim, Demirovich, Alex and Guggemoos, Michael (eds), *Kritische Theorie im gesellschaftlichen Strukturwandel*. Suhrkamp Verlag, 2004, pp. 34–64.

Hondrich, Karl Otto and Koch-Arzberger, Claudia, *Solidarität in der modernen Gesellschaft*. Fischer Verlag, 1992.

Höpner, Martin, Ist Politik gegen Verbände möglich? 25 Jahre Mancur Olsons 'The Rise and Decline of Nations', *Leviathan* 35 (3), 2007, pp. 310–347.

Houwerzijl, Mijke and Roozendaal, Willemijn, The right to strike: The Netherlands, in: Waas, Bernd (ed.), *The right to strike: A comparative view*. Wolters Kluwer, 2014, pp. 413–426.

Hyman, Richard, Understanding European trade unionism. *Between market, class & society*. SAGE Publications, 2001.

Where does solidarity end? Eurozine 2002: www.eurozine.com/where-does-solidarity-end/?pdf (20.03.2022).

Kajtár, Edit and Kun, Attila, The right to strike: Hungary, in: Waas, Bernd (ed.), *The right to strike: A comparative view*. Wolters Kluwer, 2014, pp. 285–301.

Keller, Berndt, Berufsverbände, Tarifautonomie und das System der Interessenvertretung, *Leviathan* 3 (2008), S. 364–390.

Cooperation or conflict? Occupational trade unions in the German industrial relations system, WISO-Diskurs 22/2016, online: https://library.fes.de/pdf-files/wiso/12904.pdf (22.3.2022).

Kessler, Francis, The right to strike: France, in: Waas, Bernd (ed.), *The right to strike: A comparative view*. Wolters Kluwer, 2014, pp. 207–234.

Kerr, Anthony, The right to strike: Ireland, in: Waas, Bernd (ed.), *The right to strike: A comparative view*. Wolters Kluwer, 2014, pp. 303–315.

Klindworth, Harald and Schröder, Wiebke, *Der Begriff der Solidarität in der wissenschaftlichen Literatur von 1990 bis 2009 – Bedeutung, Wandel und Schlussfolgerungen hinsichtlich der sozialen Sicherungssysteme in der BRD*. Studie im Auftrag der Rosa–Luxemburg–Stiftung, 2010.

Kock, Klaus and Kutzner, Edelgard, Solidarität im Arbeitsalltag, *WSI-Mitteilungen* 73 5 (2020), pp. 327–334.

Končar, Polonca, The right to strike: Slovenia, in: Waas, Bernd (ed.), *The right to strike: A comparative view*. Wolters Kluwer, 2014, pp. 467–476.

Kurz-Scherf, Ingrid and Zeuner, Bodo, Politische Perspektiven der Gewerkschaften zwischen Opposition und Kooperation, *Gewerkschaftliche Monatshefte*, 52 3 (2001), pp. 147–160.

Lamminen, Johannes, The right to strike: Finland, in: Waas, Bernd (ed.), *The right to strike: A comparative view*. Wolters Kluwer, 2014, pp. 193–206.

Lange, Dietrich and Thiersch, Hans, Die Solidarität des sozialen Staates – Die Solidarität des reformierten Sozialstaates, in: Böllert, Karin et al. (eds), *Die Produktivität des Sozialen – den sozialen Staat aktivieren*, Springer, 2006, pp. 211–225.

Lessenich, Stephan, Reder, Michael and Süß, Dietmar, Solidaritat – national, europäisch, global? *WSI-Mitteilungen*, 73 5 (2020a), p. 318.

Zwischen sozialem Zusammenhalt und politischer Praxis: Die vielen Gesichter der Solidarität, *WSI-Mitteilungen*, 73 5 (2020b), pp. 319–326.

Liebknecht, Karl, Zu Trutz und Schutz (1871), in: Liebknecht, Karl (ed.), *Kleine politische Schriften*. Reclam Leipzig, 1976.

Lindemann, Kai, Solidarität ist das humanistische Fundament der Arbeitswelt, *WSI-Mitteilungen*, 73 5 (2020), pp. 374–377.

Linsenmaier, Wolfgang, Kommentierung GG Art. 9 (Vereinigungsfreiheit), in: Müller-Glöge, Rudi, Preis, Ulrich, Schmidt, Ingrid, Erfurter Kommentar zum Arbeitsrecht, 22. Auflage, 2022.

Lörcher, Klaus, Anmerkung zum EGMR (Urteil vom 8. April 2014 – RMT/Vereinigtes Königreich), Newsletter zum Europäischen Arbeitsrecht 2/2014, online: www.hugo-sinzheimer-institut.de/hsi-newsletter/europaeisches-arbeitsrecht/2014/newsletter-022014.html#c5724 (22.3.2022).

Lohmeyer, Nora, Schüßler, Elke and Helfen, Markus, Can solidarity be organized 'from below' in global supply chains? The case of ExChains, *Industrielle Beziehungen*, 4 (2018), pp. 400–424.

Ludwig, Carmen, *The politics of solidarity: Privatisation, precarious work and labour in South Africa*. Campus Verlag, 2019.

Malmberg, Jonas and Johansson, Caronline, The right to strike: Sweden, in: Waas, Bernd (ed.), *The right to strike: A comparative view*. Wolters Kluwer, 2014, pp. 525–536.

Mundlack, Guy, *Organizing matters: Two logics of trade union representation*. ILERA-publication series, Edgar Elgar, 2020a, online: www.ilo.org/wcmsp5/groups/public/—dgreports/—dcomm/—publ/documents/publication/wcms_741934.pdf (1.4.2022).

On Labour representativeness: The Hidden components of the right to freely associate in trade unions, unpublished paper (2020b).

Nagel, Thomas, The problem of global justice, *Philosophie & Public Affairs*, 33 2 (2005), pp. 113–147.

Platzer, Wolfgang and Rüb, Stefan, Europäische Betriebsräte: Genese, Formen und Dynamiken ihrer Entwicklung – Eine Typologie, *Industrielle Beziehungen*, 6 4 (1999), pp. 393–426.

Pascucci, Paolo, The right to strike: Italy, in: Waas, Bernd (ed.), *The right to strike: A comparative view*. Wolters Kluwer, 2014, pp. 331–350.

Petrylaité, Daiva, The right to strike: Lithuania, in: Waas, Bernd (ed.), *The right to strike: A comparative view*. Wolters Kluwer, 2014, pp. 369–385.

Pulignano, Valeria, Ortíz Gervasi, Luis and de Franceschi, Fabio, Union responses to precarious workers: Italy and Spain compared, *European Journal of Industrial Relations*, 22 1 (2016), pp. 39–55.

Schäfer, Armin, Nach dem permissiven Konsens. Das Demokratiedefizit der Europäischen Union, *Leviathan*, 3 (2006), pp. 305–376.

Sangiovanni, Andrea, Solidarity in the European Union, *Oxford Journal of Legal Studies*, 33 2 (2013), pp. 213–241.

Schlachter, Monika, Heuschmid, Johannes and Ulber, Daniel (eds), *Arbeitsvölkerrecht*. Mohr Siebeck, 2019.

Schlachter, Monika, §6 Europarat, in Schlachter, Heuschmid and Ulber, Daniel (eds), *Arbeitsvölkerrecht*, Mohr Siebeck Publisher, 2019.

Scholz, Rupert, GG Art. 9 (commentary), in: Herzog, Roman, Scholz, Rupert, Herdegen, Mathias and Klein, Hans H. (eds), *Maunz/Dürig, Grundgesetz-Kommentar*, 90th edition. Beck Verlag, 2020.

Schubert, Jens, *Arbeitsvölkerrecht*. Erich Schmidt, 2017.

Sciarra, Silvana, *Solidarity and conflict: European social law in crisis*. Cambridge University Press, 2018.

Smith, John, The globalisation of production and the challenges facing international solidarity (with special reference to Bangladesh), in: Pradella, Lucia and Marois, Thomas (eds), *Polarising development – Alternatives to neoliberalism and the crisis*. Pluto, 2014, pp. 51–61.

Steg, Joris, Die Coronakrise als Zäsur und Chance, *Blätter für deutsche und internationale Politik*, 6 (2020), S. 71–79.

Kollektive schaffen Sicherheit in unsicheren Zeiten, *Mitbestimmung*, 3 (2020), pp. 60–61.

Waas, Bernd (ed.), *The right to strike: A comparative view*. Wolters Kluwer, 2014.

Waas, Bernd, The right to strike: A comparative view, in: Waas, Bernd (ed.), *The right to strike: A comparative view*. Wolters Kluwer, 2014, pp. 3–76.

Warneck, Wiebcke, *Strike rules in the EU27 and beyond: A comparative overview*. ETUI-REHS, 2007.

Wersig, Maria, Künzel, Annegret and Berghahn, Sabine, Ehezentrierung statt staatsbürgerlicher Solidarität der Geschlechter – wohin führen die Reformen im deutschen System der Existenzsicherung?, in: Degener, Ursula and Rosenzweig, Beate, *Die Neuverhandlung sozialer Gerechtigkeit*. Feministische Analysen und Perspektiven, 2006, pp. 301–319.

Vogt, Jeffrey, Bellace, Janice, Compa, Lanc, Ewing, K. D., Lord Hendy, Q. C., Lörcher, Klaus and Novitz, Tonia, *The right to strike in international law*. Hart Publishing, 2020.
Wirth, Carsten, *Konkurrenzen und Solidaritäten. Festschrift für Anton Kobel zum 75*. Nomos Publishing, 2021.
Zeuner, Bodo, Widerspruch, Widerstand, Solidarität und Entgrenzung – neue und alte Probleme der deutschen Gewerkschaften, in: Beerhorst, Joachim, Demirovich, Alex and Guggemoos, Michael (eds), *Kritische Theorie im gesellschaftlichen Strukturwandel*. Suhrkamp Verlag, 2004, pp. 318–353.
Zimmer, Reingard, The right to take collective action: Prospects for change in European Court of Justice case law in light of European Court of Human Rights decisions, in: Blacket, Adelle and Trebilcock, Anne (eds), *Research handbook on transnational labour law*, Edgar Elgar, 2015, pp. 194–203.
Corporate responsibility in the 'Bangladesh Accord'. Which regulations are transferable to other supply chains? Expertise on behalf of the Friedrich–Ebert–Foundation, Dezember 2016, online: http://library.fes.de/pdf-files/id-moe/13072.pdf (13.4.2022).
Legitimization: Mandate and signatory parties – the trade union side, in: ETUC (ed.), *Building an enabling environment for voluntary and autonomous negotiations at transnational level between trade unions and multinational companies*. Final Report, Brussels, 2016, pp. 18–22.
Boykottbedingte Streikaktivitäten von HafenarbeiterInnen als zulässige Arbeitskampfmaßnahme?, *Arbeit und Recht*, 11 (2018), pp. 508–513.
From international framework agreements towards transnational collective bargaining?, in: *European yearbook of international economic law (EYIEL) 2019*. Springer, 2020, pp. 167–192.
European Works Councils as participants in Euro-wide collective agreements: Analysis from a German perspective, *European Labour Law Journal*, 4 4 (2013), pp. 312–327.
Europäische Solidarität. Beispiele positive Arbeit Europäischer Betriebsräte, *Arbeitsrecht im Betrieb*, 10 (2003), pp. 620–625.
Zoll, Rainer, *Was ist Solidarität heute?* Suhrkamp Verlag, 2000.

4

Solidarity

Different Issues in a Community Perspective

Gian Guido Balandi and Stefania Buoso

Solidarity means thinking and acting in terms of community.

—Pope Francis, *Fratelli tutti*, § 16

4.1 SOLIDARITY IN SOCIAL SECURITY, IN A GENERAL AND THEORETICAL PERSPECTIVE

If one considers the social scheme that grounds social security, the principle of equality is revealed to be its core goal. Market forces, even if unavoidable, create social inequalities, and social security tends to contrast these inequalities. Equality in law does not prevent de facto inequalities – generated by the market – and social security belongs to the programme of facilitating de facto equality. A task of the Republic – according to Art. 3.2 of the Italian Constitution – which is a permanent one, because this last condition cannot be attained once and for ever, but it's the issue of a continuous struggle (Balandi 2005; Rodotà 2014).

De facto equality is not an overall condition but it is related to some values, as individuated by Art. 3.2: 'full development of the human person and the effective participation [of all workers] in the political, economic and social organization of the country'. The translation in terms of social implementation means to guarantee equality as regards education – primary but also at the highest level – healthcare, mobility and communication and other essential services. A very important instrument in furtherance of de facto equality is also income protection, the large series of monetary benefits encompassed in the social security schemes.

Solidarity plays a central role in this struggle towards de facto equality, but there is no doubt that the word solidarity is polysemic, maybe one of the most polysemic in the social arena. This characteristic implies that it's necessary to choose one possible approach and relevant notion of solidarity. Our focus is on a specific area of social security, the one that entails direct circulation of economic resources. It may provide transfer of money or services, their cost being borne, entirely or partially, by others who are not the users of the services themselves.

There are examples of costs borne by a circle of people and services – or monetary benefits – enjoyed by a wider or smaller, or in any case different, circle of citizens. One of the clearest examples is offered by some measures financed by general taxation and provided for citizens with certain characteristics: allowances for non-sufficient people (needing care for ordinary life), who might or might not be taxpayers, according to the allowance being means-tested or not. Non-contributary means-tested social pensions are another example of the same kind. As regards mandatory contributory pensions, the difference between the two circles is based on a 'generation' difference: today's workers pay for current pensioners (who in their time payed for contemporary pensioners): this is the 'pay-as-you-go' system, 'solidarity between generations' (According to EU wording).

At the very end, this is a problem of circulation of resources and the identification of its mechanisms is nothing but the identification of solidarity and of its 'quantity' or 'measure' implied in each social security institution.

Let's therefore try to answer the question whether it is possible to measure solidarity; and which instruments are to be used for this purpose.

Elements qualifying solidarity in pension systems:

a. The public mandatory system: (1) fragmentation; (2) contribution and general taxation; (3) 'capitalization' and 'pay as you go' financing; (4) calculation of benefits based on contribution or on retribution.
b. The occupational system: see later discussing the s.c. corporate welfare.

Fragmentation: legal orders where the public mandatory pension system is fragmented in a plurality of – more or less large – groups of employees, according to their belonging to a branch, or a group of enterprises or any other criterium, are exposed to a corresponding fragmentation of solidarity. Each group tends to an egoistic view and to maintain its separation, considered – frequently wrongly – a source of privilege, the bureaucracy managing the relevant institutions being particularly involved in this egoistic view, of course. The same regards the different pension schemes for self-employed workers.

Contribution and general taxation: these different sources of resources identify different measures of solidarity: universalistic the latter, variable the former, according to the amplitude of the group involved.

'Capitalization' and 'pay as you go' financing system: the latter realizes the well-known – and oft-mentioned – solidarity between generations while the former, generally speaking, distinguishes systems organized on individualistic bases. As regards the 'solidarity between generations', one must note that, in any case, the real measure of solidarity depends again on the amplitude of the group of people involved.

Calculation of benefits based on contribution or on retribution: in principle it is not easy to appreciate the different measure of solidarity implied by the two different calculation methods depending mainly on the relevant rules. For example, ceilings to contribution and/or to benefits could play a significant role: the same holds for the period of reference for calculation, between the two possible extremes: the last month of retribution vs the entire working-life contribution.

The four elements qualifying solidarity in pension schemes are of growing difficulty as regards their combined appreciation; this means that a correct evaluation of the rate of solidarity of a given scheme implies a very detailed scrutiny (which should be of great importance for any political decision in this regard).

Elements qualifying solidarity in labour market weakness protection (mandatory measures):

Unemployment insurance; short time allowances; other unemployment allowances: (1) source of resources: bilateral contribution, employers' contribution, general taxation; (2) subjective dimension (area of protection).

Source of resources: bilateral contribution, employers' contribution, general taxation: the three mentioned sources identify three different levels of solidarity from the most restricted one – being involved in the bilateral contribution and the potentially interested beneficiaries – to the universalistic one of general taxation. One must say, as regards the bilateral contribution, that actually it is difficult – and probability incorrect – to distinguish this one from the sole employers' contribution, because in any case it is considered a part of labour cost.

The recent experience of the s.c. corporate welfare: the prevision in collective agreements – both at branch and plant level – of measures of welfare, a generic definition that may include many different kinds of benefits:

a. In services directly by the company for example, nurseries and other parental aids;
b. In services payed by the employer: student fees for children of employees; summer holidays for babies; gym subscription and so on;
c. Health insurance (generic or specific: dental surgery etc.);
d. Occupational pensions.

In principle – according to the declared purposes of social partners – these measures are in addition to public welfare provisions, but in the presence of substantive cuts in public expenditure – the harmful policy of 'austerity' – they tend to substitute for them, with an evident consequence on the extent of solidarity.

The vast majority of given examples show that a social security legal order encompasses different levels of solidarity when the circulation of resources measures it. From the maximum of a universalistic benefit payed by the general taxation to zero level of an individual insurance-based pension plan (even if partially payed by the employer).

Starting from this point we are able to discuss the different role of different actors: the state, and for it the law, in the form of Acts of Parliament; the social partners, and for them collective bargaining.

The dogmatic tradition individuates the qualifying characters of Acts of Parliament to be general and abstract. The qualities of that source of regulation relate it directly with the equalitarian function of solidarity. Of course, a specialized legislation may contradict this assumption, and we have a number of examples of this in every legal order, but generally speaking, it is only an Act of Parliament that can provide for universalistic measures. Therefore, a first achievement may be as follows: ensuring the role and responsibility of the state, through legislative activity, to promote and guarantee the egalitarian function of solidarity.

The social partners, and collective bargaining, may carry on a different task. A rich company could bargain to engage in welfare programmes, like the ones mentioned above, which in principle imply a transfer of resources – from shareholders to employees – that is, fragments of solidarity. But it is a particularistic one, aimed at socially redistributing part of the market gains of that employer. What is to be checked in order to exactly qualify the relevant solidarity is the relationship with the universalistic measures in which the same subjects are involved. If the adoption of corporate welfare measures are boosted by fiscal advantages for the company – which is the case in Italy – one must consider very carefully the general balance in the circulation of resources: the part really deriving from the earning of the company (the shareholder) and the part deriving from the general taxation through fiscal exemption. Even more clear is the question of the relationship between 'general and particular solidarity' when a particular corporate welfare provision is accompanied by a – partial or total – exemption from the corresponding public general one. This is a measure that seriously hinders the general level of solidarity – and consequently of tension towards equality – of a legal system.

4.2 TRANSNATIONAL SOLIDARITY AT THE STAKE

'Transnational' solidarity is one of the possible dimensions of interest in circulation of resources that involves EU citizenship, free movement and non-discrimination (O'Leary 2005; Costamagna, Giubboni 2021).

The case of the law of the Court of Justice can be useful to better define the boundaries of the reflexion and could be interesting to signal, in particular, the changes since the early decisions: from Martinez Sala to Brey, Dano and Alimanovic cases.[1] One can appreciate a shift in the Court of Justice case law, from

[1] Court of Justice 12 May 1998, C-85/96 Martinez Sala; Court of Justice 11 November 2014, C-333/13 Dano; Court of Justice 15 September 2015, C-67/14 Alimanovic.

a protection based on the rights conferred by primary law (in ex. Art. 21 TFUE)[2] to another based on secondary law and its limitations (dir. 2004/38/EC Art. 24.2). In Brey and Dano we can analyse the possible interference between Regulation 883/2004 – that promotes a coordination rather than a harmonization of the different national social security systems – and Directive 2004/38/EC on the right of citizens of the Union and their family members to move and reside freely within the territory of the member states.

EU social coordination law can be described as 'the sum of all primary and secondary legal provisions, rules and principles that aim to remove social security barriers, which could prevent an individual from exercising his/her rights to freedom of movement' (Pennings 2015, p. 6).

At the centre of the dispute there are social non-contributory benefits and the risk of so-called 'social tourism'. Whether in Brey the Court of Justice established that national authorities have to consider special features of the specific case, considering also proportionality principle (Verschueren 2015, p. 205), in Dano the state could exclude inactive citizens who have not sufficient resources. In other words, the member state has the possibility, pursuant Art. 7 Dir. 2004/38, 'of refusing to grant social benefits to economically inactive citizens who exercise their right to freedom of movement solely in order to obtain another Member State's social assistance although they do not have sufficient resources to claim a right of residence' (pt. 78); the inactive person cannot invoke the principle of non-discrimination in Art. 24.1 of the dir. 2004/38.

Articles 4 and 70 of the Regulation n.883/2004 and 24.1 of the directive are overcome, indeed, by Art. 24.2, which establishes a derogation to non-discrimination principle. Therefore, the directive becomes an instrument of defence against the risk of social tourism and, at the same time, the circulation of resources and the freedom of movement are limited: in the European Union of the crisis, the financial stability of welfare systems prevails on transnational solidarity.

In Alimanovic, we can observe a generalized exclusion of inactive citizens, going beyond the relevance of proportionality test found in Brey: national authorities can skip the individualized control of the economic situation of the applicant. Also in *Commission* vs *UK*, the Court of Justice argues that 'the need to protect the finances of the host member state justifies in principle the possibility of checking whether residence is lawful when a social benefit is granted in particular to persons from other member states who are not economically active, as such grant could have consequences for the overall level of assistance which may be accorded by the State' (pt. 80). Again, 'in specific cases, where there is a reasonable doubt as to whether a

[2] "Union citizenship is destined to be the fundamental status of nationals of the Member States, enabling those who find themselves in the same situation to enjoy the same treatment in law irrespective of their nationality, subject to such exceptions as are expressly provided for" pt. 31. See Court of Justice 20 September 2011, C-184/99, Grzelczyk.

Union citizen or his family members satisfy the conditions set out in those articles, member states may verify if those conditions are fulfilled. Article 14(2) provides that this verification is not to be carried out systematically' (pt. 82).

There is, also, a 'new' phenomenon that deserves attention: the expulsion of EU citizens from the countries in which they are established; in Belgium, statistics show only eight expulsions in 2008 and 2,712 in 2013, with a very large increase in a few years (Gottardi 2018, p. 634): this is a sign of a silent social crisis.

The European pillar of social rights could be a possible answer on the way to re-politicize the European deliberative process. The contents of social pillar – in twenty principles – could inspire future actions and initiatives at both the EU and member-state levels: 'it reaffirms some of the rights already present in the Union acquis' but also new principles in order to address the challenges arising from societal, technological and economic developments.

We can find traces of solidarity in Chapter III about 'Social protection and inclusion', though there are no specific provisions about the level of the regulatory intervention. At point 14, we can read, 'Everyone lacking sufficient resources has the right to adequate minimum income benefits ensuring a life in dignity at all stages of life, and effective access to enabling goods and services. For those who can work, minimum income benefits should be combined with incentives to (re)integrate into the labour market'; it qualifies minimum income as 'adequate' to ensure dignity at all stages of life: it is not conditioned.

The choice to deepen the specific issue of the access to social benefits – in this general reflection – is connected to the potential conflict between the free movement of citizens and the closure of member states' welfare systems: transnational solidarity in Europe represents an open question. We think the talking point reflects, on one hand, clearly the difficulties of the growth of social Europe construction; on the other hand, the strengthening of transnational social solidarity is one of the first steps to reconstruct a real, common European social policy. Pope Francis in *Fratelli tutti* says that 'solidarity means thinking and acting in terms of community'; in the actual European Union – in particular in the COVID-19 era – there is a strong need to recognize a real solidarity community in which the social needs of persons are on the front line.

4.3 GEOGRAPHIES OF SOLIDARITY IN THE ERA OF THE GIG ECONOMY

There is a section of the present world of labour that is particularly in need of solidarity: the s.c. platform jobs. The reason is that platform workers are denied the belonging to a community or a group, they are organized – their activity is organized – as individuals, although a very powerful organization exists, coordinating the activity of those individuals.

Generally speaking, the organization pretends to be self-employed workers – small entrepreneurs – and the platform to be a commercial agent operating only for the contact between clients and suppliers of service. Some judges all over Europe have recognized that the formal and substantial reality is quite different. In Italy, some collective agreements have been bargained and concluded regulating the 'urban delivery of goods operated by transport means usable without a driving licence', a complicated jargon meaning bicycles and small motorcycles: so the special section of the national collective agreement for transport and logistics devoted to the regulation of the s.c. 'riders' (18 July 2018). In this case, the riders are considered 'employees' in all respects, and enjoy all the social security measures of 'normal' workers. But this agreement has been signed by the employers' unions organizing the big companies of transport and logistics but not by the usual 'platforms', and therefore it has no relevance for the vast majority of riders.

In May 2018, the Municipality of Bologna promoted the adoption of a Charter of fundamental rights of digital work in an urban context (Carta dei diritti fondamentali del lavoro digitale nel contesto urbano) establishing some rules defined as 'minimal standard of protection' – so Art. 2 – including information about contractual clauses, reputational mechanisms, right to fair and dignified compensation, no discrimination, health and safety, privacy, freedom of union organization and the right to strike. To be noted, Art. 7 regulates the withdrawal from the contract by the platform, lawful only in case of just cause or notable breach of contract, while the withdrawal of the worker is not clearly regulated. The Charter is formulated according to the pattern of a European Charter – several followed by chapters and articles – but it has the nature of a local collective agreement signed by a local union of riders (Bologna Riders Union), the three main confederations, CGIL, CISL, UIL, and two food delivery platforms. The local authority is committed to widen the application of the Charter by the signature of other platforms.

In the last weeks of 2019, the legislator intervened on the issue by enacting a modification of legislative decree n.81 of 2015 introducing a Chapter V *bis* devoted to the *Protection of work organized by digital platforms*. Apart from a widespread discussion about alternative self-employment vs contract of employment, or rather the boundaries of that particular self-employment in which the rules of subordinate contract are applicable, some rules are clearly stated. The right to a contract and to all information about its terms and conditions; the right not to be discriminated; the right to a fair remuneration, the right to personal data protection according to European rules. Also, the application of the rules on health and safety at work is stated by the over-mentioned legislative decree. During the COVID-19 pandemic some tribunals cleared the right of delivery riders to the same protection as employed workers (e.g., full supply of personal protection equipment) and not the more limited one reserved for the self-employed. Finally – and so I attain the main focus of this note – they have the right to social insurance for accidents at work and professional diseases, on the same grounds as normal workers.

Further evolution of the matter can be illustrated as follows: the mentioned collective agreement has been integrated – November 2020 – by a protocol stating the application to self-employed workers in the delivery sector of some wage rules of employees. Assodelivery – an association of employers – and a minoritarian union signed a very disputed agreement providing some equipment to the riders but pretending to define in any case as non-subordinated the relationship. This is contrary to a principle in civil law. Very recently, in March 2021, Assodelivery signed with the main unions – CGIL, CISL, UIL – a protocol aimed at protecting the most important rights of riders, in the field of health and safety and in general in the organization of their activity. Two important enterprise-level agreements have been signed: one obliging the company to hire riders with employment contracts, with all the consequences in terms of implied rights; the other obliging particular fulfilments as regards health protection and stipulating a private integrative insurance for illness and accidents. Moreover, some judges have recognized the subordinate character of the employment relationship of platform workers in good delivery, contributing to a case law that is spreading in different tribunals all over the country.

This complex regulation illustrates the main point of our idea about social security – as one of the most important areas in the geography of solidarity – that it should be organized with reference to the recent forms of fragmented employment. The point is that it looks to be necessary to abandon what has been for more than a century the unitary instrument of organization of social protection: social insurance. Fragmentation of employment imposes the need to articulate the answer in relation to protection. The ideal reconstruction of a universalistic system of social safeguards may be tackled from several points of view. Here I begin choosing the safeguard of 'solidarity', of its dimension, its organization, its direction: who is in solidarity with whom.

a. Dimension of solidarity. The fluidity of society – as defined in recent studies – implies a mobility of individuals, in the sense of the near impossibility of belonging to the same social group for the majority of one's life. In this way the background of solidarity within a professional group, a branch of economy or whatever other partition of society, fails. It is to be noted that, beside the fluidity already mentioned, the upward social mobility has been frustrated in many western societies: poor mobility remains within poverty, while middle classes move downward. The growth of inequality is one of the outcomes of almost forty years of neo-liberalism. That characteristic widens the dimension of solidarity towards universalism: all the citizens are involved – should be involved – in the supply and redistribution of resources.
b. Organization of solidarity. Being not any longer possible to identify the belonging to a group as the main social characteristic of a citizen, for the purpose of intervening in case of need, equally, the organization of

solidarity cannot any longer be assigned to the mechanism of social insurance, which needs exactly the previous identification of the group involved. If the citizen is relieved not as a member of a certain group but as a citizen as such, it can't be but general taxation to provide for the relevant resources.

c. Direction of solidarity. If the recipient of solidarity is the citizen in need, the provider should be, for opposition, the citizen not in need. But here time comes into play as a fundamental component of the theoretical scheme. If the collection and the redistribution of resources is in the same moment, solidarity goes from citizens not in need to citizens in need. This is the sketch of the financial system called 'pay-as-you-go'. The alternative scheme, called 'capitalization', requires resources to be collected in a period of no-need to be redistributed when in-need. This system implies an individual recording of resources and in fact was used – and somewhere still is – for old-age pensions. In this case the solidarity moves along a 'time line' and involves a limited transfer of resources between groups of citizens. If old-age pensions are at stake, in the first hypothesis, solidarity is called inter-generational, because the young people collect the resources for the retired citizens.

Besides 'solidarity', another point of view is 'responsibility'. This can be called into question when the condition of need is the result of the action of an identifiable legal entity. This is typically the case of industrial accident and diseases. In these hypotheses, a social insurance scheme could still be the instrument of solidarity, this character being revealed by some features that one can't find in commercial insurance. And it is necessary to pay attention to this issue, because the solicitation, by market forces, to solve the problems of dangerous activities with private insurance has been – and still is – very strong. A 'social' insurance should guarantee, for example, full efficacy since the very first moment of employment and, regardless of the payment of contribution by the employer, full salary replacement rate and to be inspired by the relief of the need and not by commercial profitability.

A partially analogous consideration may be developed as regards some conditions of 'weakness' in the labour market: unemployment, short time working or cases of 'poor' employment. There may be cases in which the principle of 'responsibility' should operate together with one of 'solidarity': the first period of unemployment in case of unjustified dismissal (if the law provides for its legalization by the judge, as in Italy), or of economic or technological redundancy, should remain covered by some form of contribution by the employer. General solidarity could guarantee relief in a second moment, when unemployment may be considered grounded on conditions of the labour market.

Again, a hypothesis of joint 'solidarity' and 'responsibility' is the one of old-age or retirement pensions, but here the protected citizen itself should be partially responsible for the characteristics of her or his pension benefit. Solidarity should operate in two directions: in the inter-generational system of financing and in assuring a minimum level of benefit at a fixed age; individual responsibility should emerge in the value of the contributions paid during the working life – used as a base for calculation not capitalized, being in a pay-as-you-go system – and in the choice of the retirement age (within a fixed range).

On the ground of these articulations of 'solidarity' and 'responsibility' one could think to reorganize a system of social protection capable of encompassing many of the new forms of organization of labour and human activity.

In a society that maintains the centrality of 'labour' as a source of dignity and freedom for the individual and creation of utilities and wealth for the collectivity, the income guarantee should be very carefully organized in order to avoid, on one side, leading people into deprivation but, on the other, creating a sort of forced labour.

Once gone beyond this point, which is not under discussion here, and ascertained that human activity is going to be more and more organized in fragmented individualistic portions, that will lead every citizen to carry out more than one activity, also in different fields, implying the commitment in retraining and also life-long learning, in order to avoid an individualistic drift dismantling social protection, solidarity should remain the point of reference, abandoning the unitary scheme of the Fordist twentieth century and of insurance, and adapting to the new reality.

Summarizing what we have tried to argue in these pages, the main points to adapt a social protection based on solidarity in a society maintaining 'labour' at its centre, are as follows: universalism, general taxation as the main source of resources, coordination with responsibility of employers and of individuals.

4.4 A POST SCRIPTUM DURING THE S.C. SECOND PHASE OF THE COVID-19 PANDEMIC (AUTUMN 2020)

The tragedy of the epidemic that affected – and is still and will be affecting, till a complete diffusion of vaccines – the whole world has modified, or at least should have, the perception of solidarity and of its need.

The first field is obviously the one of public health organization. The virus is attacking everybody almost in the same way even if some social differences linked to housing conditions, public transport and general availability of hygienic resources (fresh water etc.) matter significantly. But this hasn't prevented the contamination of people belonging to middle and even high social classes, politicians included. Let's put it like this: the COVID-19 virus is a universalistic one. Therefore, the response must retain the same characteristics.

A universalistic public health system involves two issues. The first one is the subjective wideness of protection: every citizen, better every single human being, present in the given jurisdiction must be eligible for intervention, without any distinction regarding her or his occupational or insurance conditions.

The second is the factual organization of the service, which must be coherent with the aforementioned principle of generalized protection: services should be diffused in the territory and not concentrated in big – even if of high quality – centres.

Universalistic protection and territorial services are a materialization of solidarity, not only because taking care of someone's health is as such solidaristic, but also because to organize it as described implies a circulation of resources – via general taxation – from those who could afford private care in excellence centres to those who will be cured in decentralized institutions. Ultimately, universalism means equality of treatment: everybody has the same right to the same quality and quantity of medical care. We should never forget the famous statement attributed to distinguished reformer Richard Titmuss at the beginning of the last century: 'Services for the poor tend to be poor services.' This is the principle that has inspired the institution of several national health services, especially in Europe: the pandemic demonstrated its necessity beyond political opportunism, to guarantee the survival of entire communities.

The COVID-19 virus is somehow contradictory: while it is egalitarian in its infection potentiality – as underlined before – it is a powerful multiplier of inequalities. Here the reference is to its social and economic effects in contemporary societies. As is well known, and deeply studied from many points of view, the last decades have been characterized by a significant increase in inequalities, a direct by-product of neoliberal policies, generally widespread in the western world and in great part in the southern one, while in the post-communist countries, like Russia – or self-pretending still communist, like China – it's a sort of hard old-fashioned capitalism that favours inequalities.

There are short-term consequences of this pandemic but also – presumably – more long-term or structural ones.

The first consequences are a temporary stop of certain economic activities, finalized to contrast the diffusion of the virus. They generate the obvious differences between workers – and small entrepreneurs – of open and closed activities or activities connected or not to certain interdictions (e.g. to travel). Under these circumstances are to be implemented and strengthened all the instruments of protection of weakness in the labour market: unemployment benefits, short time working allowances and so on. But implement and strengthen means, on one hand, to provide more substantial financial resources and, on the other, to also modify some criteria of eligibility in order to allow people irregularly attached to the labour market to enjoy that protection. Actually, it is mainly the precarious workers – employed, self-employed and also small-trade and service entrepreneurs – who suffer the activity restrictions provoked by the pandemic. And this means widening the solidarity, both in economic – more resources devoted to social protection – and legal terms by modifying the conditions of admittance.

The second consequences – long-term or structural – are connected to the fact that the pandemic acted as an accelerator of certain processes already underway: the use of ICT in the organization of goods and services production is an example. The diffusion of so-called 'smart working' – remote working – for many office tasks involved tens of thousands of employees. Probably only a portion of them will go back to the company building at the end of the pandemic: the employees – some of them – will discover that working at home is more comfortable and time saving; employers – some of them – will discover that it is resource saving for permanent structures; urban areas will discover that it's saving in transport, pollution and so on. But all the services – food but also cleaning, delivery and so on – that have grown and developed around offices in cities will lose clients and working opportunities.

This change in urban organization will involve, in turn, modifications in the scope of solidarity, always toward a universalistic dimension. Small entrepreneurs, practitioners and every kind of self-employed worker facing income precarity will deserve general solidarity.

Let's put it like this: twenty years after the publication of Bauman's *Liquid Modernity* (Bauman 2000) one can affirm that the pandemic is providing a formidable contribution to make society more and more liquid. Therefore, in this post scriptum we can confirm and specify what had already been underlined in the first part of this paper. The stability of social roles that was typical of a certain period of capitalistic modernity – working-class, employed and self-employed middle-class, capitalistic entrepreneurs – could foresee a limited solidaristic circulation of resources aiming at maintaining a certain regularity of social life. The social insurances 'invented' by Bismarck were nothing but this: a tool to keep social peace (and to 'cut socialists "nails"'), and to guarantee the access to the goods market of a fraction of the working class. In today's societies social roles and economic positions are vulnerable and insurgence of 'need' is almost always and everywhere possible. Solidarity must therefore be endowed with legal tools different from the past, what above has been mentioned as 'organization' and 'direction' of solidarity.

To complete the points, one may stress that two issues are at the core of this new pattern: the sunset of the s.c. 'social risk' and the opportunity of using services as an alternative to income transfers. In the traditional social security scheme, the 'social risk' means the individuation of a typical social situation implying the insurgence of need: for example, the industrial accident of an employee. This mechanism exonerates the victim from demonstrating the need and the administration to ascertain it. Liquidity deprived of meaning the 'social risk' and individual need – or at the family level, an extremely sensitive theme – must be precisely verified: the return, but now as a positive instrument, of means tests one century and a half later!

To offer services to citizens in need is an especially important item in a redefined notion and practice of solidarity. When healthcare is at stake, the distinction is of great relevance: money transfer means the prevalence in the system of a private market-oriented offer of healthcare, with consequences in terms of inequality of access of poor and rich people. Solidarity and equal treatment march together in general, particularly in healthcare. In other fields of social protection too, a shift from income transfer to services may better qualify solidarity. In principle this diminishes the influence of the market, which is always a source of inequality and allows to control the efficacy of measures of protection.

The new pattern of social protection in the light of a universalistic solidarity that have been sketched suggests a final reflection of the theme of the relationship between solidarity and market. Generally speaking, are solidarity and market in contradiction? Yes and no. Yes, if one considers a basic definition: solidarity as circulation of resources according to need and availability (of resources); market as circulation of resources according to interests of actors. No, from the point of view of the coexistence in the same legal order of parts bound to a solidarity pattern – a sort of solidarity agreement of the whole citizenship – and other parts left to the free market. The first part corresponds to the protection of fundamental rights, among which are health, education, employment and minimum wage, old-age care: in a word, a dignified life. The market can operate elsewhere, politics finally being in charge of controlling it and not trespassing the boundaries of fundamental rights.

The new technologies – at the ground of the gig economy dealt with in the first pages of this paper – and the pandemic are upsetting the old world and advance a strong demand for new solidarity. They may cause all the damages of an increased inequality, but at the same time they may offer the opportunity to shape a new and more inclusive model. The deal is in the hands of politics.

4.5 A BIBLIOGRAPHIC NOTE

The greatest part of the reflections on solidarity in social security schemes is based on a wide series of studies; these studies have been recently summarized in some essays: Balandi (2017, 2018, 2020) and, in collaboration with the same co-author of this contribution, Balandi and Buoso (2017).

The social protection of platform workers emphasizes all the difficulties of the transition from the twentieth-century model of the welfare state to a new already undefined model: two important recent volumes deal with the issue also with a comparative approach: Daugareilh, Degryse and Pochet (2019), and Becker and Chesalina (2020).

The Sars-Cov 2 pandemic dramatized, in a worldwide scenario, the inequalities generated by the globalized neoliberal economy. Economic and social literature has widely treated the theme: several comparative contributions collected by the Association Française de Droit du Travail et de la Sécurité Sociale under the titles *Covid-19 et droit du travail* and *Quel avenir pour l'Etat Providence après la crise du Covid ?* can be found at www.afdt-asso.fr/covid19-et-etat.

REFERENCES

Balandi, Gian Guido. 2005. 'Sulla possibilità di misurare la solidarietà', in *Rechtsgeschichte*, pp. 14–30.

2017. 'Mercato del lavoro (tutele nel)', in *Enciclopedia del diritto, Appendice* X. Milano: Giuffré, pp. 519–535.

2018. 'L'eterna ghirlanda opaca: evoluzione e contraddizione del sistema italiano di sicurezza sociale', in A' *droit ouvert Mélanges en l' honneur d'Antoine Lyon-Caen*. Paris: Dalloz, pp. 87–101.

2020. 'Del diritto del lavoro e della sicurezza sociale, del metodo e della comparazione', in *I lavoratori e i cittadini. Dialogo sul diritto sociale*. Bologna: il Mulino, pp. 9–38.

Balandi, Gian Guido & Buoso Stefania. 2017. 'Sicurezza sociale' (I aggiornamento), in *Digesto commerciale* (online), pp. 1–9.

Bauman, Zygmunt. 2000. *Liquid Modernity*. Cambridge: Polity Press.

Becker, Ulrich & Chesalina, Olga, eds. 2021. *Social Law 4.0. New Approaches for Ensuring and Financing Social Security in the Digital Age*. U. Baden-Baden, Nomos.

Costamagna, Francesco & Giubboni, Stefano. 2021. Free movement of persons and transnational solidarity, in *Rivista di diritto della sicurezza sociale*, pp. 1–31.

Daugareilh, Isabelle, Degryse, Christophe & Pochet, Philippe, eds. 2019. *The Platform Economy and Social Law: Key Issues in Comparative Perspective*. Bruxelles: ETUI.

Gottardi, Donata. 2018. 'Le modificazioni del sistema delle fonti e l'impatto delle istituzioni Ue', in *Rivista Giuridica del Lavoro*, pp. 621–642.

O'Leary, Siofra. 2005. 'Solidarity and Citizenship Rights in the Charter of Fundamental Rights of the European Union', in Grainne de Burca, ed., *EU Law and the Welfare State*. Oxford: Oxford University Press, p. 62.

Pennings, Frans. 2015. *Research Handbook on European Social Security Law*. Cheltenham: Elgar Publishing.

Rodotà, Stefano. 2014. *Solidarietà. Un'utopia necessaria*. Roma: Laterza.

Verschueren. 2015. 'Libera circolazione o turismo sociale: l'eccessivo onere nel caso Brey', in *Rivista Giuridica del Lavoro*, pp. 205–239.

5

Solidarity, COVID-19 and a New Social Contract

K. D. Ewing

Europe is in a critical situation and we need *European solidarity* now more than ever. A new *Social Contract* must be put forward which offers hope. We must not return to the failed *austerity* and policies to drive wages downwards with a view to price competition as happened during the 2008 economic crisis. These policies created fertile ground for the *far-right*.

—E. Lynch[1]

5.1 INTRODUCTION

The above observations by the Deputy General Secretary of the ETUC were expressed in 2020 at the start of the COVID-19 pandemic, a third wave of which appears to be underway at the time of writing. The pandemic is perhaps the fifth great global challenge of the last 100 years, though the others – two world wars, and two economic catastrophes – were notably much greater in scale than COVID-19 has been so far. What is striking, however, has been the EU response, which has been very different – at least in tone – from the response to the Euro-crisis and the global financial crisis. Then the talk was of financial discipline and austerity, with one British newspaper hostile to Brexit reminding us recently of Wolfgang Schauble's refusal in 2008 to contemplate any unconditional support for member states in distress. On the contrary: 'the EU went no further than the provision of emergency loans and cheap credit. The bailout money came with painful strings attached, as countries were obliged to launch deeply resented austerity programmes in order to manage their growing debt mountain.'[2]

But as the same source pointed out, the new approach is not only different, but so different as to invite parallels with Alexander Hamilton's claim in 1790 following the

[1] Lynch 2020.

[2] *The Guardian*, 25 May 2020.

US War of Independence that the pooling of debt between states would strengthen their union.[3] Such talk may be premature and exaggerated, as may be talk of a 'Marshall Plan for Europe's recovery'.[4] But hyperbole aside, the initial approach of the EU institutions to COVID-19 is nevertheless remarkable, with Ursula von der Leyen celebrating the work of delivery drivers, factory packers and care-workers. These are people rarely on the radar in such elevated quarters, yet workers to whom we are now all indebted, and to whom even the mightiest amongst us feel obliged to pay tribute.[5] We have also seen the announcement of €750 billion to be made available as part of the EU Recovery Plan to help support jobs,[6] and steps to forge ahead with the social policy agenda laid out previously in the European Social Pillar, including proposals for a new minimum wage.

But is it enough? Here we return to the observations of Esther Lynch on behalf of the ETUC above, observations informed by the trade union experience of ten years or more of austerity, and by concerns about differences within the EU and between member states about the political reactions to the economic effects of COVID-19. In the first place, Lynch makes real the need for solidarity in response to the crisis; and second, she identifies the means by which it can be achieved. Spoiler alert. There is also, however, a third dimension: whether the EU has the means constitutionally to promote a Social Contract of the kind envisaged; and a fourth dimension: whether the EU is able to rise to the challenge politically. In this chapter, I address what I understand solidarity to mean in this context; what a proposed Social Contract would look like; what are the constitutional restraints that may help to define the permissible boundaries of any response; and how that response is being defined by the Social Pillar, which at this stage seems an inadequate basis for von der Leyen's grand vision.

5.2 SOLIDARITY

Solidarity (or *solidaridad*) is a word defined narrowly in English to mean 'unity or agreement of feeling or action, especially among individuals with a common interest; mutual support within a group', illustrated with the example of 'factory workers voiced solidarity with the striking students'. The word is said to have emerged in the nineteenth century from the French word 'solidaire', which has a wider usage than the English definition would suggest, being used to mean,

3 Alexander Hamilton to Robert Morris, 30 April 1781 (US National Archives, Washington, DC, available online).

4 U. von der Leyen, 'EU Co-ordinated Action to Combat the Coronavirus Pandemic and Its Consequences', speech to European Parliament, 16 September 2020.

5 Ibid.

6 See ETUC, 'MFF and Recovery Plan: ETUC Demands Reinforcement of Social Partners Involvement', 5 August 2020 (published correspondence suggesting that up to 60 million jobs throughout Europe may be at risk).

depending on the context, 'inclusive', 'supportive', 'united', 'connected to', as well as 'solidarity'. In the sense used in English, solidarity may present in several ways, but it is often associated with empathy, compassion and altruism.[7] It may be associated with a shared commitment by those taking the action, but also by a willingness to make a sacrifice on their part as well. In this sense solidarity is conveying a message: We support your cause, we understand your struggle, and we are prepared to suffer loss as a result.

A good example attracting publicity in recent years is the support given by Scottish engineering workers who refused to repair jet engines that were being used by the Pinochet regime in Chile against its own people. This was action to support others in distress, the beneficiaries completely unknown to those taking the action in question, the latter putting themselves at risk of dismissal as a result.[8] In this sense, although a collective effort by workers acting together, solidarity is likely to be voluntary and spontaneous. Nevertheless, solidarity moved by empathy, compassion and altruism may also be moved by encouragement and leadership and may be much less tangible as a result. A good example is an inspiring speech by Nicola Sturgeon, the First Minister of Scotland, who in addressing the Scottish nation at a critical point during the COVID-19 crisis, called upon the Scottish people in language rarely heard in modern political discourse to 'be strong, be kind and let's continue to act out of love and *solidarity*'.[9]

But as English usage suggests, solidarity may be based on ideas of reciprocity as well as altruism:[10] X offers support to Y in time of need, in the expectation that Y will return the support to X when he or she needs it. In this sense solidarity may tend towards being instrumental and transactional as well as reciprocal, rather than tending towards altruism. A sense of this is encountered in one of the very few British cases where the legitimacy of solidarity action by trade unions was recognized judicially. Thus, in the war-time decision in *Crofter Hand Woven Harris Tweed* v. *Veitch*,[11] the trade union was in dispute with independent producers of Harris Tweed, in the course of which the union asked dockers not to handle supplies to, or the finished product from, the independent producers. In rejecting the claim that

7 See Titmuss 1973. In his famous study of why people donate blood without payment (as is the case in some – though not all – countries, including the United Kingdom), Titmuss identified altruism as a dominant consideration of this great act of solidarity (1973: 101).

8 The story is told in the film, *Nae Pasaran* (director, Felip Bustos Sierra, 2018). For a brief account, see the Scottish Documentary Institute, *Nae Pasaran – Feature* (2018) (available online).

9 Nicola Sturgeon, Address to the Nation, 22 September 2020 (available on Scottish government website).

10 I am grateful to Guy Mundlak for this insight. See also Titmuss 1973: although altruism is a dominant consideration of blood donors, it is also acknowledged that for some 'there may be some expectation and assurance that a return gift may be needed and received at some future time' (1973: 101).

11 [1942] AC 435. See Brodie 2007. See also on judicial blessing for solidarity action, *Conway* v. *Wade* [1909] AC 606 (esp. per Lord Loreburn).

the union action was unlawful at common law, it was acknowledged by the court that by taking action of a kind that now has no legal protection in British law,[12]

> In the present case the pressure was applied by means of action by the dockers, who were in no sense employees in, or directly connected with, the trade in Harris tweed; but employees in this trade were members of the same union, and the interest of the dockers and the trade employees in the union and its welfare were mutual, and I can see no ground for holding that it was not legitimate for the union to avail itself of the services of its docker members to promote the interests of the union.[13]

In this context the conduct of the dockers – or some of them – may have been moved by altruism, though being directed by the union it is unlikely to have been spontaneous as was the case of the engineering workers supporting Pinochet's victims. Indeed, it is equally possible that the dockers were moved not only by a sense of reciprocity, but also by a sense of expectation, obligation or even coercion. There would be coercion if providing mutual support on the instruction of the union was – directly or indirectly – a condition of membership of the union. That coercion would be underpinned by law, in the sense that the duty to provide mutual support would be legally binding as a contractual obligation to the union, failure to comply with which could lead to the offender's discipline and expulsion. And where closed-shop arrangements operated,[14] that coercion would be reinforced by the ostracism by co-workers, and the risk of dismissal by an employer if a worker lost his or her union membership. For some, that would be an industrial death sentence.

What are the implications of this for the state? The foregoing would suggest that if solidarity is a principled basis for public policy, then the state at least has a negative duty to refrain from any regulatory or other activity that would undermine solidarity as a principle. In the case of labour law, this would mean avoiding steps taken to restrict trade union freedom and the capacity of trade unions to engage in solidarity activities. But it also suggests a positive role for the state, in terms of a duty to encourage, facilitate and promote solidarity activities, whether by (i) voluntary institutions such as trade unions and employers' associations or (ii) the state acting through its institutions as an agent independent of workers, citizens, trade unions and civil society organizations. Solidarity as an instrument of public policy promoted by the state – in fields such as healthcare or social insurance – is likely to be based on reciprocity rather than altruism. Perhaps requiring a sharing of financial resources, it is also likely to be obligatory rather than voluntary, and indeed coercive in terms of sanctions for failure to comply with solidarity obligations.

12 See *RMT* v. *United Kingdom* [2014] ECHR 366.

13 [1942] AC 435, p. 460 (Lord Thankerton).

14 At that time there would be closed-shop practices in operation by means of which workers would be required to be in membership of the union as a condition of employment, either formally or informally. See McCarthy 1964.

As we have seen, Ursula von der Leyen invoked the spirit of the Marshall Plan as part of her vision for a post-COVID-19 world. Only a few months earlier, Kristalina Georgieva, Managing Director of the IMF, spoke of the need for a Great Reset (notably not a Great Reversal) to deal with the consequences globally of COVID-19.[15] Addressing the need to focus on 'the social fabric of our societies' and 'the expansion of social programs so we take care of the most vulnerable people', so that in turn 'we can have a world that is better for everyone',[16] Georgieva invoked the memory of another iconic text of post-war Europe, albeit one that that was forged in the heat of war. This was Sir William Beveridge's eponymous report in 1942,[17] which is said to have been one of the foundations of the modern European welfare state.[18] Along with his work on *Full Employment in a Free Society*,[19] Beveridge's work has been described as 'the most authoritative historical starting points for the welfare state', it being noted also that

> The Western-European Welfare state can be seen as an organized system of solidarity, historically grown from group solidarity among workers, later between workers and employers, moving towards solidarity between larger social groups: between healthy people and the sick, between the young and the elderly, between the employed and the unemployed.[20]

The seventieth anniversary of the Beveridge Report led to many tributes, recognising what was at the 'high-water mark of British solidarity', and the epitome of 'social solidarity'.[21] Invoking the solidarity of Beveridge in the midst of the COVID-19 pandemic is remarkable, not only because 'the conditions of society which informed Beveridge's conclusions have fundamentally altered',[22] but also because Beveridge – a liberal, not a socialist, though a liberal with a strong commitment to a strong state – had views on free enterprise that would not endear him to the IMF.[23] So far as his famous report is concerned, however, Beveridge proposed that there should be 'substituted for all the anomalies and inadequacies of the existing arrangements, which had grown up in a haphazard way to meet ad hoc needs, a unified "pooling of risks", which, being firmly based on insurance, removed all taint of poor law or means test and yet ensured adequate support in times of need'.[24]

15 Georgieva 2020.
16 Ibid.
17 Sir William Beveridge, Social Insurance and Allied Services, Cmnd 6404, 1942.
18 Schuyt 1998.
19 Beveridge 1943.
20 Schuyt 1998: 297.
21 Fabian Society 2012.
22 Rethinking Poverty 2014.
23 Beveridge 1943: 'private control of the means of production, with the right to employ others at a wage in using those means, whatever may be said for or against it on other grounds, cannot be described as an essential liberty' (p. 49).
24 Bruce 1972: 306.

But while it may be true that 'the solidarity that underpinned the post-war settlement has been eroded',[25] solidarity has nevertheless evolved from being (i) a principle of altruistic or mutual support between workers, and subsequently (ii) a principle of public policy informing government programmes, to what is now (iii) a constitutional principle. That principle is to be found in the TEU, where it is referred to on fifteen occasions in the treaty and its protocols, the term being used in multiple different ways to express a foundational value of the EU, solidarity between people and generations, and solidarity between member states. The principle also finds expression in the EU Charter of Fundamental Rights, with a chapter on solidarity consisting of twelve separate articles of varying degrees of precision. But although haphazard, wide-ranging and opaque, *it is nevertheless crucial that in both the TFEUTEU and the EUCFR we can find solidarity as a constitutional principle to mean both the negative and positive obligations of the 'state' and its constituent parts*, to the significance of which we return.

5.3 SOLIDARITY AND THE SOCIAL CONTRACT

Before dealing with solidarity as a constitutional principle, it is necessary first to address the Social Contract that Esther Lynch and others have identified as a means for its development and delivery. Here we find that the ETUC and its leading officials are not alone in using the language of the Social Contract as a basis for resetting global, European and national political economies.[26] At this point, however, the term Social Contract invites two preliminary comments. The first is that the term is not used quite as it was by Rousseau in 1762, though modern authors of the term claim nevertheless to draw inspiration from Hobbes, Locke and Rawls as well as Rousseau to inform their own understanding about 'the basis of state authority over citizens'.[27] Thus, according to the ILO Global Commission on the Future of Work: 'Individuals agree to certain limits on their inalienable freedoms in exchange for protection of their rights and satisfaction of the interests of society.'[28]

The second point is that although the appeal to a new Social Contract has been used as a basis for responding to COVID-19, it is an idea advanced in recent times pre-pandemic in response to the earlier crisis of globalization and austerity. Thus the ILO Global Commission on the Future of Work starts with the claim that there is a need 'on the part of governments as well as employers' and workers' organizations' to 'reinvigorate the Social Contract that gives working people a just share of economic progress, respect for their rights and protection against risk in return for their

[25] Rethinking Poverty 2014.

[26] See also Rodgers 2021 for a thoughtful and more rigorous analysis of some of the issues explored in the pages that follow.

[27] ILO Global Commission on the Future of Work 2019: n. 13.

[28] Ibid. The agreement is presumed; no one is asked.

continuing contribution to the economy'.[29] Notably, the Commission claims that to be successful, 'such efforts demand solidarity among people, generations, countries and international organizations'.[30] Located very firmly in the values and aspirations of the ILO Constitution,[31] and offering significant 'resistance' to prevailing orthodoxy,[32] the Commission proposed a Universal Labour Guarantee, expanding time sovereignty, and revitalizing collective representation.[33]

It is commonplace that the Commission's recommendations failed to cut through, and that the ILO Centenary Declaration failed to reflect the Commission's ambitions. On the contrary, the ILO Declaration is a paean to globalization and economic liberalism, reflecting the triumph of the values of the latter over the social democratic values of the Declaration of Philadelphia, which it remains necessary to revisit.[34] Nevertheless, by locating its proposals for a radical reset in the idea of 'Social Contract', the ILO Global Commission on the Future of Work was not alone. Lynch's proposals for a new Social Contract appear as a response to growing concerns about the rise of the far-right, and illiberal democracy. It is a plea for a social democratic turn to counteract the populist movements now appearing throughout Europe. While – like the ILO Global Commission on the Future of Work's proposals – Lynch's demands are given added poignancy by the COVID-19 crisis, it is an idea articulated in the ETUC's Vienna Manifesto, published on 28 May 2019.[35] This was four months after the ILO Global Commission on the Future of Work published its report, and almost a year before the COVID-19 crisis began to seriously to emerge.

Like the ILO Global Commission on the Future of Work's proposals, however, the ETUC Manifesto of 28 May 2019 has proved to be very prescient. It is also very measured, and carefully set in the context of the TEU, Art. 3, which refers to the EU's commitment to a 'social market', a commitment which notably has also been acknowledged by von der Leyen. According to the ETUC,

> What is needed is a renewed Social Contract for Europe setting out the relationship between three different groups in society: the state, labour and capital. Institutions have to take responsibility for reinforcing the social market economy. Companies

[29] Ibid., p. 10.
[30] Ibid., p. 54.
[31] Ibid., p. 39.
[32] Novitz 2020.
[33] Ibid., pp. 37–42.
[34] See Ewing 2019.
[35] ETUC 2019–2023. For a different more broadly based EU-wide manifesto, see Countouris and Freedland 2013, epilogue by the editors. Note the especially powerful observation that 'Europe must find again the path to economic growth and the respect of fundamental rights, but it must also rediscover new and old ways to redistribute more equally the wealth that it is still capable of creating and – no less importantly – the wealth that is embedded in what remains one of the most prosperous regions of the world' (p. 495). This has never been more urgent.

should not be able to profit from the single market and at the same time undermine it by exploiting labour or avoiding paying taxes and social contributions.[36]

In responding to this 'need', the ETUC Manifesto contains proposals for macro-economic change, constitutional reform, economic governance reform, as well as 'rebuilding the European social model, by reinforcing and implementing the principles of the European Pillar of Social Rights through policies, legislation, social regulation, collective agreements and sound measures for redistribution and upward convergence'.[37]

The re-emergence of a Social Contract in these ways perhaps has two dimensions especially relevant in the context of solidarity. The first relates to Rousseau's point not addressed in either of the foregoing texts (the ILO Global Report or the ETUC Manifesto), which reminds us that the Social Contract is rooted in equality. This is his plea for 'a large measure of equality in social rank and fortune, without which equality in rights and authority will not last long'.[38] The second dimension takes us back to the duty of the state proposed above, 'to encourage, facilitate and promote solidarity activities, whether by (i) voluntary institutions such as trade unions and employers' associations or (ii) the state acting through its institutions as an agent independent of workers, citizens, trade unions and civil society organisations'. Both of these dimensions are captured by the ILO Declaration of Philadelphia and by the ILO Global Commission on the Future of Work (though not the ILO Centenary Declaration), but most famously by the Declaration of Philadelphia.

Indeed, particularly notable about the Declaration of Philadelphia are two core provisions in the Bill of Social Rights in Part III,[39] which play to each of these duties of the state. These are first the solemn obligation to promote 'the effective recognition of the right of collective bargaining, the cooperation of management and labour in the continuous improvement of productive efficiency, and the collaboration of workers and employers in the preparation and application of social and economic measures' (which plays to the first duty of the state). The second is a solemn obligation to promote 'policies in regard to wages and earnings, hours and other conditions of work calculated to ensure a just share of the fruits of progress to all, and a minimum living wage to all employed and in need of such protection' (which plays to the second duty of the state). It is a striking feature of the ETUC Manifesto in contrast that it is very light in terms of the second dimension, heavily dominated by demands/proposals for 'state' support for trade union autonomy.[40]

36 Ibid., p. 2.

37 Ibid., p. 3 (Manifesto, para. 4).

38 Rousseau 1976: 113.

39 See Supiot 2012. On the idea of a Bill of Social Rights, see also Gurvitch 1946.

40 It is striking for example that the only substantive as opposed to procedural claims are those relating to equality and the protection of precarious workers. Both might be seen as relating to inclusivity and effectiveness of labour law, rather than the improvement of standards. It may be

By trade union autonomy what is meant for this purpose is trade union engagement in social dialogue, economic governance and collective bargaining; in other words rebuilding what Ruth Dukes has characterized as *The Labour Constitution*.[41] This relates to what Julia López López has referred to as the role of the ETUC as 'an actor in the regulation of labour rights'.[42] The key word here is 'regulation', which points to the trade union role in participating at multiple levels in determining with governments and employers the rules governing working conditions. That regulatory role is the apotheosis of trade unionism,[43] though it is a role that has been displaced in some jurisdictions by economic liberalism, with trade unions performing increasingly a role as service and representative organizations. The ETUC Manifesto nevertheless places emphasis on the role of trade unions rather than the state as a key element in developing the Social Contract as an instrument of solidarity, justified by the need for better trade union integration if their equalizing potential is to be fully realized.

What does this tell us about and how does it relate to Rousseau's underpinning vision for 'a large measure of equality in social rank and fortune', as a precondition of 'equality in rights and authority'? Notably, Rousseau was writing in a pre-democratic era, and suspicious of representative government, as well as 'special interests'. He makes no reference as to how that 'equality in social rank and fortune' is to be secured, whether (i) directly by the state, (ii) by autonomous processes encouraged by the state, or (iii) by a combination of both. But returning to the ILO Global Commission's vision of the Social Contract as 'the basis of the legitimacy of state authority over citizens', whereby 'individuals agree to certain limits on their inalienable freedoms in exchange for protection of their rights and satisfaction of the interests of society',[44] the implicit focus on the state to some extent misses the point, which in contrast is plainly visible in the ILO Constitution itself.[45] As the ETUC Manifesto reminds us, the Social Contract is not only about ends, but just as importantly about means, and the democratization of both the economic and the political spheres.

5.4 SOLIDARITY AND THE SOCIAL CONSTITUTION

The ETUC Manifesto and the case for it reinforced by COVID-19 raises questions about the capacity of the EU to respond, and in particular the capacity of the EU

of course that the support for the Social Pillar meets the demand for better substantive standards (pay and dismissal) to be delivered by the 'state'.

41 Dukes 2014.

42 López López 2013: 354.

43 See the discussion in Ewing 2005.

44 ILO Global Commission on the Future of Work 2019: n. 13.

45 And indeed is recognized elsewhere by clear implication in the ILO Global Commission's Report: 'The Constitution of the ILO remains the most ambitious Social Contract in history' (2019: 23, immediately before cue 13). See also ITUC 2019.

Constitution to respond, in a way that would bring the solidarity principle to life. The starting point for this purpose, however, is the TEU which sets out in Art. 2 the founding values of the EU as being values 'common to the Member States in a society in which pluralism, non-discrimination, tolerance, justice, *solidarity* and equality between women and men prevail' (emphasis added). Thereafter, Art. 3 not only provides for a single market but also includes a commitment to 'work for the sustainable development of Europe based on balanced economic growth and price stability, a highly competitive *social market economy*, aiming at full employment and *social progress*'.

So far so good, though it is not clear in this context what solidarity means. Nor is it clear what the social market economy means, though it is notable that it was referenced by Ursula von der Leyen as 'unique', enabling the EU to respond effectively to the COVID-19 crisis.[46] As pointed out above, however, the term solidarity is used multiple times in the TEU, but in different contexts to mean different things:

- Solidarity as a founding value of the EU (TEU, Art. 2);
- Solidarity between generations (TEU, Art. 3);
- Solidarity among member states (TEU, Arts 3, 24, 31, 32);
- Solidarity of member states with the EU (TEU, Art. 24);
- Solidarity among peoples worldwide (TEU, Art. 3); and
- Solidarity in external relations (TEU, Art. 21).

What is striking by its omission from this list is the absence of any social or economic solidarity with or between workers, apart from the oblique and opaque references in TEU Arts 2 and 3. Rather, the focus is principally on the solidarity obligations of member states towards each other and to the EU, with solidarity between workers to be found in the CFR EU, an altogether different conception in an altogether different kind of text.

Solidarity as deployed in the TEU paradoxically has been *wholly destructive* of any notion of a Social Contract of the kind proposed particularly in the ETUC Manifesto. This is to be seen most vividly of course during the eurozone crisis and the solidarity of the European Commission with the workers and citizens of Greece.[47] In a speech in 2012 rooted in TEU, Art. 2, Herman van Rompuy (then President of the European Council) referred to the eurozone crisis as 'the very first real test of solidarity in the history of the Union'.[48] In the same speech, however, van Rompuy gave examples of the benefits of European solidarity, which included labour market efficiencies 'already showing in lower labour costs' in Spain and

[46] Von der Leyen 2020.
[47] See ILO 2011.
[48] Rompuy 2012.

Portugal.[49] This is a theme he had developed on a number of occasions to explain the support for Greece in particular,[50] which revealed the tensions in our understanding of solidarity, and the conflict of solidarity interests. Solidarity *between* states is not necessarily synonymous with solidarity between – or with – workers and citizens *in* states.

That said and as already pointed out, the obligations of EU solidarity are being deployed in a radically different way during the COVID-19 crisis, in a way designed to preserve and protect rather than to degrade and destroy, as we saw in so many countries with MOUs and Country-Specific Recommendations.[51] This difference in approach is to be seen in von der Leyen's State of the Union Address:

> When I took office, I vowed to create an instrument to protect workers and businesses from external shocks. Because I knew from my experience as a Minister for Labour and Social Affairs that these schemes work. They keep people in jobs, skills in companies and SMEs in business. These SMEs are the motor of our economy and will be the engine of our recovery. This is why the Commission created the SURE programme. And I want to thank this House for working on it in record time. If Europe has so far avoided mass unemployment seen elsewhere, it is thanks in large part to the fact that around 40 million people applied for short-time work schemes. This speed and unity of purpose means that 16 countries will soon receive almost 90 billion euros from SURE to support workers and companies. From Lithuania to Spain, it will give peace of mind to families who need that income to put food on the table or to pay the rent. And it will help protect millions of jobs, incomes and companies right across our Union.[52]

As von der Leyen says, 'this is real European solidarity in action'. But although a very different kind of solidarity from the solidarity of van Rompuy and although very welcome, it is nevertheless a limited and particular form of solidarity: it is episodic, operating at a governmental level, which is 'state' driven and controlled. It is not using state power to encourage or promote the solidarity institutions of civil society.

This is not the solidarity or the Social Contract sought by the ETUC. Herein lies one problem. The EU Social Constitution is ill-equipped to deliver the type of Social Contract sought by the ETUC Manifesto, to the extent that the latter is based on trade union integration into the structures of political and corporate governance. As the ETUC has suggested, the case for such integration is reinforced by COVID-19, which has led the ETUC's Deputy General Secretary to propose that collective bargaining should be the cornerstone of rescue and recovery plans, highlighting a

[49] Ibid.

[50] BBC News, 24 May 2012: 'We want Greece to remain in the Euro area while respecting its commitments', he told a news conference. 'The eurozone has shown considerable solidarity having already disbursed, together with the IMF [International Monetary Fund] nearly 150bn euros [£120bn; $188bn] in support of Greece since 2010.'

[51] See Bogg and Ewing 2019.

[52] Von der Leyen 2020.

comprehensive list of ways by which this could be done.[53] But how can it be done under existing constitutional arrangements? And how can it be done when the proposal is to respect the right to organize for collective bargaining,[54] as well as ensuring that 'necessary institutions are in place to support collective bargaining, in particular sectoral collective bargaining and cross-sectoral bargaining, along with resources and legal backing especially protecting workers and their unions'?[55]

In assessing the deliverability of a Social Contract in which the EU encourages autonomous activity rather than takes responsibility itself, it is important to distinguish between measures (such as the TFEU, Title X) based on solidarity, which help to construct a Social Contract, from measures based on solidarity (such as CFR EU, Chapter IV) that help to protect solidarity measures in place, however constructed. But therein lies the real heart of the problem, in the sense that the TFEU, Title X (the Social Policy Title) falls a long way short of the expectations set by the Community Charter of the Fundamental Social Rights of Workers in 1989, which an earlier European Commission president (Jacques Delors) had falsely promised British trade unionists (then suffering from Mrs Thatcher's onslaught) would guarantee that every worker would be covered by a collective agreement.[56] The reality has been a patchwork Social Europe with limited means constitutionally to contemplate a Social Contract of the kind proposed by the ETUC.

Apart from the limited legislative powers to advance social solidarity in the form of a Social Contract, a related concern is the contradictory orientations tailored into the EU constitutional texts. Writing in 2012 at the time of the austerity programmes in response to the financial crisis, Julia López López observed the contradiction between the social rights agenda of the EU on the one hand, and the economic policies pursued by the EU in response to the financial crisis in 2008 on the other.[57] That contradiction reflects a number of constitutional contradictions that we see played out in litigation (most famously in *Viking* and *Laval*, though elsewhere as well),[58] but also in the TEU and TFEU themselves. So, while the TEU, Art. 3(3) refers to a 'social market economy', the TFEU, Title VIII (Economic and Monetary Policy) refers to an 'open market economy with free competition', which sounds very different, suggesting an ideological tension at the heart of the EU project

[53] Lynch 2020. For an outstanding analysis of the extent of the problem from a legal perspective with comprehensive proposals of how to respond, see Novitz 2020.

[54] Including a right of access to the employer's premises.

[55] Lynch 2020: 4.

[56] Delors 1998, where he referred to 'three proposals, which were designed to clearly show the social dimension of the European construction'. They included a 'platform of guaranteed social rights, containing general principles, such as every worker's right to be covered by a collective agreement'. Since 1988 collective bargaining has collapsed in the United Kingdom. People remember the failure to keep false promises.

[57] López López 2013.

[58] See Case C-426/11, *Alemo-Herron* v. *Parkwood Leisure Ltd*, 18 July 2013.

tailored into constitutional arrangements, which hitherto has seen the subordination of social rights.

The foregoing tension between the social-market and open-market orientations of the European constitutional order is revealed in the outputs of the European Semester, which at least for the best part of a decade operated in a way that was extremely hostile to the idea of a progressive Social Contract and the underlying principle of solidarity.[59] As Silvana Sciarra noted in 2014, 'the European Semester does not interact in a constructive way with Social Dialogue and in some cases puts severe limits to it',[60] while others have documented how the European Semester was instrumental in stripping out collective bargaining systems operating in member states, by requiring the decentralization of collective bargaining arrangements and the deregulation of employment conditions. With its hitherto economically liberal and open-market focus, it is difficult not to be sceptical of current constitutional arrangements as a basis for rebuilding a model in the destruction of which they have played such a conspicuous part. But in view of the constitutional constraints referred to above, there may be no other option.[61]

5.5 SOLIDARITY AND THE SOCIAL PILLAR

So, if the ambition is to build solidarity through a Social Contract moulded by a constitution of limited and contradictory formal powers, how is to be done? The answer from the Commission pre-pandemic is by implementing the European Social Pillar, which has been hailed by Sacha Garben (writing on leave from the European Commission) as

> a high-profile political reaffirmation of a broad set of social rights and principles, which in line with the Rome Declaration could be taken as an indication that in the future post-Brexit EU27, there may be a stronger commitment to EU social policy. The Pillar's implementation envisages the deployment of the full array of EU governance instruments: regulations and directives, recommendations and communications, the creation of new institutions, funding actions, and country-specific recommendations. As such, the static imagery evoked by the notion of a 'pillar' arguably does not capture the true nature and potential of the initiative, which is dynamic and fluid, wide-ranging, and permeating.[62]

59 See Bogg and Ewing 2019. But with brilliant insight, Nicola Countouris may have found a way to unravel the constitutional problems by 'accommodation' of different constitutional objectives rather than the perpetual dominance of one ideological vision: Countouris 2020.

60 Sciarra 2014.

61 Quite apart from the outcomes of the European process, there are serious concerns about the process and its compatibility with the rule of law (on which, see TEU, Art. 2). The latter is a principle designed not only to protect judicial independence (I am thinking here about concerns with Hungary and Poland), but also with wider questions about the nature of a legal system (Lord Bingham 2007; Bingham 2011).

62 Garben 2019.

Yet although Professor Garben also claims that 'an equation of the Pillar with the core set of twenty social rights and principles it proclaims similarly fails to capture its true legal and political significance, which lies mainly in its programmatic nature',[63] it is nevertheless surprising that the ETUC Manifesto should propose as one of its flagship initiatives 'Rebuilding the European social model, by reinforcing and implementing the principles of the European Pillar of Social Rights through policies, legislation, social regulation, collective agreements and sound measures for redistribution and upward convergence.' Despite the applause from Professor Garben and others, the Social Pillar is a regressive measure, a pale shadow of the Community Charter of the Fundamental Social Rights of Workers published in 1989, which began expressly by acknowledging the inspiration of the ILO and the Council of Europe's Social Charter, and includes clear commitments to freedom of association and the right to bargain collectively, two preconditions of solidarity institutions.[64] The Social Pillar in contrast pitches the commitment as an afterthought in this way:

> The European Pillar of Social Rights shall not prevent Member States or their social partners from establishing more ambitious social standards. In particular, nothing in the European Pillar of Social Rights shall be interpreted as restricting or adversely affecting rights and principles as recognised, in their respective fields of application, by Union law or international law and by international agreements to which the Union or all the Member States are party, including the European Social Charter signed at Turin on 18 October 1961 and the relevant Conventions and Recommendations of the International Labour Organization.[65]

And what was previously a '*right* to negotiate collective agreements under the conditions laid down by national legislation and practice'[66] is now diluted so that the social partners 'shall be *encouraged* to negotiate and conclude collective agreements in matters relevant to them, while respecting their autonomy and the right to collective action'.[67] The 1989 Charter in contrast did not simply seek to 'respect' the right to collective action but purported to embed the *right*.

It is true nevertheless that the Social Pillar has produced already an important Directive on Transparent and Predictable Working Conditions,[68] and that there are now serious proposals for an instrument on the minimum wage. The latter seems designed to implement the ambiguous commitment in the Social Pillar which provides that

[63] Ibid.
[64] Bercusson 1990.
[65] European Social Pillar, Preamble, para. 16.
[66] Community Charter of the Fundamental Social Rights of Workers, para. 12.
[67] European Social Pillar, Preamble, para. 8(a).
[68] Directive (EU) 2019/1152 of the European Parliament and of the Council of 20 June 2019 on Transparent and Predictable Working Conditions in the European Union.

> Workers have the right to fair wages that provide for a decent standard of living. Adequate minimum wages shall be ensured, in a way that provide for the satisfaction of the needs of the worker and his/her family in the light of national economic and social conditions, whilst safeguarding access to employment and incentives to seek work. In-work poverty shall be prevented.[69]

This is ambiguous in the sense that while there is a 'right' to a decent standard of living, only an 'adequate minimum' will be ensured, a distinction reflected in proposals from the Commission at the time of writing for a Directive on adequate minimum wages that fails to guarantee a standard consistent with the European 'decency' threshold.

As it stands, the commitment to minimum wages reinforce the regressive nature of the Social Pillar: an 'adequate minimum' based on the satisfaction of need is an early twentieth-century standard, and as such a significant departure from the ILO Declaration of Philadelphia, which refers to a 'just share of the fruits of progress' (which I assume is more than a subsistence wage); the Council of Europe's Social Charter, which refers to remuneration that will guarantee a 'decent standard of living'; and the Community Charter of the Fundamental Social Rights of Workers of 1989, which requires all employment to be 'fairly remunerated', to which end workers are to be guaranteed an 'equitable wage', defined in turn to mean 'a wage sufficient to *enable* them to have a decent standard of living'. At their best, current proposals from the Commission for a Directive on adequate minimum wages refer to an 'adequate wage' that is 'guided by criteria set to promote adequacy with the *aim* to achieve decent working and living conditions'.[70]

There is, however, a more serious concern about the minimum wage proposal based on the Social Pillar, and the potential adverse effect 'on the six member states which set wages exclusively through collective bargaining – Austria, Cyprus, Denmark, Finland, Italy and Sweden'.[71] Ursula von der Leyen was required to address this latter concern directly in the Swedish press, where she wrote that 'The Commission will never request Sweden to introduce a statutory minimum wage', and that 'Instead, we want to strengthen collective agreements in countries that have a lot left to do, and we want to do it without disturbing well-functioning systems, such as that in Sweden.'[72] This is curious in light of the steps that had recently been taken by the Commission to require or encourage the dismantling of collective bargaining systems by means of either MOUs or Country-Specific

69 European Social Pillar, para. 6.

70 Proposal for a Directive of the European Parliament and of the Council on adequate minimum wages in the European Union, COM (2020) 682 final, Art. 5(1).

71 Von der Leyen 2020.

72 ETUC 2020.

Recommendations.[73] Nevertheless, the commitment was repeated in von der Leyen's State of the Union Address where she said that

> Dumping wages destroys the dignity of work, penalises the entrepreneur who pays decent wages and distorts fair competition in the Single Market. This is why the Commission will put forward a legal proposal to support Member States to set up a framework for minimum wages. Everyone must have access to minimum wages either through collective agreements or through statutory minimum wages. I am a strong advocate of collective bargaining and the proposal will fully respect national competencies and traditions. We have seen in many Member States how a well-negotiated minimum wage secures jobs and creates fairness – both for workers and for the companies who really value them. Minimum wages work – and it is time that work paid.[74]

So far as von der Leyen's assurances are concerned, it is true that they were welcomed by the ETUC as providing 'much needed clarity about her plans'.[75] It is also true that at the time of writing we now have a proposal for a Directive on adequate minimum wages. It is a matter of some concern, nevertheless, that although there are proposals to promote collective bargaining, the Draft Directive otherwise expresses no preference for collective bargaining over legislation for setting wages, Article 1(2) providing that member states may choose whether to 'set statutory minimum wages or promote access to minimum wage protection provided by collective agreements'. Surprisingly, those countries that have adopted the latter will not be required to 'make the collective agreements universally applicable'.[76] In line with von der Leyen's assurances, however, the proposed Directive by Article 1(3) makes clear that it is not to be construed as requiring a statutory minimum wage to be introduced in those handful of countries 'where wage setting is ensured exclusively via collective agreements'.

Nevertheless, the provisions designed to promote collective bargaining are otherwise consistent with the weak commitment in the Social Pillar, whereby member states 'shall be *encouraged* to negotiate and conclude collective agreements in matters relevant to them, while respecting their autonomy and the right to collective action'.[77] Hugging very closely to this text, the proposed Directive includes obligations to 'promote', 'encourage' and in extreme cases (which would have included

[73] In the case of Greece, it was said famously by the ILO Committee of Experts to have had 'a severely detrimental impact upon the entire foundation of collective bargaining in the country': ILO Committee of Experts, Right to Organise and Collective Bargaining Convention, 1949 (No. 98) – Greece, Observation, Adopted 2012, Published 102nd ILC (2013).

[74] Von der Leyen 2020.

[75] ETUC 2020.

[76] Proposal for a Directive of the European Parliament and of the Council on adequate minimum wages in the European Union, Art. 1(3).

[77] European Social Pillar, Preamble, para. 8(a).

the UK) 'provide for a framework of enabling conditions'.[78] There are no methods prescribed, no rights created and no obvious means of effective enforcement, other than through the Semester process. At best this seems likely to maintain the status quo whereby a small number of states have a preference for collective bargaining over legislation for the regulation of wages, while others continue to rely on an inadequate statutory model that so far has led to a situation in which 'national statutory minimum wages are lower than 60% of the gross median wage and/or 50% of the gross average wage in almost all Member States'.[79]

So while there are doubts about the proposed Directive's commitment to collective bargaining, there are also doubts about the commitment to a statutory minimum wage.[80] Intervention is conveniently constrained by treaty restrictions,[81] with the result that it is proposed member states will be required by Art. 5(1) as already pointed out simply to take 'the necessary measures to ensure that the setting and updating of statutory minimum wages are guided by criteria set to promote adequacy with the aim to achieve decent working and living conditions, social cohesion and upward convergence'.[82] Writing in 1913, Lenin condemned a statutory minimum wage for one million or so British coal miners as 'a mere deception of the workers',[83] having written a few months earlier that it 'cannot bring about any appreciable improvement in their conditions'.[84] It is not necessary to be a disciple of Lenin to understand that little has happened since to redeem the strategy,[85] confidence in

[78] Proposal for a Directive of the European Parliament and of the Council on adequate minimum wages in the European Union, Art. 4.

[79] Ibid., Explanatory Memorandum.

[80] This is despite claims that adoption and implementation of the Directive will lead to a pay increase for 24 million workers: ETUC, '24m could get pay rise under EU directive', 18 February 2021 (available online).

[81] See TFEU, Art. 153. See further, European Commission, Second Phase Consultation of Social Partners under Article 154 TFEU on a Possible Action Addressing the Challenges Related to Fair Minimum Wages, COM (2020) 3570 final, pp. 16–17. The Commission acknowledges that the EU could not 'take away the freedom of Member States and social partners to set the level of minimum wages' (p. 17).

[82] See Muller and Schulten 2020. As the authors point out, although the minimum decency threshold of 60 per cent of the gross median wage and 50 per cent of the gross average wage is referenced in Art. 5(3) as a factor to be taken into account in setting the minimum wage at national level, it is not included 'as a binding criterion'.

[83] Lenin 1970a: 233.

[84] Lenin 1970b: 229. See generally Arnot 1953 on the Coal Mines (Minimum Wage) Act 1912.

[85] See European Commission, Recommendation for a Council Recommendation on the 2020 National Reform Programme of the United Kingdom, COM(2020) 528 final: 'Real wage growth has also remained slow. Many parts of the United Kingdom are relatively poor with comparatively low levels of investment in skills and infrastructure. Limited career progression prospects for people in low-wage jobs negatively affect both productivity and poverty. This condition is set to continue and may even be exacerbated in the light of the Covid-19 crisis' (para. 20). The United Kingdom has had a statutory national minimum wage since the National Minimum Wage Act 1998.

which is likely to be diminished still further by a weak Commission proposal that appears to add nothing of substance to existing practice.[86]

5.6 CONCLUSION

The concern in this chapter has been to examine the 'principle' of solidarity in the context of 'state' action. The role of the state in promoting solidarity is twofold: first to support and encourage solidarity through autonomous institutions (trade unions) and processes (collective bargaining, collective action and Social Dialogue); and second to initiate its own solidarity measures and programmes. The concern has also been to examine that 'principle' in the context of proposals for renewing the 'Social Contract', highlighting different conceptions of the Social Contract, but focusing mainly on that proposed by the ETUC. It is argued, however, that there are both constitutional and institutional problems in relation to EU support for a Social Contract of this kind, these problems relating to an over-rigid constitution and a weak political programme, both of which predate COVID-19, and both of which seem ill-equipped to meet the challenges presented by the pandemic.

The EU constitution is perhaps one of the most economically liberal constitutions in the developed world, consolidated with wretched bad timing on the eve of the global financial crisis, in a period of uncontained confidence in globalization. But as a deeply ideological constitution (despite impressive social democratic values laid out in TEU, Arts 2 and 3) it is also rigid, cumbersome and inflexible, difficult to engage at speed.[87] The weak political programme is the European Social Pillar, which defines institutional policy until 2023 regardless of what gets in the way between its conception in 2016 and its designated delivery date. True, COVID-19 has added urgency to implementation of its twenty principles, which are the consequence of the damage caused by austerity rather than the challenges presented by COVID-19. True too, the final version of the Social Pillar is a marked improvement on the original version which was a hymn to the commodification of labour and the worship of labour markets.[88] But it still falls a long way short of the war-time responses invoked recently from improbable quarters as an indication of the challenges that lie ahead.[89]

[86] See European Commission, Recommendation for a Council Recommendation on the 2019 National Reform Programme of Italy and delivering a Council Opinion on the 2019 Stability Programme of Italy, COM(2019) 512 final, para. 18.

[87] For a less pessimistic view of constitutional possibilities, see Countouris 2020. See also Vergis 2020.

[88] See Bogg and Ewing 2019.

[89] I am thinking here of Kristalina Georgieva (IMF) and Ursula von der Leyen (European Commission), referred to above. Even Boris Johnson in the United Kingdom has been heard to say that 'In the depths of the Second World War, in 1942, when just about everything had gone wrong, the government sketched out a vision of the postwar new Jerusalem that they

The Social Pillar certainly falls a long way short of the ETUC's Social Charter, and of what is perhaps the most significant war-time response with which policy-makers are yet to engage, namely the Bill of Social Rights in Part III of the Declaration of Philadelphia. But for all that, there are nevertheless signs of optimism, with Silvana Sciarra rightly applauding what she sees as 'pathways to new solidarities'. These include the EU's job support programmes (delivered at speed it ought to be said), and the synergies that COVID-19 has created between the EU and member states for renewed social dialogue.[90] It is notable nevertheless that at the time of writing, the EU solidarity interventions – most notably the SURE programme referenced by von der Leyen in her State of the Union Address – are designed mainly to maintain rather than change the status quo, however impressive and welcome they may be. It thus remains to be seen whether such optimism in the face of the pandemic is justified, or whether because of legal constraints and multiple political failures, COVID-19 takes us closer to a world in which solidarity has an altogether more sinister meaning.[91]

REFERENCES

Arnot, P. R., *The Miners: Years of Struggle*. George Allen & Unwin, 1953.

Bercusson, B., 'The European Community's Charter of Fundamental Social Rights of Workers' (1990) 53 *Modern Law Review* 624.

Beveridge, Sir William, Social Insurance and Allied Services, Cmnd 6404, 1942.

Beveridge, W. H., *The Pillars of Security*. George Allen & Unwin Ltd, 1943.

Bingham, T., 'The Rule of Law' (2007) 66 *Cambridge Law Journal* 67.

The Rule of Law. Penguin Books, 2011.

Bogg, A. and Ewing, K. D., 'Tale of Two Documents: The Eclipse of the Social Democratic Constitution', in E. Nanopoulos and F. Vergis (eds), *The Crisis behind the Eurocrisis*. Cambridge University Press, 2019.

Brodie, D., 'The Scottish Case: Crofter Hand Woven Harris Tweed v Veitch', in K. D Ewing, J. Hendy and C. Jones (eds), *The Right to Strike: From the Trade Disputes Act 1906 to the Trade Union Freedom Bill 2006*. Institute of Employment Rights, 2007.

Bruce, M. *The Coming of the Welfare State*. Batsford, 1972 reprint.

Delors, J., '1992: The Social Dimension': Address by President Delors at the TUC – Bournemouth, 8 September 1998.

Countouris, N., 'The Narrowing Constitution: European Constitutionalisms, the Social Market Economy, and the Principle of Accommodation', in A. Bogg, J. Rowbottom and A. Young (eds), *The Constitution of Social Democracy*. Hart Publishing, 2020, ch 19.

wanted to build.' Less plausible is his claim 'that is what we are doing now – in the teeth of this pandemic' (*The Guardian*, 6 October 2020).

90 Sciarra 2020. Sciarra also welcomes the minimum wage initiative as 'a remarkable step, because it revived social dialogue' on 'a very sensitive theme'. The British experience has been different, with trade unions having minimal impact after a period of successful engagement with government at the beginning of the COVID-19 pandemic. See Ewing and Hendy 2020.

91 Mosley 1934; Schmitt 2001 (first published 1926). See esp. the second edition of the latter.

Countouris, N. and Freedland, M. (eds), *Re-socialising Europe in a Time of Crisis*. Cambridge University Press, 2013.

Dukes, R., *The Labour Constitution*. Oxford University Press, 2014.

ETUC, *Manifesto 2019–2023* (available online).

'MFF and Recovery Plan: ETUC Demands Reinforcement of Social Partners Involvement', 5 August 2020.

'ETUC Welcomes von der Leyen Vow to Protect Collective Bargaining', *Press Release*, 14 September 2020.

European Commission, Recommendation for a Council Recommendation on the 2019 National Reform Programme of Italy and delivering a Council Opinion on the 2019 Stability Programme of Italy, COM(2019) 512 final.

Recommendation for a Council Recommendation on the 2020 National Reform Programme of the United Kingdom, COM(2020) 528 final.

Ewing, K. D., 'The Function of Trade Unions' (2005) 34 *Industrial Law Journal* 1.

'Reflections on the ILO Centenary', in C. Kelly, J.-C. Tham and J. Sempill (eds), *Papers from the Symposium on the Centenary of the ILO: Democracy, Labour Law and Trade Unions*. 2019.

Ewing, K. D. and Lord Hendy QC, 'Covid-19 and the Failure of Labour Law' (2020) 49 *Industrial Law Journal* 497.

Fabian Society, *Beveridge at 70*, 1 December 2012 (available online).

Garben, S., 'The European Pillar of Social Rights: An Assessment of its Meaning and Significance' (2019) 21 *Cambridge Yearbook of European Legal Studies* 101.

Georgieva, K., 'The Great Reset', Remarks to World Economic Forum, 3 June 2020 (available online).

Gurvitch, G., *The Social Bill of Rights*. International Universities Press, 1946.

ILO Global Commission on the Future of Work, *Work for a Brighter Future*. ILO, 2019.

ILO, *Report of the High Level Mission to Greece*. Athens, 19–23 September 2011. ILO, 2011.

ITUC, 'ITUC takes demand for a New Social Contract to the UN General Assembly', 11 April 2019 (available online).

Lenin, V. I., 'The British Labour Movement in 1912', *Pravda*, 1 January 1913, reprinted in V. I. Lenin, *On Trade Unions: A Collection of Articles and Speeches*. Progress Publishers, 1970a.

'On Britain', *Pravda*, 12 August 1912, reprinted in Lenin, *On Trade Unions: A Collection of Articles and Speeches*. Progress Publishers, 1970b.

Leyen, U. von der, 'EU Co-ordinated Action to Combat the Coronavirus Pandemic and its Consequences', *Speech to European Parliament*, 16 September 2020.

López López, J., 'Solidarity and the Re-socialisation of Risk: Analysing ETUC Strategies to Face the Crisis', in N. Countouris and M. Freedland (eds), *Re-socialising Europe in a Time of Crisis*. Cambridge University Press, 2013.

Lynch, E., 'A New Social Contract to Resist the Rise of the Far-Right' (2020) 1/2 *International Union Rights* 3.

McCarthy, W. E. J., *The Closed Shop in Britain*. Basil Blackwell, 1964.

Mosley, O., *The Greater Britain*. British Union of Fascists, 1934.

Muller, T. and Schulten, T., 'The European minimum wage will come – but how?' Social Europe, 15 September 2020 (available online).

Novitz, T., 'Past and Future Work at the International Labour Organization: Labour as a Fictitious Commodity, Countermovement and Sustainability' (2020) 17 *International Organisations Law Review* 10.

'The Perils of Collective Begging: The Case for Reforming Collective Labour Law Globally and Locally Too' (2020) 44 *New Zealand Journal of Employment Relations* 3.

Rethinking Poverty, *Beveridge at 70*, 18 March 2014 (available online).

Rodgers, L., 'The ILO, Social Contracts and the Human-Centred Approach to Work' (2021) 32 *King's Law Journal* 207.

Rompuy, H. van, A *Test of Solidarity* (Speech at the Ambrosetti Forum, 8 September 2012).

Rousseau, J.-J, *The Social Contract*. M. Cranston tr. Penguin Books, 1976 ed.

Schmitt, C., *The Crisis of Parliamentary Democracy*. MIT Press, 2001 printing, 2nd ed., first published 1926.

Schuyt, K., 'The Sharing of Risks and the Risks of Sharing: Solidarity and Social Justice in the Welfare State (1998) 1(3) *Ethical Theory and Moral Practice* 297.

Sciarra, S., 'European Social Policy in the Covid-19 Crisis', IACL-IADC Blog, 14 May 2020 (available online).

'Social Law in the Wake of the Crisis', *WP CSDLE 'Massimo D'Antona'* Int-108/2014.

Scottish Documentary Institute, *Nae Pasaran – Feature* (2018) (available online).

Supiot, A., *The Spirit of Philadelphia: Social Justice vs the Total Market*. Verso, 2012.

Sturgeon, N., Address to the Nation, 22 September 2020 (available on Scottish government website).

Titmuss, R. M., *The Gift Relationship: From Human Blood to Social Policy*. Penguin Books, 1973.

Vergis, F., *Collective Labour Rights as an Element of the Substantive Constitutionalisation of EU Law after the Treaty of Lisbon*. PhD thesis, University of Cambridge, 2020.

6

Solidarity in the City

Scott L. Cummings

6.1 OVERVIEW

This chapter explores the concept of solidarity in the city – its sources, meaning, and function in relation to worker movements challenging the rise of inequality in urban spaces resulting from decades of neoliberal policy.[1] The contribution is built upon an empirical study of legal mobilization to redesign labor law in Los Angeles – and thus examines solidarity from a US perspective. The study analyzes local government as a labor battleground, which necessarily depends on understanding the city itself as a site of solidarity – not just among workers but among broader progressive movements, which come together around campaigns to reshape low-wage work, while also promoting related goals like immigrant inclusion, affordable housing, and environmental justice. As such, the project is fundamentally about labor law's relation to power in a multi-level system and how to build decentralized forms of solidarity in a political context where there is an absence of opportunity for moving labor policy at the national level. Building decentralized solidarity in the city, as this chapter suggests, requires conceptualizing solidarity along two dimensions: *external solidarity across movements*, that is, solidarity *between* labor and allied movements like immigrant rights and environmental justice; and *internal solidarity within the labor movement itself*, specifically *among* workers fighting for better lives. The relationship, and tension, between these conceptions is the focus of this chapter. It begins by introducing the idea of local solidarity as a response to political challenges to labor law. It then traces the origins of neoliberalism and community–labor solidarity in Los Angeles, using the city as a case study of the opportunities for and constraints on solidarity projects. After providing a summary of

[1] This chapter is adapted from *An Equal Place: Lawyers in the Struggle for Los Angeles* (New York: Oxford University Press, 2021).

LA's seminal community–labor campaigns, the chapter concludes by reflecting on lessons for the study of labor solidarity at the local level and beyond.

6.2 THE COMMUNITY–LABOR CHALLENGE TO NEOLIBERALISM: A LOCALIST PERSPECTIVE

Over the past quarter-century, labor scholars have argued over the appropriate regulatory framework for collective rights, and the appropriate strategies for collective action against the backdrop of labor law's 'ossification' and the changing nature of the workplace (Estlund 2002; Stone 2004). As statutory revisions and judicial interpretations have limited the utility of the federal labor law system of collective bargaining for promoting employee interests, and corporate practices have placed a growing number of workers beyond the 'reach and grasp' of employment and labor law altogether (Zatz 2008), scholars and practitioners have searched for alternative structures of protection and mobilization. A fundamental question has been the degree to which the traditional regulatory framework and organizational structures (i.e., unions) are worth salvaging or whether the future of workers' rights lies in 'reimagining' labor law in relation to different legal regimes, forms of mobilization, and scales of intervention (Fisk 2014).

Underlying this question are several important trends. One is the changing demographics of low-wage work, particularly the growth of immigrant workers (some undocumented) (Milkman 2006), which has occurred alongside ongoing racial division in the low-wage marketplace. Working-class whites have become deeply disaffected from the labor movement's historical political home, the Democratic Party, and black workers are often left out of the conversation about the problem of low-wage work and how to address it. In addition, the development of new forms of organization designed to channel the 'hydraulic pressure' of worker organizing into substantive workplace gains (Sachs 2008) – like worker centers and community–labor groups (Fine 2006; Working for Justice 2010) – has continued to run up against the limited power of nonunionized workers to challenge industry employment practices and respond to the rise of independent contracting and other forms of risk-shifting in the new "gig" economy (Dubal 2017). Finally, the hostility of conservatives to the enforcement and expansion of labor rights has resulted in federal gridlock on issues as basic as an increased minimum wage and has succeeded in producing an entrenched majority against labor rights on the Supreme Court. For organized labor, this has spurred efforts to identify and build on opportunities for state and local labor reforms – like the $15 minimum wage – which have resulted in important successes but continue to beg critical questions about how to bridge gaping conservative-liberal state divides and translate local energy into a broader national resurgence of the US labor movement.

To illuminate these issues, I conducted a study of the movement to challenge economic inequality in one of America's most unequal cities: Los Angeles.

Covering a transformative period of city history – from the 1992 riots to the 2008 recession – the study examines how law has been used, and what it has achieved, in the struggle to improve conditions for workers in the low-wage economy. Encountering Los Angeles at the crossroads of change, the study provides an original history of five high-profile campaigns to reform legal rules – and thereby enhance labor conditions – in vital industries. Each campaign emerged from the profound realignment of Los Angeles's economy beginning in the 1980s, marked by the growth of service employment, labor flexibility, and immigration. Within each industry, law shaped the structure of low-wage work through employer practices (e.g., contracting out and wage theft) and governmental policies (e.g., deregulation and underenforcement). In response, the campaigns sought to build alternative legal frameworks to reconstruct a foundation for greater solidarity to mobilize workers and extend unionism. Taken together, the campaigns have enacted new legal formats for worker protection and organizing – and pointed to a new localist regime for workplace regulation that has important implications for solidarity-building.

Studying these campaigns illuminates central dynamics of "labor activism in local politics" (Stone & Cummings 2011). For the purposes of this chapter's examination of solidarity, I spotlight the evolving relationship between worker organizing and labor's *political strategy*, in which organizing success is translated into policy reform and greater influence by the labor movement in local politics. This feeds into my specific analysis of solidarity, which I explore in relation to the unstable *alliance* between labor and other progressive movements, particularly immigrant rights and environmental justice, which are key partners in many campaigns, but which also have to navigate labor's growing political influence in ways that create challenges to sustained solidarity in pursuit of economic equality. This last point raises important questions about how community–labor solidarity is promoted and persists – and what it means for the power of the labor movement to organize and raise standards in low-wage industries.

6.3 THE RISE OF NEOLIBERALISM AND THE ORIGINS OF COMMUNITY–LABOR SOLIDARITY IN LOS ANGELES

To answer these questions, it is useful to situate the development of community–labor solidarity in relation to the evolution of neoliberalism, and the activism it spawned, in Los Angeles during a pivotal period in the city's evolution: from the 1992 civil unrest through the 2008 recession. During this less than two-decade span, the city confronted the consequences of tectonic demographic, economic, and political shifts – the roots of which had been growing for some time. Compared to the postwar period, Los Angeles in the early 1990s was a city with more racial diversity, more immigrants, and more income inequality (Gottlieb et al. 2005). The changing demography and economy spawned new demands for representation and redress, dramatically shifting local politics, which moved from a business friendly, tough-on-crime conservatism to a pro-labor, more inclusive progressivism. The struggle to reclaim the dignity of work, led by low-income communities of color, was a product of this shift and contributed to its velocity.

On April 29, 1992, in Simi Valley northwest of Los Angeles, the jury foreman in the prosecution of five police officers charged with the brutal videotaped beating of a handcuffed black man, Rodney King, uttered words that would ignite the city: "Not guilty. Not guilty. Not guilty. Not guilty . . ." Protests erupted immediately, exposing long-seething anger in the black community over police abuse in South Los Angeles (Understanding the Riots 1992). In 1965, protesters in Watts had chanted "burn baby burn" after highway patrolmen arrested a woman on suspicion of drunk driving and then proceeded to arrest her mother and brother in the ensuing scuffle. This was followed by a continuous scourge of unchecked police brutality, which regularly broke into public view: the 1978 killing of a black woman triggered by an unpaid utility bill; the 1989 killing of a black Muslim man after a traffic stop; and untold killings of purported gang members in the name of Operation Hammer instituted by reviled police chief Daryl Gates. After the 1992 riots ended, the city took stock of its toll: 60 dead, 2,383 injured, roughly 10,000 arrested, 623 fires, and $1 billion in total damage (ibid. 25, 31, 130). In the aftermath, city and community leaders looked backward and forward: analyzing the causes of the unrest and taking tentative steps toward reconciliation and rebuilding.

Looking back with the perspicuity of hindsight, it was clear that, through the 1992 unrest, South LA residents were uncorking years of frustration over joblessness, inadequate schools, and discriminatory housing practices that segregated African Americans in less desirable neighborhoods close to freeways and other environmental hazards. As the Civil Rights movement revealed the intransigence of segregation, efforts to address some of these problems seemed to only make things worse. School integration provoked acrimonious boycotts from white parents, who kept ten thousand children home on the first day of the LA busing plan in 1978 and increasingly abandoned the school system altogether, draining resources from central city schools and the city's economic infrastructure (Schneider 2008).

Frustration in the black community was also a product of shifting economic fortunes. World War II had brought African Americans to Los Angeles from the South in search of opportunity, which many found in military-related industries (Von Hoffman 2003: 210). After World War II, the city experienced tremendous economic growth. Wartime production of military airplanes and other manufacturing items was retooled for postwar civilian production, galvanizing a manufacturing boom, particularly in the aerospace, electronics, and automotive industries, which were all heavily unionized. In addition, light manufacturing industries – like garment production – and some service industries – notably construction, janitorial services, and trucking – were important growth sectors with high union density in the postwar period (Milkman 2006: 85–86). Despite persistent inequalities based on race and immigration status, a diverse middle class emerged in Los Angeles, bolstered by the heavy manufacturing sector (which employed one in five county residents in 1970 (Grant 2000)), as well as the unionized service industries.

The foundation of middle-class Los Angeles crumbled as quickly as it had been built. The manufacturing base that powered Los Angeles's mid-century growth began to decline in the 1970s and 1980s. Trade liberalism and workplace restructuring produced Los Angeles's own version of deindustrialization, shifting the economic balance toward low-wage service industries. Between 1978 and 1982, the city lost nearly one hundred thousand manufacturing jobs, primarily in the automobile industry (Soja 2010: 125). As Edward Soja (ibid.: 126) describes, one consequence was the westward migration of African Americans from South Los Angeles to places like Inglewood, which were closer to the airport and the still-strong aerospace industry. However, recession in the early 1990s decimated aerospace as well, causing the loss of three hundred thousand more manufacturing jobs. Between 1990 and 1994, the largely unionized durable goods manufacturing sector declined by one-third (Gottlieb et al. 2005: 85). A critical pillar of middle-class Los Angeles was irreversibly degenerating.

In its place, the economically bipolar service sector rose to dominate the LA economy, distributing enormous wealth at the high end and economic insecurity at the low end. As an emerging global city, Los Angeles developed a dense economic network of finance, real estate, and professional service industries like law and accounting that reshaped the market, creating a new class of professionals connected to the central city who relied on cheap labor, often accessed through the informal economy, to provide the food, child care, maintenance, and other services that facilitated their lives (Sassen 1991). Low-end service sector jobs – in growth industries like retail sales and hospitality – lacked the high wages, labor protections, and job security that had undergirded the postwar middle class. Abuse was rampant in the burgeoning informal economy, while even in the formal economy, there were increasing rates of labor violations.

In addition, corporate strategies to restructure work undermined union density and degraded labor standards. Companies in previously unionized industries (such as janitorial services and garment production) launched subcontracting practices – outsourcing work to small independently owned companies – that broke the unions, drove down wages, and promoted exploitation while shielding those with economic power from legal responsibility. Although Los Angeles still remained the manufacturing capital of the United States in the 1990s, the bulk of those jobs were in light manufacturing – like garment and furniture production – which were not unionized and paid low wages (Gottlieb et al. 2005: 56). The labor movement's decline in Los Angeles was part of a national corporate strategy to undermine unions' economic standing and political clout. Labor protections atrophied. As a prominent symbol of labor's weakened state, the federal minimum wage declined by nearly 40 percent in real terms from the late 1960s to the late 1980s (Pollin & Luce 1998). Added to this was a shrinking safety net, culminating in the 1996 federal welfare reform law, forcing more people to rely on precarious work.

It was in this context that income inequality surged in Los Angeles – built on the backs of the new working poor (More et al. 2000). By the end of the 1990s, over 40 percent of Los Angeles County residents lived below the needs-based poverty threshold (200 percent of the federal poverty level) and roughly two-thirds of them lived in a household with at least one full-time worker. More than one million individual workers in Los Angeles County earned less than the needs-based income threshold, nearly 80 percent of whom worked full time. These working-poor Angelenos were disproportionately Latinx and foreign-born.

Beginning in the 1980s, with job growth exploding in the low-wage market, immigration to the region expanded as employers took advantage of workers forced to accept degraded conditions in newly restructured workplaces (Milkman 2006). As immigration increased, particularly from Mexico and other Latin American countries, the demography and residential patterns of Los Angeles shifted. Attracted by the promise of prosperity, immigration to the LA metropolitan area grew sharply, from roughly half a million in 1984, to a peak of 1.8 million in 1991 (Bobo et al. 2000). In 1994, one-fifth of immigrants to Los Angeles came from Mexico, with significant proportions also coming from Russia, the Philippines, China, and El Salvador. A large number of entrants were undocumented immigrants – with estimates of Los Angeles County's undocumented population ranging from 533,000 to 1.5 million in 1992. As a result of migration, the overall demographic composition of Los Angeles shifted toward a higher proportion of Latinx and foreign-born residents. By the start of the new millennium, the city of Los Angeles was 47 percent Latinx, 30 percent white, 10 percent Asian American, and 11 percent African American (Gottlieb et al. 2005: 78). Reflecting this overall trend, between 1970 and 1990, the composition of the workforce changed dramatically, from 75 percent white to less than 50 percent; while African Americans held constant at 10 percent, "the Latino and Asian workforce grew by more than 300 percent and 463 percent, respectively" (Grant 2000: 58). The foreign-born population in the region rose from 1 million in 1970 to nearly 4 million in 1990 (with 54 percent of Latinx residents foreign-born) and close to 5.5 million by 2010, as the overall population increased from 11 to 17 million over the same forty-year span (Soja 2010 121–122).

The 1992 riots constituted a pivot point in LA politics. The Civil Rights era saw the rise of black political power in the city, culminating in the election of Tom Bradley as mayor in 1974. Yet as the city's composition changed, so did its politics. The most immediate consequence of the riots was backlash. After five terms as mayor, Bradley declined to seek reelection in 1993, opening the door for Republican lawyer and businessman Richard Riordan to claim a resounding victory built on promises to promote economic development and crack down on crime (his campaign slogan was "Tough Enough to Lead L.A."). Yet the Riordan interregnum served as a bridge between the Bradley era and the rise of Latinx political influence.

Although the City Council was never as pro-business as Mayor Riordan, by 2003, it had shifted more forcefully toward organized labor, symbolized by the election of Antonio Villaraigosa (who had been an organizer for United Teachers Los Angeles) to the fourteenth district, and Martin Ludlow (a former organizer for the Service Employees International Union (SEIU)) to the tenth.

The election of Villaraigosa and Ludlow, along with the broader ascendance of pro-worker politics, was the product of labor's own reinvention. As Ruth Milkman documents, organized labor in Los Angeles had followed an atypical path that made it well positioned to respond to the growth of service industries and immigrant workers (Milkman 2006). Unionism during Los Angeles's postwar period occurred primarily in "older, occupationally based, nonfactory unions" affiliated with the American Federation of Labor (AFL), which used a sectoral strategy of taking wages out of competition by pressuring and negotiating with employers industry-wide, rather than mobilizing workers on the shop floor – the strategy adopted by Congress of Industrial Organizations (CIO) unions (ibid.: 38, 74). Through the 1950s, AFL unions achieved notable success organizing janitors, truck drivers, garment workers, and construction workers, and by 1955, 37 percent of LA workers were unionized – the vast majority in AFL unions (ibid.: 45–70). As elsewhere, deindustrialization and neoliberal restructuring hit the LA labor movement hard. By 1986, union density had dropped sharply to 22 percent and was concentrated in heavy manufacturing (ibid.: 79). In former labor strongholds like construction, janitorial services, and trucking, "deunionization and employment restructuring" was "followed by an exodus of native-born workers, [and] an immigrant influx" (ibid.: 7). By the mid-1980s, organized labor had gone into steep decline, hemorrhaging members and resources (ibid.: 84–87).

Nevertheless, in the seeds of decline were sown labor's rebirth, which it achieved by building solidarity with Los Angeles's burgeoning community groups and committing to organize new immigrants in the precise service industries where AFL unions had historic strength. The LA model of community–labor solidarity was a product of deliberate union strategy – innovation born of desperate times and guided by organizers who had cut their teeth as architects of earlier efforts by the United Farm Workers to mobilize low-wage immigrants against contract-based corporate farmers. Perhaps no other campaign heralded the renaissance of the LA labor movement more than Justice for Janitors (JfJ), led by SEIU Local 399, which put Los Angeles on the map by showing that unions could win collective bargaining agreements in the new environment of subcontracting and immigrant work (Erickson et al. 2002).

The JfJ campaign had powerful ripple effects, not the least of which was to reshape the labor movement's approach to local politics. Throughout the tenure of Mayor Bradley, organized labor continued to exercise significant local political influence through the vaunted Los Angeles County Federation of Labor (County Fed), whose close relations with city officials permitted union members, particularly in the building trades, to benefit from city-sponsored redevelopment projects in the 1980s (Frank & Wong 2004). However, the 1992 riots and the end of Bradley's reign left the County Fed at a crossroads – with the critical issue of how to deal with Los Angeles's growing population of immigrant workers unresolved. At the national level, the AFL-CIO had endorsed the 1986 Immigration Reform and Control Act (IRCA), which imposed sanctions on employers for hiring undocumented immigrants – signaling that the union movement did not envision a future partnership with immigrant workers. Although the County Fed did not explicitly co-sign the national labor movement's support for IRCA, there was significant local disagreement over whether to embrace organizing immigrant workers, who many viewed as unorganizable (Milkman 2006: 114). This debate reached a crescendo after JfJ, leading to the narrow 1996 election of a new leader of the County Fed, Miguel Contreras, who had built his reputation organizing Latinx immigrant workers for the Hotel Employees and Restaurant Employees (HERE) Local 11 union.

Contreras's election cemented the County Fed's movement toward building solidarity with the immigrant community, punctuated two years earlier by the County Fed's agreement to co-sponsor a 100,000-person march against anti-immigrant state Proposition 187 – demonstrating a "new and powerful political alliance between Labor and the Latino community" (Frank & Wong 2004: 157). Contreras led a shift away from the County Fed's Bradley-era insider politics, rebuilding labor's power through a sophisticated get-out-the-vote operation predicated on an innovative strategy of mobilizing occasional voters, securing the elections of Villaraigosa and Ludlow to the City Council in 2003 – and paving the way for Villaraigosa's successful bid for mayor in 2005 (ibid.: 161). The County Fed was also instrumental in engineering the national AFL-CIO's 2000 decision to reverse its previous stance on immigration policy and support a pathway to citizenship for undocumented workers.

In addition to fostering political realignment, JfJ also underscored the power of community partnerships, helping galvanize a new brand of community–labor solidarity in Los Angeles that sought to connect labor's resurgence with efforts to promote cross-racial collaboration in the wake of the riots. This new solidarity reshaped progressive political and legal advocacy while challenging the underlying structure of low-wage work. At the grassroots level, the new activism built on Los Angeles's base of community organizations, some dating back to the 1960s and others emerging out of 1980s restructuring (Soja 2010: 133). The Watts Labor Community Action Committee was established just before the Watts riots to address the lack of economic opportunity in South Los Angeles. It became the model for other community development corporations that followed: CHARO Community Development Corporation (1967), the East Los Angeles Community Union, or TELACU (1968), and Little Tokyo Service Center (1979). Esperanza Community Housing Corporation, located in an immigrant-dense neighborhood adjacent to the

University of Southern California (USC) just south of downtown, was started in 1985 by a nun from the local Catholic parish, Sister Diane Donoghue, who worked to stop resident displacement by a proposed garment sweatshop (Von Hofman 2003: 218). Esperanza grew rapidly to support the neighborhood's immigrant community, mostly from Mexico and Central America, providing English-language and other classes, and beginning in 1994, building much-needed affordable housing (ibid.: 218–220).

As Martha Matsuoka (2005) shows, these community development groups were initially place-based, but soon engaged in new forms of regional organizing that responded to the same forces of economic restructuring and demographic change that reshaped the labor movement. By adopting cross-sectoral, multiracial approaches, these groups sought to address the widening chasm of inequality that cut across neighborhood lines. One effort that reflected the potential of sectoral initiatives was the 1998 Alameda Corridor Jobs Coalition (ACJC) campaign to win local hiring and other community benefits in connection with the billion-dollar expansion of the Alameda Corridor rail line linking the ports to downtown Los Angeles – at the time the largest public works project in the United States. ACJC also demonstrated the importance of legal partnerships in sectoral initiatives as the final agreement codifying the coalition's gains was negotiated and drafted by lawyers from the Los Angeles Legal Aid Foundation and San Francisco's Employment Law Center.

The new wave of aggressive, coalition-led organizing to promote equitable development ran counter to the city-sponsored effort to subsidize industry in the aftermath of the 1992 civil unrest. The city's official program, dubbed Rebuild LA (RLA), was launched by Mayor Bradley and Governor Pete Wilson, who persuaded Peter Ueberroth, who had organized the 1984 LA Olympics, to lead the effort. Ueberroth's approach was to "use his considerable skills to influence the heads of corporations to donate money, people, and equipment to RLA and persuade large businesses, especially chain retail outlets, to open branches in South Central and other inner-city areas. He also hoped to coordinate large amounts of government funds" (Von Hoffman 2003: 228). When this failed, new RLA leadership focused on "bottom-up" development, mapping existing economic assets in South Los Angeles and working to support their expansion based on "competitive advantage" (ibid.: 237). Mirroring the federal movement to provide business incentives through "Empowerment Zones," RLA sought to channel resources and information, through conferences and networking opportunities, to strengthen extant industries in the inner city: garment, furniture, food, and toy manufacturing – the very light manufacturing industries contributing to the rise of low-wage work. In parallel, the Riordan administration pushed initiatives to cut business regulation and promote city-subsidized retail redevelopment in the downtown area, which further added to the glut of low-wage jobs.

In 1992, students from the UCLA Department of Urban Planning's nascent Community Scholars program conducted a research project, led by Professor Gilda Haas, which critiqued the city-sponsored expansion of tourism-related industries and offered a plan for growth that focused on equity for workers (Ansell et al. 1992). Their report, titled "Accidental Tourism," was the template for what would become LAANE (founded in 1994 as the Tourism Industry Development Council), which won its first victory – the nation's second living wage law in 1997 – by convincing the City Council to override a veto by Mayor Riordan. The seminal Bus Rider's Union (BRU) campaign was also launched in 1992, organized by the Labor/Community Strategy Center, whose founder, Eric Mann, had been involved in the General Motors plant closing movement a decade earlier. The BRU – a multiracial coalition of low-income, largely immigrant workers – targeted the linked problems of transit racism and pollution, provoked by the Metropolitan Transportation Authority (MTA) decision to raise bus fares and reduce routes to poor neighborhoods. Teaming up with the LA branch of the NAACP, the BRU filed a civil rights lawsuit that resulted in a 1996 consent decree in which the MTA promised affordable and accessible service for Los Angeles's working poor (Rice 2003). Two years later, protests at USC over outsourcing janitorial and food service workers launched a grassroots movement that coalesced around another new group, Strategic Actions for a Just Economy (SAJE), started by Haas, which spearheaded an alliance between labor and community members concerned over gentrification and displacement (Wilton & Cranford 2014).

Into this welter of activity entered a small but influential number of worker centers: grassroots groups experimenting with new ways of organizing and protecting worker rights outside of traditional unionism. As they evolved, worker centers focused on immigrants, emphasizing policy advocacy and legal redress for labor abuse. One of the earliest worker centers in Los Angeles was Korean Immigrant Workers Advocates (KIWA, which later changed its name to the Koreatown Immigrant Workers Alliance). Founded in 1992, just before the Rodney King verdict, KIWA gained notoriety by helping Latinx and Asian American workers receive compensation from stores shut down by the unrest. Its major campaign was an effort started in 1997 to organize Latinx and Asian American workers fighting wage theft by Korean-owned restaurants and groceries (Gottlieb et al. 2005). The campaign, in partnership with local unions and civil rights organizations, combined boycotts with legal action – taking a stand for cross-racial workers' rights over ethnic solidarity, winning back pay and living wage agreements from employers, and bringing public attention to the problem of labor abuse in Koreatown.

In 2002, the UCLA Labor Center, established nearly forty years earlier to promote research and policy development on workers' issues, opened its flagship downtown office overlooking MacArthur Park in a bustling community of Latinx immigrants. The Downtown Labor Center (DLC) aimed to build bridges between worker centers, organized labor, and immigrant communities in the surrounding neighborhood and beyond. It was there that the National Day Laborer Organizing Network (NDLON) and the Community Labor Environmental Action Network (CLEAN) Car Wash Campaign were officially launched as the DLC became a key meeting place and strategic headquarters for the worker center movement, strengthening ties to organized labor while also helping establish networks of movement lawyers, like the Coalition of Immigrant Workers Advocates. Crucially, the DLC also sought to build bridges to African American workers concerned about being marginalized by organized labor's growing focus on Latinx workers. This effort to promote multiracial solidarity, albeit not without friction, was reinforced by partnerships between the County Fed and groups like Action for Grassroots Empowerment and Neighborhood Alternatives, which advocated for better jobs for black workers in South Los Angeles and teamed up with the County Fed to mobilize black voters in support of progressive political leaders. From the ashes of the LA riots, a new foundation for progressive activism in Los Angeles was thus built – one that weaved together multiple strands of community–labor solidarity into a coordinated challenge to inequality.

6.4 COMMUNITY–LABOR CAMPAIGNS TO CHALLENGE INEQUALITY IN LOS ANGELES

The campaigns recounted in this study grew out of the emerging community–labor challenge to inequality after the 1992 unrest and fundamentally contributed to its rise. The campaigns targeted industries that, in general, were disproportionately comprised of Latinx immigrant workers and thus the theme of immigrant worker organizing featured prominently. However, low-wage work cut across race and the campaigns themselves aspired to be self-consciously cross-racial, attending to the varied racial composition of different industries. In doing so, the campaigns fused different types of organizing approaches (inside and outside of unionism) and social movements (labor, immigrant rights, environmental justice, and others), while also creating a central role for lawyers and law. I summarize them here.

First came the anti-sweatshop campaign that woke the city (and nation) to the severe exploitation of immigrant workers – and created a new model for change. Launched in 1995 with the discovery of more than seventy enslaved Thai workers in a suburban apartment complex surrounded by barbed-wire fence, the campaign – led by the Asian Pacific American Legal Center – pioneered the integration of strategic litigation and worker organizing, marking the emergence of a movement to contest garment sweatshops. The sweatshop regime was built on a legal foundation of subcontracting: insulating retailers and manufacturers, which sold and created clothes, from the contractors actually producing them. At its most ambitious, the campaign sought to make legal responsibility follow economic power, rupturing the legal fiction that protected retailers and manufacturers from labor abuses such as those uncovered in the Thai worker case. Through the campaign, lawyers built a powerful alliance with labor and grassroots organizers, won important legal victories in court, and achieved passage of a landmark state law creating manufacturer liability for contract labor violations. It then turned to a fierce fight against retailer Forever 21, which showed the power of industry countermobilization and ultimately marked the end of the litigation campaign. This outcome underscored a central lesson of the new economy: Individual enforcement and litigation strategies, even when paired with innovative organizing and media campaigns, confronted formidable barriers in challenging abuse enabled by extensive contracting and – crucially – the threat of global outsourcing. Nonetheless, in fusing law and organizing to mount this challenge, the anti-sweatshop campaign marked a new beginning in the movement against low-wage work – one in which lawyers and activists would apply the tools honed in the manufacturing context to target Los Angeles's immobile service industries.

The next pivotal battle in this new movement involved the two-decade-long legal campaign led by the Mexican American Legal Defense and Educational Fund (MALDEF) to contest anti-solicitation ordinances – local laws prohibiting the public solicitation of work by day laborers. The relationship between day laborers and those who use their labor is defined through contracting, with day laborers negotiating for daily rates and often experiencing labor abuse. Although part of the underground economy, during the 1990s, day laborers became some of the most visible immigrant workers, standing on the corners in affluent communities to find jobs. They also became the target of legal backlash, with nearly forty anti-solicitation ordinances passed by cities in the greater LA area by 2000. The legal campaign to challenge these ordinances began with the alliance between MALDEF and NDLON, which together created a litigation model built around organizing worker committees to be plaintiffs in federal First Amendment lawsuits. This model created legal standing while protecting workers from intrusive discovery. After a series of legal battles, joined by the American Civil Liberties Union, the campaign won a monumental Ninth Circuit Court of Appeals ruling striking down the Redondo Beach anti-solicitation ordinance as an overbroad regulation of commercial speech. The ruling had the effect of invalidating similar ordinances and thus preserving significant parts of the region's sidewalks for day laborers to seek work. It therefore showed the power of litigation to create the conditions for collective action by sweeping aside barriers to its realization. It also underscored litigation's limits: Although the campaign succeeded in protecting the "corner" as a place for contracting work, it could not prevent the labor abuse that followed – or stop the creation of the next generation of anti-solicitation ordinances tailored to circumvent the Ninth Circuit's ruling.

The community benefits campaign emerged at the intersection of Los Angeles's living wage movement and efforts to challenge gentrification. Led by LAANE and SAJE, the campaign sought to leverage community benefits from publicly subsidized development, particularly in gentrifying neighborhoods where displacement of low-income residents was occurring. These developments produced significant numbers of retail and hospitality jobs (along with jobs in ancillary industries like janitorial services and security); a primary goal of the campaign was to ensure these jobs would go to local residents and pay a living wage. The benefits strategy was advanced through interlocking coalitions that negotiated with developers to create contracts – known as community benefits agreements (CBAs) – that traded developer promises to provide specific benefits (living-wage guarantees, job training programs, local hiring, and affordable housing) for coalition promises to support the projects. The first campaign, targeting the development of a sports and entertainment complex in downtown Los Angeles, won a multimillion-dollar package of benefits, including an agreement by the developer to ensure that retailers ultimately occupying the complex as tenants would pay workers at the living-wage rate. This filled a gap in the LA Living Wage Ordinance, which excluded tenants in publicly subsidized commercial projects. It also laid the foundation for two other major CBAs: a half-billion-dollar agreement with Los Angeles International Airport (LAX) in relation to airport expansion, and a CBA with the developer of a transformative mixed-use downtown development known as the Grand Avenue Project. Both of these were significant for different reasons: The LAX agreement showed the power of a nascent labor–environmental or "blue–green" alliance to negotiate a monumental benefits package with a public entity, whereas the Grand Avenue CBA revealed how organized labor's growing power permitted it to achieve community benefits through insider political strategies while community groups focused on affordable housing continued to pursue CBAs through outsider challenges. Overall, the CBA campaign was important for its innovative use of private contracting mechanisms to promote labor standards and unionization – through living wage, card check neutrality, and local hiring provisions – which were ultimately embedded in local policy.

Growing out of the CBA campaign was the community–labor challenge to the retail giant Wal-Mart, whose announced plan in 2002 to bring forty Supercenters into California threatened to undercut wages in the unionized grocery sector. The campaign focused on LAANE's confrontation with Wal-Mart in the separately incorporated city of Inglewood, a historically working-class African American community in South Los Angeles. It centered on the labor-backed campaign to stop the development of the Inglewood Supercenter through legislative and legal challenges – a technique known as a "site fight" because of its focus on blocking Wal-Mart at a specific location. In the site fight, labor and community groups enlisted legal advocacy to mobilize community opposition to Wal-Mart's Inglewood initiative and later to craft a Superstores Ordinance that conditioned Wal-Mart's ability to enter the Los Angeles market on undergoing a community impact assessment, which gave labor unions leverage to negotiate agreements on workplace standards. The study traces the story to Wal-Mart's effort to circumvent that ordinance, which only applied to big-box stores, by opening a small-format grocery store in the historic Chinatown neighborhood in downtown Los Angeles.

The final case study examines the campaign to raise work and environmental standards at the ports of Los Angeles and Long Beach – known as the Campaign for Clean Trucks. This blue-green campaign, led by LAANE and the Teamsters union (on the labor side) and the Natural Resources Defense Council (on the environmental side), emerged as a fight over air quality, but developed as a struggle over the conditions of short-haul truck drivers, whose misclassification as independent contractors contributed to poorly maintained trucks viewed as a key cause of air pollution, while precluding labor organizing. The campaign rested on an innovative legal foundation: the port, as a publicly owned and operated entity, had the power to define the terms of entry for trucking companies through concession agreements. The campaign therefore hinged on how those agreements treated truck drivers and what types of environmental standards they set. In 2006, labor unions, environmental activists, and community residents formed the Coalition for Clean and Safe Ports, which passed a Clean Truck Program two years later through the LA Board of Harbor Commissioners. The program conditioned port concession agreements on two requirements: first, that trucking companies convert their fleets to low-emissions vehicles, and, second, that they convert all their drivers to employees. Under this new program, the environmental movement advanced a long-standing goal – "greening" the port – while the Teamsters could pursue driver unionization. It was a win-win designed to take maintenance out of the low-paid drivers' hands, making companies internalize the costs, thus creating a sustainable foundation for clean trucking over time. Lawyers working with the coalition crafted the program to minimize the legal risk that it would be preempted by federal law, all the while planning for a federal preemption legal challenge by the American Trucking Associations. That lawsuit came quickly, resulting in a Ninth Circuit ruling invalidating the program's requirement of employee drivers. As a result, the labor–environmental alliance's joint policy victory was torn asunder through litigation – with port truck drivers forced to carry the economic burdens of heightened environmental compliance without the economic benefits of enhanced labor standards. The ports campaign thus presents a cautionary tale – demonstrating law's potential to build coalition-led reform but also to split it apart. It further highlights the power of movement resilience: tracing how organized labor responded to legal setback through an innovative new strategy to maneuver around preemption and reassert its challenge to driver misclassification.

6.5 LESSONS FOR SOLIDARITY IN THE CITY: AND BEYOND

This study's temporal focus – tracing the labor movement's response to neoliberalism and the ascent of the service economy in Los Angeles – precisely tracks the scholarly response to the same structural transformation, which has interrogated the legal and economic underpinnings of the labor movement's decline, while debating strategies for labor law's revitalization (Estlund 2002; Stone 2004; Sachs 2007).

A central claim in this debate is that the old federal labor law paradigm, codified in the 1935 National Labor Relations Act, is "failing" (Andrias 2016), which raises the question of whether it should be defended, revised, or scrapped (Estlund 2006).

By tracing the longer arc of "labor activism in local politics," my study of Los Angeles provides a critical perspective on the claim that local labor struggle, both as a descriptive and normative matter, contains a vision of labor law that transcends the framework inherited from the New Deal. Instead of marking a rupture with the past, the LA campaigns reveal an essential continuity: demonstrating the labor movement's sustained effort to foster new forms of solidarity in order to establish and strengthen legal rules – at all levels of government – that allow unions to effectively use the established federal labor law system to organize in favor of better working conditions. This last section presents lessons from Los Angeles on building external and internal solidarity toward the goals of building union density and promoting social inclusion in the city.

6.5.1 *Seeking Legal Foundations of Solidarity outside of Labor Law*

One important lesson from the LA campaigns is to reveal how labor law necessarily interacts with other legal regimes in ways that make any affirmative unionization strategy intrinsically interdisciplinary. This interdisciplinarity is both tactical and substantive. Tactically, labor groups turn to legal strategies – litigation and legislative initiatives – as a way to mobilize workers and enhance labor standards adjacent to the federal collective bargaining framework. Indeed, legal strategies constitute an essential element of comprehensive labor campaigns, responding to the legal underpinnings of de-unionization and labor abuse. Critical scholars have cautioned that rights-based advocacy coopts labor struggle, arguing that the legalization of collective bargaining and the pursuit of rights-based employment claims have weakened the labor movement (Lichtenstein 2002). However, the LA campaigns mobilized rights as a pragmatic response to constraints on the traditional union organizing paradigm: for example, supporting misclassification litigation in an effort to restore port drivers to the baseline of employee status. Similarly, rather than coopting labor activism, local legislative initiatives, such as the LA Living Wage Ordinance, established legal frameworks designed to incentivize bargaining in which labor groups can effectively negotiate benefits for workers.

Substantively, labor law's interdisciplinarity hinges on alternative legal frameworks to facilitate its aims. Contemporary labor law has been inexorably pulled in two directions – both of which offer legal benefits while also presenting significant trade-offs. In one direction, labor law, which governs collective bargaining, increasingly interacts with employment law, which governs individual worker rights (Sachs 2008). While the line between these two legal regimes has long been blurry, the rise of contracting has pushed them together more forcefully because organizing under labor law depends on fortifying employment law concepts of joint employership and misclassification to succeed. Thus, mobilization to strengthen these concepts has become an essential element of local labor campaigns, which are forced to fight over the basic terms of employment status in order to reestablish the baseline right to organize.

Moving in a different direction, labor law has been pulled toward and melded with quite distinct regulatory regimes embedded in local land-use law. Here, too, labor's interdisciplinarity adds legal strength while carrying trade-offs. To work, these local policies must avoid preemption by labor (and other higher-order) law, instead framing their objectives in terms that fit neatly within justifications for the exercise of local land-use power. For example, the Superstores Ordinance – which was designed in part to give unions leverage to negotiate wage standards with Wal-Mart – was framed around eliminating economic "blight" (a land-use concept), while the Clean Truck Program emphasized the need for trucking firms to hire employee drivers as a way to internalize the costs of compliance with environmental regulation. However, by nesting labor-enhancing policy in local laws framed around land-use planning and environmental mitigation, such policy becomes accountable to a different set of legal standards that constrain its scope and does not ensure protection against federal preemption challenges (as in the case of the Clean Truck Program). As this suggests, labor's engagement with local land-use law is both necessary in an era of federal constraint and second-best relative to restoring the federal labor system to full strength.

6.5.2 *The Role of Unions in Building External and Internal Solidarity*

The labor movement's investment in the city as the key battleground for rebuilding American unionism speaks directly to ongoing debates about the political role of unions, and connections between their efforts to promote external cross-movement solidarity and internal workplace solidarity. As the LA campaigns underscore, in addition to being an economic bargaining agent, unions are inherently political actors seeking to represent workers in the public domain in order to design legal frameworks within which to effectively advocate for workers' economic interests. Precisely because there is no dividing line between the market and politics in American capitalism, unions are constantly required to play dual roles: bargaining for workers in the private sector to enhance workers' rights and engaging in politics in the public sector to defend and extend the rules of the game within which bargaining occurs. These dual roles must interlock for the labor movement to be successful. It is only through economic representation that unions are able to generate the resources and standing to engage politically, and political engagement is essential for long-term economic success. Labor's local turn is a product of this dual role because, for the time being, it is primarily in big cities with favorable political environments where unions can exercise political power.

Historically, unions' political engagement has been important not just for protecting union bargaining rights, but for advancing broader redistributive policy – from minimum wage to welfare – serving as the foundation for America's shared postwar prosperity. This is one reason why corporate interests have targeted union representation, through right-to-work laws depriving unions of membership dues and the evisceration of nonmember "fair share" fees. Corporate success in undercutting union density has contributed to weaker economic regulation and the rise of inequality throughout the American economy that labor's efforts in cities like Los Angeles have sought to address. It is against this backdrop that scholars have debated the nature of labor's political role and how it should relate to unions' core function of workplace organizing.

In this regard, the LA experience makes a strong case that union efforts to promote local policy benefiting community members outside of the workplace – enlarging the sphere of solidarity with movements like immigrant rights – may pay direct union organizing dividends inside the workplace. This occurs both through changing the public perception of unions and by embedding specific mechanisms in local policy that directly support unionization. From a normative standpoint, by demonstrating that they can deliver benefits to low-income communities and communities of color around issues like housing and environmental justice, unions may overcome the negative stereotype of labor as a special interest group and improve long-term prospects for increasing union density. However, in order to continue promoting wider redistributive reform, labor's local policies – even as they aim to transcend unionism – must still provide a means to directly strengthen collective bargaining in order to maintain unions' political power under the current system of campaign finance, which depends on dues collection. In Los Angeles, the paradigm of this type of reform – simultaneously promoting unionism while benefiting workers outside its scope – was the Living Wage Ordinance, passed in 1997, which contained an opt-out for companies with unions, under which employers could pay the living wage *or* accept a union – an option that motivated many employers to accept a union because it lowered overall costs while ensuring labor peace. Unions leveraged this opt out provision to pressure firms employing retail, security, and janitorial workers at the Los Angeles International Airport and hotels in the airport zone to accept collective bargaining. The important point is that the Living Wage Ordinance benefited many workers outside of the union movement, which promoted external solidarity. But it also increased union density in the retail and hospitality industries in particular and was thus essential to building local labor power, which ultimately led, two decades later, to successfully passing a $15 city minimum wage (roughly twice federal minimum). In this way, the labor movement leveraged the benefits of external solidarity to promote more internal solidarity. Although such opt-outs have been controversial, portrayed as a retreat from the principle of minimum labor standards (Andrias 2016: 7), and therefore cutting against the goal of promoting a positive public image for unions, from a long-term perspective, they serve as critical tools to increase the union density necessary to empower unions to provide broader community benefits.

The development of local policies like the living wage also illuminates a representational division of labor: While community–labor alliances play a vanguard role in politics, unions remain central in the workplace. This division of labor spotlights a final point about political unionism, which is that while it fundamentally depends on solidarity across movements – community–labor solidarity – in the public domain, it must nonetheless continue to fight for a traditional notion of worker solidarity in private firms or industry sectors in order to maintain and potentially strengthen union density. Trying to mediate between these different forms of solidarity creates synergies and tensions for the labor movement.

In terms of synergies, the study shows how labor's political resurgence in Los Angeles has relied on identifying and capitalizing upon interest convergence with other social movements, which have contributed the resources, power, and legitimacy necessary to build credible political organization and enact labor-friendly law. This interest convergence was the essential predicate for inter-movement solidarity, while also testing its limits. For example, a powerful labor–environmental alliance converged around overlapping interests in the city to create the Clean Truck Program, which banned environmentally polluting trucks and, importantly for labor, converted truck drivers who had been illegally misclassified as independent contractors into employees organizable under labor law. However, an industry-backed preemption lawsuit (supporting clean trucks while attacking employee drivers) drove a wedge that broke the coalition apart. Labor partnerships with housing advocates produced important CBAs, but also flared over the optimal distribution of limited developer funds, revealing how labor's growing political clout was a double-edged sword: reducing incentives for solidarity with movements, like housing and environmental justice, whose aims could be perceived to conflict with job growth. Scaling up to the national level, in a conservative political environment in which opportunities for policy success by progressive movements across issue areas are highly constrained (and thus victories may appear to create zero-sum trade-offs), one would expect inter-movement solidarity to remain difficult to forge, and yet crucial to achieve, in order to rebuild labor's political power.

6.6 CONCLUSION

In conclusion, I spotlight two major challenges to labor solidarity in the current moment. The first challenge is how to connect alternative forms of labor solidarity to unions' efforts to effectively fight for worker power in the rapidly changing labor market. In pursuit of community relevance and policy influence, unions have supported new forms of worker collectivism that break the traditional mold. Early worker centers, like that in the garment industry, originated outside the labor movement. Over time, organized labor came to appreciate the potential of worker centers to foster organizing and thus took on a stronger role incubating and financially supporting them. Despite worker-center growth, however, and wider discussion of more flexible forms of workplace representation, unions have continued to assert their primacy as the only vehicles capable of winning employer recognition and bargaining for stronger worker rights because worker centers and other community-based labor groups have not shown themselves capable of achieving an influential voice in the workplace. Perhaps as the workplace itself fractures in the contemporary market, traditional unions will prove less important, and sectoral policy strategies will take precedence. However, unions have not been willing to bet the future of American workers' rights on ceding control to unproven alternatives, and – particularly so long as unions' political effectiveness depends on density – alternative representational forms may risk undermining the labor movement's political potency. How to mobilize labor solidarity outside of unions to strengthen worker representation in the workplace – and unions themselves – is a key challenge.

A second challenge to labor solidarity is scale: How to move beyond the successful examples of solidarity and policymaking in cities like LA to reshape federal labor law and rebuild the faltering labor movement nationwide? Although there are new opportunities for influence in the relatively prolabor Biden administration, efforts to change federal labor law to overcome problems like employee misclassification and employer abuse during union campaigns continue to be blocked by Republicans. Breaking this blockade requires moving beyond effective movement-building efforts in progressive cities to foster a prolabor consciousness among the predominately white workers in conservative cities and states, who are hostile to unions and continue, against their economic interests, to vote in favor of political representatives opposed to expansive labor rights. Finding a pathway to fundamentally reform labor law thus requires building power to influence federal political decision-makers in conservative parts of America (or making those areas less conservative), which hinges on transforming the relationship between the white working class and the labor movement. . In short, changing the trajectory of the American union movement depends on solidarity among workers from different places, of different races, and of different political views. This requires that the labor movement adopt a multivocal strategy in which it sends different messages to different groups to illuminate shared economic interests and create unity across cleavages of identity and ideology.

In the face of these challenges, my study offers reasons for optimism. Real change has occurred in LA that demonstrates what labor solidarity can achieve: reclaiming the city as a space for greater equality and social innovation. This success has deepened local commitments to equity and inclusion beyond the workplace – visible in labor-supported policies to promote sanctuary for undocumented immigrants and to combat climate change through environmentally friendly reforms. It is precisely the arduous, bottom-up effort to weave together strands of progressive activism into a larger movement to challenge the rise of inequality, and the forces of racism and division it inflames, that makes the example of solidarity in Los Angeles an enduring symbol what it takes for labor resurgence to happen – and why it is so crucial to the future of democracy.

REFERENCES

Andrias, Kate, The New Labor Law, 126 *Yale Law Journal* 2 (2016).

Ansell, Phill et al., Accidental Tourism: A Critique of the Los Angeles Tourism Industry and Proposals for Change. Masters thesis, UCLA, 1992.

Bobo, Lawrence D., Melvin L. Oliver, James H. Johnson, & Abel Valenzuela, Jr., Analyzing Inequality in Los Angeles. In *Prismatic Metropolis: Inequality in Los Angeles*, ed. Lawrence D. Bobo, Melvin L. Oliver, James H. Johnson, Jr., & Abel Valenzuela, Jr. New York: Russell Sage Foundation Press, 2000.

Dubal, Veena, Winning the Battle, Losing the War? Assessing the Impact of Misclassification Litigation on Workers in the Gig Economy, 239 *Wisconsin Law Review* (2017).

Erickson, Christopher L., Catherine L. Fisk, Ruth Milkman, Daniel J. B. Mitchell, & Kent Wong, Justice for Janitors in Los Angeles: Lessons from Three Rounds of Negotiations, 40 *British Journal of Industrial Relations* 543 (2002).

Estlund, Cynthia L., The Ossification of American Labor Law, 102 *Columbia Law Review* 1527 (2002).

The Death of Labor Law?, 2 *Annual Review of Law & Social Science* 105 (2006).

Fine, Janice, *Worker Centers: Organizing Communities at the Edge of the Dream*. Ithaca, NY: Cornell University Press, 2006.

Fisk, Catherine L., Reimagining Collective Rights in the Workplace, 4 *UC Irvine Law Review* 523 (2014).

Frank, Larry, & Kent Wong, Dynamic Political Mobilization: The Los Angeles County Federation of Labor, 8 *Working USA* 155–157 (2004).

Garea, Susan, & Sasha Alexandra Stern, From Legal Advocacy to Organizing: Progressive Lawyering and the Los Angeles Car Wash Campaign. In *Working for Justice: The L.A. Model of Organizing and Advocacy*, ed. Ruth Milkman, Joshua Bloom, & Victor Narro. Ithaca, NY: ILR Press, 2010.

Gottlieb, Robert, Mark Vallianatos, Regina M. Freer, & Peter Dreier, eds., *The Next Los Angeles: The Struggle for a Livable City*. Berkeley: University of California Press, 2005.

Grant, David M., A Demographic Profile of Los Angeles County, 1970 to 1990, in *Prismatic Metropolis: Inequality in Los Angeles*, ed. Lawrence D. Bobo, Melvin L. Oliver, James H. Johnson, Jr., & Abel Valenzuela, Jr. New York: Russell Sage Foundation Press, 2000.

Lichtenstein, Nelson, *State of the Union: A Century of American Labor*. Princeton, NJ: Princeton University Press, 2002.

Matsuoka, Martha, From Neighborhood to Global: Community-Based Regionalism and Shifting Concepts of Place in Community and Regional Development. PhD thesis, UCLA, 2005.

Milkman, Ruth, *L.A. Story: Immigrant Workers and the Future of the U.S. Labor Movement*. New York: Russell Sage Foundation Press, 2006.

More, Paul et al., *The Other Los Angeles: The Working Poor in the City of the 21st Century*. Los Angeles, CA: The Los Angeles Alliance for a New Economy, 2000.

Pollin, Robert, & Stephanie Luce, *The Living Wage: Building a Fair Economy*. New York: The New Press, 1998.
Rice, David R., The Bus Rider's Union: The Success of the Law and Organizing Model in the Context of an Environmental Justice Struggle, 26 *Environs* 187–197 (2003).
Sachs, Ben, Employment Law as Labor Law, 29 *Cardozo Law Review* 2685 (2008).
Labor Law Renewal, 1 *Harvard Law & Policy Review* 375 (2007).
Sachs, Ben I., Employment Law as Labor Law, 29 *Cardozo Law Review* 2685 (2008).
Sassen, Saskia, *The Global City: New York*. Princeton, NJ: Princeton University Press, 1991.
Schneider, Jack, Escape from Los Angeles: White Flight from Los Angeles and Its Schools, 1960–1980, 34 *Journal of Urban History* 995 (2008).
Soja, Edward W., *Seeking Spatial Justice*. Minneapolis: University of Minnesota Press, 2010.
Stone, Katherine V. W., *From Widgets to Digits: Employment Regulation for the Changing Workplace*. New York: Cambridge University Press, 2004.
Stone, Katherine, & Scott Cummings, Labor Activism in Local Politics: From CBAs to "CBAs", in *The Idea of Labour Law*, ed. Guy Davidov & Brian Langille. London: Oxford University Press, 2011.
Understanding the Riots: Los Angeles Before and After the Rodney King Case. Los Angeles, CA: Los Angeles Times Syndicate Books, 1992.
von Hoffman, Alexander, *House by House, Block by Block: The Rebirth of America's Neighborhoods*. New York: Oxford University Press, 2003.
Wilton, Robert D. & Cynthia Cranford, Toward an Understanding of the Spatiality of Social Movements: Labor Organizing at a Private University in Los Angeles, 49 *Social Problems* 374 (2014).
Working for Justice: The L.A. Model of Organizing and Advocacy, ed. Ruth Milkman, Joshua Bloom, & Victor Narro. Ithaca, NY: ILR Press, 2010.
Zatz, Noah D., Working Beyond the Reach or Grasp of Employment Law, in *The Gloves-Off Economy: Workplace Standards at the Bottom of America's Labor Market*, ed. Annette Bernhardt, Heather Boushey, Laura Dresser, & Chris Tilly. Champagne, IL: Labor and Employment Relations Association, 2008.

7

Regulation of the Access of Undocumented Migrants to Social Protection

Exploring the Boundaries of Solidarity

Alexandre de le Court

7.1 INTRODUCTION: UNDOCUMENTED MIGRANTS, ORGANISED SOLIDARITY, AND FACTORS OF INCLUSION

The evolution from nationality to residence as factor for inclusion in systems of social protection has shaped undocumented immigrants into an exclusionary category, with the view to bring social law in line with goals of immigration control. However, undocumented immigrants have access to social protection in certain circumstances.

Systems of social protection are generally construed as the expression of the concept of solidarity or as governed by a principle of solidarity considered as a core value of democratic states, with constitutional relevance (Becker 2007: 1). However, solidarity is an elusive, difficult and poly-semantic concept (Supiot 2015). In this chapter, I refer to solidarity above all as state-organised, compulsory redistribution of resources related to the notion of welfare state, sometimes also referred to as 'coerced collective action' (Kolers 2012), or to use Durkheim's concept, an imposed form of organic solidarity. This form of redistribution is regulated by a legal concept of solidarity, among other principles. But from a political point of view, it must base its legitimacy on the understanding of solidarity by those who are part of it (van der Veen et al. 2012).

But this also poses the question of the boundaries of solidarity. Who can be part of that system of solidarity? In exploring that question, this chapter uses the notions of exclusive and inclusive solidarity as loosely based on the work of Hannah Arendt. She defines exclusive solidarity as a shared experience of oppression leading to interdependence and a shared understanding of the rationale of action and organisation. And inclusive solidarity is present where the experience of oppression is not shared but where action and organisation arise from the 'judgment that certain factual conditions involved in the situation of a ... group of persons constitute an affront to the dignity of humankind' (Reschaur 1992: 728).

For practical reasons, this chapter translates those concepts into a form that would structure the analysis around its objective. Therefore, inclusive solidarity would refer to organised solidarity that goes further than the boundaries of the group of solidarity defined around the concept of citizenship and legal residence. Redistribution of resources to cover social risks within that group of solidarity would be referred to as exclusive solidarity, involving a communitarian understanding of solidarity (Misic 2018: 271). Even if those translations do not contain the same meaning as in their use by Arendt as dynamics of solidarity, it is contended that the concepts of exclusive and inclusive solidarity have those logics at their core, even if some aspects of solidarity within the community of nationals and immigrants with authorised residence are funded on the logic of inclusive solidarity, and some aspects of the access of undocumented immigrants to organised social protection find their explanation in logics of exclusive solidarity. This would show the inherent lack of coincidence between the logics of immigration law and social protection law.

As even in the EU the subject still pertains to the core competences of the Member States (excepting within the sphere of the right to free movement), and in the presence of only very timid specific international standards on the matter (O'Cinneide 2020: 58), the chapter analyses four cases pertaining to the Continental Welfare State group (and its Mediterranean derivative), Germany, The Netherlands, France, and Spain. Their systems of organised solidarity rely on a combination of employment-related social insurance systems and more universalistic complementary systems of protection.

Core to the analysis are the concepts of responsibility, reciprocity, dignity, and vulnerability as factors of inclusion in the circle of solidarity, reflecting different 'dimensions of solidarity' (Supiot 2015), which are also factors of legitimation of the institutionalisation of solidarity in the form of those social protection systems (van Oorschot and Roosma 2015).

Before starting the analysis, and given the extremely complex character of the question, some limitations to the study must be explained. The notions of undocumented worker or undocumented immigrant are complex and represent various realities of precarious statuses of residence in a host country: refused asylum seekers, non-citizens with expired authorisations, immigrants with short-term authorisation without work permits, persons in a situation of transition between authorisations, victims of human trafficking, and so on. The analysis developed here eludes that complexity to a certain extent, as its objective is to focus above all on the regulation of social rights, rather than be a study of the notion of undocumented migrant. This is also the reason why it does not consider the different regulations of the residence and work authorisation policy or the different openings towards regularisation of immigration status, relating to immigration law, even if they are important factors of access to solidarity that allow one to qualify that solidarity around the inclusive–exclusive spectrum.

This is because the purpose of the chapter is to explore the legal boundaries of the systems of social protection as defined by social law, and critically analyse the exclusion of undocumented migrants from those systems, drawing on the different rationales legitimising being on the receiving end of solidarity, other than nationality or legal residence. While the first section focuses on the discussion of exclusion from the point of view of the equality principle, the following sections analyse the system of benefits in case of work-related accidents as a system based on the responsibility of the employer, employment-related insurance as a system based on reciprocity, social assistance as a system guaranteeing dignity as well as evolving around the idea of vulnerability, and, finally, healthcare as having essential links with core fundamental rights.

7.2 EXCLUSIVE SOLIDARITY AS INSTRUMENT OF IMMIGRATION POLICY AND THE PROBLEMATIC FRAMEWORK OF EQUALITY LAW

The French or Dutch cases clearly show that the exclusion of undocumented immigrants from organised systems of solidarity should not be considered as an absolute constant, but rather the culmination of a process accompanying or following the extension of social security systems and gradual substitution of nationality by residence as a criterion of inclusion (Isidro 2016: 106; Kapuy 2011: 271).

Since the Dutch Linkage Act of 1998, Section 10 of the Act on Foreign Nationals (Vreemdelingenwet) provides that a foreigner without authorisation to stay has no right to benefits or advantages conceded by an administrative authority. Exceptions are possible for benefits related to education, necessary medical care, the necessity to protect public health, or legal assistance.

In France, authorised residence as a condition of access to social insurance was generalised by the Act of 24 August 1993 on Control of Immigration and Conditions of Entry, Reception and Stay of Non-Nationals in France, after a process of affirmation by administrative courts and the Conseil Constitutionnel of a principle of equal treatment between nationals and non-nationals in terms of social security (Michelet 2007: 82–83). Since then, section 115–116 of the Social Security Code only allows inclusion of foreign citizens in obligatory social insurance if they are in order with legislation on residence and work of non-nationals. Access to retirement, invalidity, maternity, and sickness benefits became likewise limited. Exclusion of undocumented immigrants from social assistance was culminated in 1998 (Isidro 2016).

The Spanish case is one of central regulation, but with precepts left open to interpretation. Act 4/2000 of 11 January on the rights and freedoms of foreigners in Spain and their social integration provides that those foreigners with residence in accordance with the legal provisions have the right to develop a professional activity as employee or self-employed person as well as the right to access the social security system. They also have the right to social assistance and social services in the same conditions as Spanish citizens. Undocumented immigrants could be therefore considered as excluded *a contrario*. However, the Act also provides that non-nationals, whatever their administrative status (including thus undocumented immigrants) have the right to basic social services and benefits. Also, the Act specifies that the absence of authorisation to reside or to work 'shall not be an obstacle for the access to benefits deriving from circumstances provided by international treaties for the protection of workers, or other [benefits] to which [the worker] could have right, whenever they are compatible with his or her situation'. The open wording of the provision seems to be in line with the statement of the Tribunal Supremo in a judgment recognising the right to benefits in case of industrial accident, according to which one cannot ignore 'the progressive evolution towards the social protection of immigrants who provide services as employees without counting with the preceptive authorisations' (González Ortega 2008).[1] However, in a later judgment of 2008 on access to unemployment benefits, the same Court put the brakes on the expansive jurisprudence of lower courts that was being built on that idea.[2] It considered that such an approach would imply the lack of different treatment between authorised and non-authorised residents, a movement that would go against the aim of disincentivising non-authorised immigration. Therefore, a restrictive interpretation was needed, and the Court seemingly limited the 'benefits compatible with the situation of the worker' to the basic social assistance benefits expressly authorised by the Act.[3]

The German case is one based on more complex legislation and a different tiers system. Section 30 of the 1st Book of the Social Code (*Sozialgestezbuch* I, or SGB I) provides that the Social Code, as an expression of the responsibilities of the Social State, applies to all those who have their domicile or habitual residence in Germany (Mimentza Martin 2011: 125). As undocumented immigrants are considered by definition to have a provisional residence, because of the lack of authorisation, they are excluded from said scope (ibid.: 126).[4] However, section 37 SGB I provides that the specific regulation in other books of the Social Code can make exceptions to the principle of section 30, enlarging or reducing said scope. As such, inclusion in obligatory employee social insurance depends on legality of employment (even if in some cases employment can be legal even without authorisation to stay and exceptions are made under the regulation of specific social risks). Inclusion in the system

1 González Ortega (2008) cites the Judgment of the Tribunal Supremo of 7 October 2003 to ground this assumption.

2 Judgment of the Tribunal Supremo of 18 March 2008.

3 Montoya Medina (2009: 863) criticises that interpretation by stating that a systematic and teleological interpretation of the provision and the Act does not permit such a far-reaching limitation, giving rise to the possibility of access to employees' social insurance benefits 'compatible with the workers' situation'.

4 This would thus include in the scope of application those undocumented workers who have not (yet) been ordered to leave the country.

of social assistance benefits in cash for employable persons (Hartz IV) also depends on habitual residence. But the Act on Asylum's Seekers Benefits, which provides for a system of social assistance calculated and organised differently, also applies to those who are 'obliged to leave the country', and therefore undocumented immigrants (ibid.). This involves thus the existence of a different tiers system, the content of which varies in function of administrative status, but which guarantees, in theory, a minimum of subsistence to all.

The logic of subservience of solidarity to immigration policy is expressed thus under different forms of intensity in function of the case. In a particular case it has been pushed to the extreme through the appearance of what has been called a 'solidarity crime'.[5] Section L622-1 of the French Code for Entry and Residence of Foreigners and the Right of Asylum forbids any person to facilitate or try to facilitate the irregular entry, circulation, or stay of a non-citizen. The interpretation of this vague definition by Criminal Courts ended considering various forms of individual, private help towards undocumented migrants as an offence, and prohibited thus solidarity in its most unorganised version: direct empathy and defining a category of persons not even deserving private help for a supposed common good (Cinalli and De Nuzzo 2018: 295 and 298).

However, in the context of appeal procedures against those judgments, the Conseil Constitutionnel recognised for the first time in an explicit manner the principle of fraternity as constitutional principle, which involves the guarantee of 'the liberty to help others, with a humanitarian goal, without consideration of the regularity of their stay within the national territory'. As a response to the public debate, an amendment was introduced in the law in September 2018 that created immunity from prosecution in case of free help to move within the territory or in providing shelter, except if the help is provided for passing the border. This brought French law more in line with article 1 of Directive 2002/90/EC, which requires financial gain for the assistance to undocumented immigrants to be an offence. Before the entry into force of that law, the Cour de Cassation already annulled judgments in application of the jurisprudence of the Conseil Constitutionnel and ordered the persons to be judged again before the Court of Appeal of Lyon, which absolved them from prosecution in May and October 2020.[6]

However, it is not only in its extreme expressions that the limitation of solidarity as a mechanism at the service of immigration policy has been brought before the

[5] The notion of 'solidarity crime' starts being used in several countries to conceptualise the criminalisation of individuals and organisations helping migrants and refugees. This can happen through direct means, like in the French case, but also through indirect means, like in the case of the prosecution of ship captains helping refugees crossing the Mediterranean in Italy for supposed complicity with immigration mafias (and there are other cases in Switzerland, Belgium, and the USA), contributing to the forming of an imaginary where a fundamental value ends being criminalised.

[6] The Prosecution, however, appealed the judgment of 18 May 2020 so that the case is again pending before the Cour de Cassation.

Courts. In the four analysed cases, the legal configuration of exclusive solidarity systems in function of the necessities of immigration policy has been challenged on the grounds of the equality principle, without, however, any real success.

The Centrale Raad voor Beroep[7] had to decide upon several requests for non-application of the Dutch Linkage Act for being contrary to the equality principle of article 26 of the International Covenant on Civil and Political Rights. The Court found that there was no violation because the purpose of the Act as well as its means were sufficiently justified: the Act contributed to a coherent migration policy that had among its goals that persons who are not authorised to stay would be made to leave. In this context, access to social benefits could give rise to extension of unauthorised stays and the creation of a situation of 'apparent legality' possibly affecting the qualification of the residence.

The French Conseil Constitutionnel approved the 1993 reform by merely and very succinctly stating that it did not violate the principle of equal treatment, because undocumented immigrants were not in a similar situation when compared to nationals or non-nationals with authorisation to reside or work.[8] As such the Conseil did not even proceed to assess if the difference of treatment was adequate to the purpose of the law. This does not seem to be in line with the traditional doctrine on equal treatment principle. It would be difficult to sustain that the adequate character of exclusion from social insurance is sufficiently evident for the Court not to even mention it (Michelet 2007: 84).

Even if there are no judgments of the Spanish Constitutional Court on the specific provisions regulating inclusion in social security, the application of the equality principle between nationals and non-nationals has been configured with the occasion of a 1984 judgment on the compatibility with the right to work of the existence of a work authorisation as condition for valid employment. Starting from the premise that section 14 of the Constitution limits the application of the general principle of equality of treatment to Spanish nationals, it states, however, that the use of nationality as a criterium to limit access to a right is not allowed if this would be prohibited by law or an international treaty, or in case it would affect those fundamental rights that are necessary for the guarantee of human dignity and which the Constitution generally states that they belong to anyone, and not only to Spanish citizens.[9] But the right to work does not belong to that second category.

The more complex character of the legislation in the German case might explain that there does not seem to exist judicialised controversies on the exclusion of undocumented immigrants from the general scope of the Social Code. However, segmentation of social assistance rights in function of the type of residence authorisation (or the absence of authorisation) has been discussed under the

[7] The highest appeal court in matters of social security.

[8] Conseil Constitutionnel, Decision 93-325 DC of 13 August 1993, at 118.

[9] Tribunal Constitucional, judgment 107/1984 of 23 November, legal ground no. 3.

equality principle of section 3 of the German Federal Basic Law. Benefits under the Asylum Seekers' Benefits Act are more limited, can be paid in kind,[10] and are not based on an individualised approach. However, in a Judgment of 13 November 2018, the Bundessozialgericht found that this did not involve a violation of the equal treatment clause of section 3 paragraph 1 of the Federal Constitution. Considering the wider margin of appreciation of the legislator when regulating social benefits linked to the needs of the beneficiaries, the Court found that the justification for the unequal treatment (reducing economic migration and avoiding social benefits from being incentives for the extension of the stay of beneficiaries) was to be considered in adequate proportion to the affectation of the fundamental right. And one of the main reasons for that is that basic needs are guaranteed in all cases. Here thus, the existence of a multiple-tier system guaranteeing basic needs allows to consider as justified the exclusion of access to 'general' social rights in the name of migration policy. Another argument that was used, and reminds of the reasoning of the Dutch courts, is the necessity to avoid factual statuses that might be considered hidden regularisation processes.

A look at the jurisprudence of the European Court of Human Rights (ECtHR) also shows the limitations of the non-discrimination framework in challenging restrictive legislation in the international sphere. However, it allows for the addition of new elements to the debate.

The European Convention on Human Rights has, according to its article 1, the vocation of applying to 'all persons' under the jurisdiction of the ratifying parties, including undocumented immigrants (Da Lomba 2014), and the ECtHR has forbidden unequal treatment between nationals and non-nationals in the access to social security rights in the absence of sufficient justification.[11] However, in *Ponomaryovi* v. *Bulgaria* (judgment of 28 November 2011), the Court considered that 'a State may have legitimate reasons for curtailing the use of resource-hungry public services – such as welfare programmes, public benefits and healthcare – by short-term and illegal immigrants, who, as a rule, do not contribute to their funding. It may also, in certain circumstances, justifiably differentiate between different categories of aliens residing in its territory.' In the case at hand, the Court found a violation of article 14 taken in conjunction with article 2 of Protocol no. 1 (right to education), considering the circumstances of the case, which excluded the application of 'any consideration related to the need to stem or reverse the flow of illegal immigration' or that it could not be said that the applicant tried to abuse the Bulgarian education system. The Court seems thus to connect on the one hand the right of access to public benefits to the level of contribution to the system, and on the other does not rule out the objectives of immigration policy or the limitation of abuse of the system as possible justification of unequal treatment on grounds of the

[10] Even if in general beneficiaries are given cash benefits, except in Bavaria.

[11] ECtHR, judgment of 16 September 1996, *Gaygusuz* v. *Austria*, and subsequent jurisprudence; for a critical appraisal of the significance of the judgment, see Dembour (2012).

immigration status. The Court confirmed in *Bah* v. *United Kingdom* that limiting 'access of certain categories of aliens to resource-hungry' public services could be justified, where it considered that excluding access of a mother and her son to social housing and housing assistance because the residence authorisation of her son was delivered on the condition that he would have no recourse to public funds, pursued the legitimate aim of allocating a scarce resource fairly between different categories of claimants.[12] The means were also considered to be proportionate to the aim given the specific circumstances of the case, because there would have been an obligation of the municipal authority to intervene if the threat of homelessness had materialised, even if temporarily.

Those decisions show the lack of effectiveness of the equality framework in advancing inclusive solidarity in the field. But this lack of effectiveness could not be said to be due to an intrinsic problem with the principle of equality, or the weakness of possible justifications against exclusion versus those in favour. What the analysis reveals is the general unwillingness of Courts to proceed to a weighted analysis of the different countervailing arguments, taking subjective legislative assumption generally for granted. On the other hand, they do not seem to go as far as ruling out immigration status as a possible ground for discrimination. As such, there is a formal adherence to the right of undocumented migrants to equality, but in practice, the margin of appreciation given to the Member State or the legislative power 'dilutes the impact of this formal universalism', without forgetting the weaker protection generally given to social fundamental rights (O'Cinneide 2020: 58).[13]

However, the underdevelopment of that area of human rights law does not mean that there can be no evolution towards more universalism (ibid.: 64). When focusing on social protection, one element to be considered is the internal logic of the regulation of access to those systems. In addition to treating that aspect, the following sections also show that there are cases where exclusionary systems are not as tightly closed as one would assume.

7.3 THE CASE OF INDUSTRIAL ACCIDENTS: INCLUSIVE SOLIDARITY AND EMPLOYERS' RESPONSIBILITIES

In all the cases of the analysis, whatever the restrictive character of their social insurance system towards undocumented workers, exceptions are made for benefits related to industrial accidents.

[12] The Court also considered that, while immigration status is to be considered an aspect of personal status for the purpose of article 14, despite being granted by law, the element of choice as to the status is important to determine the scope of the margin of appreciation to be accorded to the state. It reminded that the applicant was not a refugee, and could thus return to her country of origin, and chose to have her son join her in the United Kingdom.

[13] This also confirms to some extent the observation of Dembour (2012), according to whom there is a refusal to address the liberal contradiction between universalism of rights and particularism in access to resources.

The Dutch case is one where inclusive solidarity in the matter is technically explained by the classification of the question as part of the realm of labour law, rather than social security. Pursuant to article 629 of the 7th Book of the Dutch Civil Code on the regulation of the employment contract, in case of incapacity to work due to illness (including accident, industrial accidents and professional diseases), pregnancy or childbirth, the employer has the obligation to pay the employee 70 per cent of the salary during a maximum period of 104 weeks.[14] As employment contracts celebrated with a worker without authorisation to work or stay are considered valid as to their effects, independently of the responsibility of the workers for the situation, the system of wage continuation applies also to undocumented workers (Kapuy 2011: 513). Here thus, it is the formal qualification of the coverage of a social risk as a right under labour law (as opposed to a social security right) for which the employer is solely responsible, which serves as system of extension of solidarity.[15]

In the other cases, the link with the employment contract is more tenuous, even if material or formal connections are clearly present. The definition of industrial accident by section L-411-2 of the French Social Security Code applies to 'all employees or person providing work, wherever and under which title ever'. This has been traditionally interpreted as including undocumented workers under the principle that 'no distinction has to be made when the law does not make any'.[16] The origin of the definition of professional disease in the Labour Code and its treatment under the same Book of the Social Security Code also involves inclusion of undocumented workers under its scope.

Obligatory inclusion in the Unfallenversicherung (German Insurance in case of Industrial Accidents, SGB VII) depends only on the material characteristics of being employed, without consideration to the declared or undeclared character of the work, or the residence status. In this line, the law explicitly provides for the payment of benefits also when the habitual residence is in another country (Mimentza Martin 2011: 174). The insurance institutions can, however, recover the costs of their intervention towards the employer in case of absence of declaration and payment of contributions.[17]

[14] In case of permanent incapacity to work, however, most undocumented workers will not be covered as they will not be considered as employees under the Sickness Benefits Act and the Work and Income According to Labour Capacity Act (Kapuy 2011: 518).

[15] In case of permanent incapacity due to industrial accident, there is also an obligation under labour law to compensate the worker for the loss of salaries. Permanent incapacitation in case of illness or non-industrial accident is covered under the Social Security Law, involving exclusion of undocumented non-citizens. However, the *Besluit aanspraken bij beroepsziekten van niet op grond van de* WAO *of de Wet* WIA *verzekerden* provides for an exception in case of certain professional diseases, even if payment of benefits is made dependent on the proof of establishment in another country.

[16] Cour de Cassation, judgment of 4 May 2016, Case 15-12.237.

[17] §110 SGB VII.

The Spanish Tribunal Supremo, in its judgment of 9 June 2003, based its favourable interpretation of existing norms (ILO Convention 19 on Equality of Treatment (Accident Compensation) and Order of 1966 on the extension of the scope of social security) on the idea that 'a worker cannot be deprived of an element of protection which in our system of labour relations always has been inherent to the employment contract'. Therefore, the principle of automaticity of benefits and presumed registration with the social security system in case of industrial accidents should apply, even in case of nullity of the employment contract. As explained hereunder, those principles involve payment of benefits by the social security administration also in case of undeclared work, and repetition of the benefits from the employer by the administration.

Benefits in case of industrial accidents are thus an important exception to the exclusion of undocumented workers from social protection. This could be explained by the close historical links this form of worker protection has with the contract of employment. In the analysed cases, absence of work and/or residence authorisation does not invalidate the contract, or if it does, the effectiveness of most rights the employee has under the contract is not affected. Moreover, rooted in the traditional concept of objective liability of the employer for industrial accidents, the cost of that social insurance is generally fully borne by the employer, and it is less the community of nationals and authorised residents that bears the costs of redistribution. This is also expressed by the right to repetition that the state has towards employers whose undocumented workers are to be covered by state benefits. One could therefore discuss whether this system of social protection is to be grounded on principles at the basis of organised solidarity, or rather pertains to the scope of responsibility and liability from one contracting party to the other, even if the mechanisms of application of that private liability have been collectivised.

7.4 EMPLOYMENT-BASED SOCIAL INSURANCE SYSTEMS: EXCLUSIVE SOLIDARITY DESPITE RECIPROCITY

Undocumented workers are generally excluded from employment-based social insurance, whether as part of the general exclusion like in the Dutch[18] and French cases,[19] or through a more complex configuration in the German and

[18] As a complement to the Linkage Act, the different acts regulating the branches of employment-based social insurance (Health Care Act – Ziektewet, Unemployment Act – Werkloosheidswet, Work and Income according to Labour Capacity Act – Wet Wia – and the Work and Care Act – WAZO) all provide for the explicit exclusion of undocumented workers from the notion of employee under their application. Also, without authorised residence, non-nationals who are receiving benefits would see their right suspended, suspensions that would be lifted in case of a new authorisation or once residence has been established abroad in the EU/EEA or in a country with which a bilateral agreement has been concluded (Kapuy 2011: 482–483).

[19] Up to 2017, section L161-8 of the Social Security Code provided that in case of loss of conditions to be covered by a regime of social insurance (which the Council of State extended to the loss

Spanish cases. However, if undocumented workers are excluded from benefits, social contributions generally remain due by the employer for the period of unauthorised employment. The connection of those contributions with the principle of reciprocity as an important element at the basis of (and legitimisation of) redistribution of resources through solidarity allows us to question the coherence of the exclusion.

The German case is one of generally explicit exclusion from the right to perceive benefits. Undocumented workers are also excluded from unemployment benefits, due to their impossibility to be able to enter the labour market, one of the main conditions of the benefit. And considering healthcare, sickness benefits, and support in case of care needs, the inclusion of undocumented immigrants within the special healthcare and social assistance benefits of the Benefits for Asylum Seekers Act involves their exclusion from those social insurances.

As seen above, the Spanish case is one where access to social insurance benefits seems not to be necessarily prohibited to undocumented workers. However, a general condition for the access to benefits in the case of the occurrence of a social risk is that the worker be registered with the social security system, an administrative act that can only take place upon the communication by the employer of the hiring of the worker, which involves the communication of the authorisation to work in the case of non-nationals. However, in case of undeclared work, section 166.4 of the Basic Social Security Act provides that, with respect to benefits in case of unemployment, industrial accident, and healthcare benefits in case of maternity, common accident or common illness, workers will be presumed being registered by law if they fulfil the other conditions to receive those benefits. And because the payment of contributions is a responsibility that pertains to the employer, the lack thereof cannot be opposed to the worker by the social security administration. This construction has been extended to undocumented workers in the case of industrial accidents, as seen above, but the Tribunal Supremo refused to extend it to unemployment benefits. Claims to other benefits have not been brought before courts.

On the other hand, despite the exclusion from the reception of benefits, all cases provide for the obligation of the employer to pay the social contributions related to the period of (most probably) undeclared employment, based on the responsibility for the employer for their payment,[20] except in the case of The Netherlands,[21] were

of authorisation to work/reside), the right to sickness, maternity, invalidity, and benefits in case of decease would be maintained during a period determined by decree (one year in 1998). However, the provision was amended in 2017 and now excludes expressly undocumented workers from its application.

[20] France: section 115-6 Social Security Code. In Germany, this obligation is generally submitted to a prescription period of thirty years (Tangemann and Grote 2017).

[21] With some exceptions for the employer and in the case of social insurance not related to employment, like the basic pension insurance (Kapuy 2011: 490).

payment of an amount equivalent to unpaid contribution is legally conceptualised as a fine.

As seen above, the Spanish Tribunal Supremo has put the question of the obligation of payment of social contributions despite the unauthorised character of the employment in the middle of its legal reasoning for the recognition of some categories of social insurance benefits to undocumented workers.

The payment of contributions can be connected to the insurance logic behind earnings-substituting benefits. But it is also closely connected to the idea of reciprocity or the interdependency logic behind those forms of organised solidarity. Social contributions can be considered as a tax on the salary with the objective to finance specifically the benefits paid to the other members of the group of solidarity (in the future or at the time of payment) and involve therefore 'membership elements' (Spiegel et al. 2015: 11). Therefore, their payment is the fulfilment of the primary condition of reciprocity to be able to be part of the system.

In the four analysed cases, it is the employer who bears the responsibility to pay social contributions to the administration, both those that are detracted from the workers' salary in a legal sense and those the employer has the obligation to pay, and which are part of the salary as labour cost. And in case of irregular employment the employer will bear liability for the lack of payment. But it is important to conceptualise that liability as not related to the obligation of the employer to contribute to the system, but to the employer being the instrument through which contributions are collected, because the employer is the party to the employment contract with the most means. And because the liability of the employer in case of non-payment of contributions is thus a practical means guaranteeing that contributions will be recovered, the absence of their payment during the employment relationship should not exclude the fact that the undocumented worker contributed to the system through his or her employment, and as such fulfilled, at least to a certain extent, the condition of reciprocity at the basis of his or her membership of the community of solidarity.[22]

Under that perspective, the obligation to pay contributions in case of employment of undocumented workers is not to be construed as a penalty on the employer (or at least not exclusively), but as materialisation of the contribution of the worker to the social security system in parallel with his or her contribution to society and/or the economy through his or her activity. It could thus justify their right to access to benefits under the idea of reciprocity as legitimisation of social insurance systems. From that perspective, in those cases where undocumented workers would have

[22] The open clause of section 36.5 of the Spanish Act on Foreigners, granting access to benefits 'compatible' with the situation of the undocumented migrant should thus be read in this light.

worked sufficiently to build up rights to social benefits, the justification for excluding undocumented migrants from social protection brought forward by the EctHR under *Ponomaryovi* v. *Bulgaria* should not stand.[23]

7.5 SOCIAL ASSISTANCE AND OTHER FORMS OF PROTECTION OF THE RISK OF POVERTY: DIGNITY AND VULNERABILITY AS FACTORS OF INCLUSIVE SOLIDARITY

Legal discussion around access of undocumented migrants to social assistance and other subsidiary systems concerns less the principle of equality (except maybe in the German case, to a certain extent, as discussed in Section 7.2) than the existence of a positive obligation of the state to maintain the dignity of all those who find themselves on its territory, with special emphasis on the most vulnerable.

In France, the introduction in 1993 of the authorisations of residence and/or work as condition for access to social benefits also extended to social assistance. Exceptions were made for social assistance benefits for children (extended by jurisprudence to other forms of social aid for children, like school meals); social assistance in case of admission in a shelter for social reinsertion (victims of violence, toxicomania, ex-convicts, and so on); and some social assistance benefits for elderly people (linked with a duration of residence requirement). The Conseil Constitutionnel did not see any infringement of the right, enshrined in the Preamble to the Constitution, 'of any human being to obtain means for an acceptable existence from the community when, for reason of age, physical or mental state, or economic situation he or she is incapable to work'. According to the Conseil, it pertains to the legislative and executive powers to determine the modalities of exercise of that right. And the law restricting access to social assistance provided for the possibility to derogate from the principle of authorised residence by governmental decision. The Conseil recognised this element of proportionality as sufficient not to have to review the law.[24] It is, however, important to point out that the possibility for the government to provide for 'inclusive' exceptions has never been exercised, reinforcing the purely theoretical character of the proportionality test in this case.

Social assistance is also a domain where the open character of definitions in the Spanish case leaves important questions unresolved. Act 4/2000 provides that any non-national, independently of his or her administrative status, has the right to basic social services and benefits. Those concepts are, however, not further defined. Moreover, except for the so-called non-contributory benefits of the social security

[23] It is also important to consider that if undocumented workers do not formally contribute to the social security system, it is because the immigration regulation does not allow them to, despite providing effective work and (even modestly) contributing to the economy or providing valuable services to the community.

[24] Decision 93-325 DC of 13 August 1993, paras 125–127.

systems and the newly implemented Vital Minimum Income, to which undocumented immigrants have no access, social assistance is regulated at the regional level. But regional legislations do not necessarily define benefits or services under categories that would refer to the term 'basic'. The lack of clarity involves a certain leeway for regional laws to remain confusing on the subject and exclude undocumented immigrants for those schemes.

The explicit exclusion of undocumented immigrants to social assistance in the case of The Netherlands gave rise to several challenges based on international law. The Centrale Raad van Beroep recognised in 2010 that in certain circumstances, exclusion from social assistance benefits could violate Art. 8 of the ECHR (right to respect for private and family life, home, and correspondence). In the case at hand, it was recognised that an undocumented migrant with serious health problems that could not be remedied without shelter had a right to the latter in application of the positive obligation of the state to guarantee a person's dignity. However, so as not to 'contradict the migration policy of the government', this does not necessarily mean that those persons have access to social benefits in application of the general social assistance act (WWB, now Participation Act). It first must be ascertained if the positive obligation under Art. 8 ECHR can be assumed by the administration competent for immigration (which provides some benefits or services to some categories of immigrants, like victims of human trafficking or refugees).[25]

The question of exclusion of social assistance to undocumented migrants in The Netherlands was brought to the attention of the European Committee of Social Rights (ECSR) through a collective complaint brought by the Confederation of European Churches for violation of the European Social Charter for the lack of emergency assistance and shelter given to adult undocumented immigrants.

In its decision of 1 July 2014,[26] the ECSR reminded its decision in *FIDH* v. *France*, where it considered that, even though the first paragraph of the Appendix to the ESC apparently limits its scope to foreign nationals of contracting parties when they are residing or working lawfully in the concerned state, the limitation of the scope by the Appendix must be interpreted restrictively to preserve the essence of the rights of the Charter, and would not apply when rights are at stake that have to be considered a prerequisite of human dignity, a fundamental value or the core of positive European human rights law.[27] The ECSR also reminded that already in its 2009 Conclusions it found The Netherlands being in breach with

[25] Centrale Raad van Beroep, judgment of 19 April 2010.

[26] ECSR, Decision on the Merits of 1 July 2014, complaint number 90/2013.

[27] ECSR, Decision on the merits of 3 November 2004, complaint number 14/2003 (*International Federation of Human Rights Leagues* v. *France*). In the case at hand, the ECSR did not find a violation of article 13 of the Charter, as the French system of State Medical Aid (commented hereafter) provided a form of medical assistance to undocumented migrants, even if with imprecise concepts and difficulties of implementation. It found, however, a situation of non-conformity with article 17 as the same conclusions could not be attained when children, to which the UN Convention on the Rights of the Child applies, are concerned.

article 13-4 (right to social and medical assistance to nationals of other Parties to the Charter) and 31-2 (right to housing) of the ESC – because 'it has not been established that all persons without resources, whether or not legally present in The Netherlands, have a legally recognised right to the satisfaction of basic human material need (food, clothing, shelter) in situations of emergency'.[28] Moreover, the Committee considered that emergency assistance 'cannot be made conditional upon the willingness of the persons concerned to cooperate in the organisation of their own expulsion', decoupling thus the limited right to access to solidarity from its submission to immigration policy.

In a judgment of 26 November 2015, the Centrale Raad van Beroep followed only partially the decision of the ECSR. It acknowledged that Art. 3 and Art. 8 of the ECHR could impose, in specific circumstances, the obligation on a state to provide minimal assistance to undocumented immigrants, and that emergency assistance in the form of food and shelter should thus be given. However, it considered that this possibility already existed in the form of the existing shelters for asylum seekers. In the case at hand, the claimant had been offered continued shelter by the Immigration Administration once his authorisation had expired, but on the condition that he would cooperate to his return to his country of origin. The municipality had refused to give assistance under social assistance laws because of the existence of the latter alternative. The Court found that the obligation to cooperate to his return did not invalidate the legitimacy of that alternative (contrary to the position of the ECSR on the obligation to cooperate),[29] for which the refusal of the municipality was in accordance with the law.[30] In a judgment delivered on the same day,[31] the administrative section of the Council of State considered that the cooperation of an undocumented immigrant with his or her return as a condition for providing emergency shelter and assistance did not violate the obligation of the state under the ECHR,[32] provided that exceptions could be made in particular circumstances.[33]

[28] In a Recommendation of 19 January 2000, the Committee of Ministers of the Council of Europe adopted a Recommendation already on 19 January 2000 where it stated that the right to basic material needs 'should be open to all citizens and foreigners, whatever the latter's position under national rules on the status of foreigners'.

[29] The Court stated that the European Social Charter did not have direct applicability and that the decision of the ECSR, while authoritative, did not bind national courts.

[30] Subsequently, the applicant brought a complaint before the ECtHR, which in its Decision of 5 July 2016 (*Hunde* v. *The Netherlands*) acknowledged the decision of the ECSR, but refused to consider that the violation of the ECS in the case would automatically involve a violation of article 3 of the ECHR, and declared the application manifestly ill-founded, refusing to compare the situation to that in *M.S.S.* v. *Belgium and Greece*.

[31] And referred to by the Centrale Raad van Beroep, which shows the judicial cooperation between both Courts on the case.

[32] It also denied direct applicability of the ESC.

[33] It is important to point out that the concerned shelter facilities involve limitation of freedom of movement of their inhabitants, an element that reduces the incentives of undocumented migrants to claim emergency assistance, and that has not been discussed, neither by the ECSR nor by national jurisprudence.

After those decisions governmental negotiations have been slowly going on to develop a 'Bed, Bath and Bread' policy, which for the moment has included the pilot project 'Landelijke Vreemdelingenvoorziening', an agreement between the government and municipalities to develop the first shelters for undocumented immigrants. More than 40 per cent of the persons welcomed in those institutions ended receiving authorisations of residence after a certain time, despite not having authorised residence when they claimed the right to shelter and food (Mack et al. 2020). This shows again the complexity of the categorisation of undocumented immigrants as well as the lack of immutable character of their status, reinforcing the argument for more generous perspectives on their right to access solidarity systems.

The German case is also of particular interest, since the Federal Constitutional Court recognised for everyone the fundamental right to a benefit guaranteeing the minimum of existence arising out of the social state principle and the right to dignity in its 'Hartz IV' judgment of 2010. The object of the constitutional challenge was the system of social assistance benefits for employable persons (ALG II), discussed in Section 7.2.[34] The question soon arose if such right would also apply to foreigners without resources, including undocumented migrants. With its judgment of 2012 the Court declared the fundamental right to a minimum of existence applicable to all non-citizens falling under the scope of the Benefits for Asylum Seekers Act and that the level of benefits provided at that time involved a manifest violation of the right. The Court explicitly stated that

> Migration policy considerations to keep the benefits for asylum seekers and refugees low to avoid incentives for migratory movements due to a possible comparative high level of benefits, cannot justify a lowering of those benefits below the physical and socio-cultural subsistence level from the outset . . . The human dignity guaranteed in Section 1, Paragraph 1 of the Basic Law cannot be relativized for reasons of migration policy.[35]

According to some authors, section 1a of the Asylum Seekers' Benefits Act, which reduces the range of benefits guaranteeing the minimum of existence to undocumented migrants who act to impede their return to their home country to cover only food, housing and personal hygiene (excluding clothing, consumer goods and other daily needs), could be considered as violating the fundamental right (Kanalan 2018), reflecting the position of the ECSR on the unconditionality of social assistance for undocumented migrants.

[34] Concerning access of undocumented migrants to social assistance in Germany, next to the benefits of the Asylum Seekers' Act, it is also important to point out that, pursuant to section 2 of the Act, after an uninterrupted stay of eighteen months that would not have been influenced by a behaviour constituting an abuse of right, benefits will be paid in application of the XIIth Book of the Social Code (social assistance for non-employable persons). This means that a more 'generous', individualised approach, with benefits in cash, would be applied in cases of long-term stay in 'precarious' authorisation circumstances.

[35] Bundesverfassungsgericht, judgment of 18 July 2012 (1 BvL 10/10), para. 95.

When analysing social assistance or non-employment-related systems of social protection, it is more difficult to integrate the logic of contribution as expression of the idea of reciprocity to argue for inclusive solidarity, even if the logic of reciprocity is invading the logic of social assistance through its 'workfarisation' or its increasing conditionality (de le Court 2016; Hoop 2014). This does not mean that the rationale behind social assistance cannot relate to the idea of solidarity. In this case, the jurisprudence of the German Federal Constitutional Court on the right to a minimum existence is a strong example of legal recognition of the link between the human right and the fundamental value of dignity and the right of access to organised solidarity with only potential residual conditions of reciprocity for undocumented immigrants.

Another element that is present in those decisions making exceptions to the exclusion of undocumented workers is the vulnerability of the specific persons affected,[36] or the conceptualisation of undocumented migrants as a particularly vulnerable group (Krause 2008). The same idea is also expressed by the Inter-American Court of Human Rights in its advisory opinion OC-18/03 of 17 September 2003 on the Legal Condition and Rights of Undocumented Migrants. It has been the main argument for the ECSR to extend application of the European Social Charter to persons 'unlawfully present' on the territory of a contracting party, despite the wording of paragraph 1 of the Appendix. It also surrounds the justification of a more generous regime for children of undocumented migrants, under the influence of the UN Convention for the Rights of the Child.[37] This is an element of much relevance when considering the point of view of solidarity (Reshaur 1992: 728). One cannot deny that undocumented migrants are to be categorised as a particularly vulnerable group, and that this vulnerability is greatly increased by the lack of access to social rights on the one hand, and the difficulties to access them in those cases where they have a right in principle. One of the aspects of the latter problem is that contact with social protection institutions involves visibility and the consequent increase of chances to be expelled or be notified of the obligation to leave the country, above all given the obligation of those institutions to communicate irregularities to the immigration administration. To the extent such obligations can be conceptualised as covert obligations for undocumented migrants to cooperate with their return, they should be considered as highly suspicious under the right to housing or social assistance, as developed under the European Social Charter. This should also be considered when analysing data protection rights of undocumented migrants.

[36] Centrale Raad van Beroep, judgment of 19 April 2010, case 09-1082 WMO.

[37] See for example European Committee of Social Rights, *DIH* v. *The Netherlands*, 20 October 2009, and the subsequent decision of 21 September 2012 of the Hoge Raad der Nederlanden (highest cassation court in civil, criminal and tax matters).

7.6 HEALTHCARE: DIGNITY AND PUBLIC INTEREST AGAINST AUSTERITY

The case of healthcare seems to have been a more fertile terrain for inclusive solidarity, even if sometimes only circumscribed to emergency healthcare. Here the concept of dignity can be found to be a justification, however mixed with the necessity to protect the health of the public in general. On the other hand, the reasons accepted by jurisprudence to justify restrictions to access seem to focus more on the costs of healthcare, rather than the necessity to guarantee a 'coherent' immigration policy.

The Spanish case might be considered as an exception within the scope of this chapter. Section 3 of Act 16/2003 on the cohesion and quality of the National Health System provides explicitly that undocumented immigrants have the right to healthcare in the same conditions as Spanish citizens. This has, however, not always been the case. In 2012, the right to healthcare for undocumented workers had been restricted to urgent healthcare in case of serious illness or accident and assistance in case of pregnancy before or after childbirth, as well as healthcare for minors. The Tribunal Constitucional considered that these restrictions did not violate the constitutional duty to develop a healthcare system and to guarantee fundamental rights of foreigners where their dignity is affected.[38] By permitting access to healthcare in situations of emergency, the Act guaranteed interventions in those cases more closely connected with the right to health and the right to life, 'taking into account the objective of the law which is the preservation of the public health system taking into account the possibilities of the system in a moment of intense economic complication, respecting the proportionality principle as well as its international obligations'.[39]

In any case, the situation was reversed by the newly formed socialist government by urgent Decree-Law 7/2018 of 27 July, appealing, according to its preamble, to the special vulnerability of undocumented immigrants and the fact that international law recognises the right to health without discrimination based on the authorised character of the residence.

In the three other cases, special systems of access to healthcare for undocumented migrants have been created, with various degrees of generosity.

While since 1998, the absence of residence authorisation does not allow undocumented non-nationals to be included in Health Care Insurance under the Dutch Health Care Insurance Act (Zorgverzekeringswet), section 10 of the Dutch Act on Foreign Nationals provides an exception to the 'linkage principle' in case of

[38] Tribunal Constitutional, judgment 140/2016 of 21 July, legal ground no. 10.

[39] It is interesting to observe that the Court also cites the jurisprudence of the CJUE commenting on the 'need to protect the finances of the host Member State' when assessing the right of residence of non-economically active EU citizens for access to social benefits (Case C-308/14, 14 June 2016).

necessary medical care or for the protection of public health. The term 'necessary healthcare' is quite broadly defined under section 122a of the Health Insurance Act as care, covered by the Act (or the Long-term Care Act), which the provider (e.g., doctor, hospital) considers to be necessary (with the possibility for the government to exclude some interventions). However, even in those cases, costs are to be borne by the patient. But the Centraal Administratie Kantoor (CAK) covers 80 per cent of the costs of the intervention when those cannot be recovered from the patient (100 per cent for intervention related to pregnancy and childbirth). This means, however, that 20 per cent of the costs remain for the account of the undocumented immigrant, generally to be paid by way of payment plans (Hendriks and Toebes 2015). It has been detected however, that financial considerations might influence the interpretation by healthcare providers of the notion of necessary medical care, excluding access altogether to avoid the risk of non-payment (Hendriks and Toebes 2015; Nationale Ombudsman 2013; Commissie Medische Zorg voor (Dreigend) Uitgeprocedeerde Asielzoekers en Illegale Vreemdelingen 2007).

The different tier system of the German case is also present for healthcare. Undocumented migrants have access to healthcare under the conditions of the Benefits for Asylum Seekers Act. As such, they are not obliged to have healthcare insurance, like the rest of the population. Section 4 of the Benefits for Asylum Seekers Act provides for healthcare and medication, including dental care, necessary for recovery, improvement, or alleviation of 'acute illnesses or painful conditions' or for pregnant women, before and after childbirth. It is also important to point out that in case of admission to a hospital for urgent reasons, migrants are covered by the continued prohibition of disclosure of their personal data. Therefore, the general obligation of any administration providing social benefits to communicate situations of unauthorised residence to the immigration administration under section 87 of the Act on Residence (Aufenthaltsgesetz), does not apply.

The French case is known for having a specific healthcare system for undocumented immigrants, who are explicitly excluded from general social healthcare insurance. The system of State Medical Aid (Aide Médicale de l'État) is regulated by Section L251-1 of the Code for Social Action and Families. It provides an important range of healthcare benefits to those undocumented migrants with resources below a certain level, for a period of one year from the application. The Conseil Constitutionnel, in its already mentioned 1993 decision, considered that exclusion form general healthcare did not violate the right of all to the protection of their health contained in the Preamble to the Constitution, as the latter was guaranteed by the existence of this alternative system of access to healthcare.

The access to State Medical Aid has been further restricted in 2003 (introduction of a waiting period of three months of prior residence, except urgent medical aid) and 2019 (prior residence must have been unauthorised; application cannot be filed through social services anymore; possibility to subject non-urgent interventions to a waiting period of nine months). Both reforms were adopted in annual budgetary laws in the name of the fight against abuses and the need to control costs. On the other hand, the 2019 reform was adopted in a context where almost half of the undocumented immigrants who need healthcare are not covered by the AME or by health insurance (Jusot et al. 2019) and was met with harsh criticism from a great number of healthcare organisations.[40] However, both reforms were unsuccessfully challenged before the Conseil Constitutionnel.

In the first case, the Conseil repeated its 1993 position on the existence of alternatives in case of urgent need to find no violation of the right of all to protection of their health. However, it assumed (without expressly stating it) that the restriction, introduced in a law regulating budgetary matters, was sufficiently connected to the objective of the law (financial considerations related to the necessity to curb costs),[41] accepting as such without reservation a legislative assumption of a highly subjective character (Michelet 2007: 85). In the second case, the Conseil Constitutionnel considered that the measures involved a conciliation between the right to health and the constitutional requirement of a good use of public money and the need to combat fraud in matters of social protection, which was not manifestly disproportionate.[42]

In those countries where the two-tier systems of healthcare (or the limitation to emergency healthcare) have been subjected to legal review, under the right to health, the restrictions were declared justified based on the combination of the arguments of cost control (or fighting abuse) and the existence itself of a two-tier system providing for a last-resource intervention.

However, those arguments (or at least the acceptance, without reservation, of those legislative assumptions under the proportionality principle) are highly questionable. No consideration was given by the concerned Courts to the fact that restricting access could contribute to possible degradation of the health of undocumented immigrants, which goes against elementary principles of public health. Moreover, the costs of treatment once medical interventions become urgent are higher than at the initial stages of an illness (Michelet 2007: 85).[43]

This can be illustrated by the dissenting opinion to the judgment of the Spanish Tribunal Constitucional on the matter, which saw no sufficient connection between the limitation of healthcare to a situation of emergency and the goal of the measure (preserving financial sustainability of the system). Excluding persons who in general are part of a particularly vulnerable collective and have more difficulties to pay private healthcare will inevitably lead to their need to receive

[40] Presse release of 31 October 2019, www.aides.org/communique/le-gouvernement-sapprete-degrader-la-sante-des-personnes-etrangeres-le-cri-dalarme-des.

[41] Conseil Constitutionnel, Decision 2003-488 DC of 29 December 2003, paras 18–20.

[42] Conseil Constitutionnel, Decision 2019-796 DC of 27 December 2019.

[43] A parallel reasoning can be found in the dissenting opinion to the 2016 decision of the Spanish Constitutional Court on the restriction of access to free public healthcare, mentioned just before.

(free) urgent public healthcare when their situation has degraded. In that light, the sole declaration of the legislator of the adverse effect of free public healthcare for undocumented immigrants on the sustainability of the system, without more concrete elements, cannot be accepted as sufficient justification,[44] above all because the 2012 modification is to be considered as a regressive measure in the meaning of the International Covenant on Economic, Cultural and Social Rights.

Finally, it should be mentioned that the availability of generalised access to free public healthcare has been used as a reason by the Spanish authorities not to proceed to a campaign of regularisation of undocumented migrants during the COVID crisis, contrary to what happened in Portugal and Italy,[45] where lack of access to healthcare (and the consequences for the spread of COVID) was the main reason behind those campaigns.[46] However, the Spanish experience shows that not only the access of vulnerable immigrants (undocumented or no) to healthcare is a condition for better control of the spread of the pandemic, but other elements of social protection, like the right to health at work or the right to housing, are important in that respect.

7.7 INSCRIBING SOLIDARITY WITH UNDOCUMENTED IMMIGRANTS: RECIPROCITY, DIGNITY AND VULNERABILITY AS BUILDING BLOCKS FOR INCLUSION

During the development of the post-war welfare state, residence has slowly taken the place of nationality as the element of definition of the community within which solidarity as redistribution of resources is organised (Isidro 2016: 106). This could be said as a movement in line with an idea of inclusive solidarity and centred around the extension of the principle of equal treatment between nationals and non-nationals, which, in the field of access to social security under the perspective of human rights law seems to have been affirmed in 1996 by the judgment of the ECtHR in *Gaygusuz* v. *Austria*. Therefore, one could say that social aspects of citizenship have been extended altogether with civil and political rights to non-citizens (lawfully) present in the territory. Social security rights that are strongly based on reciprocity as a source of solidarity, generally through social contributions, have been fully extended. According to Oosterlynck et al. (2015) this corresponds to the idea of organic solidarity. Some restrictions remain in terms of access to

44 Interestingly, the dissenting opinion also reinforced its argument by stating that the 2012 modification was to be considered as a regressive measure in the meaning of the International Covenant on Economic, Cultural and Social Rights, and should thus have been subjected to closer scrutiny.

45 In the latter case, regularisation was also driven to the necessity of declared work in essential sectors.

46 Declaration of the Minister of Social Security and Immigration of 19 May 2020 before the Senate.

solidarity systems, like social assistance, which show fewer tangible elements of reciprocity. There, minimum length of residence is a criterion generally used, whether inscribed in social assistance laws or through conditioning the authorisation of residence to the prohibition to resort to it.

From a negative perspective, the latter restrictions are supposed to combat welfare tourism.[47] But from a positive perspective, they can be considered as translating the need to strengthen the links with the host community before accessing solidarity, reinforcing belonging to that community, reminding the idea of shared norms and values as a source of solidarity (Oosterlynck et al. 2015: 6) as well as building interdependency.[48] However, in most of the analysed cases, this move towards extending solidarity to foreign residents has been accompanied by the introduction of the category of authorised residence (or authorised work) as a new definition of the personal boundaries of solidarity within a national territory. A parallel can be found with what happened to the social protection rights of non-working EU citizens. While in the *Grzelczyk* case the CJUE granted access to social benefits decoupling social rights for EU citizens from the notion of authorised residence,[49] this initial jurisprudence has been restricted with the 'unreasonable burden test' and the 'real link/integration formula' (Thym 2015: 17) moving back towards a more communitarian approach to solidarity with other EU citizens (Schwiertz and Schwenken 2020).

However, this chapter shows that despite the principle that access to social solidarity systems is conditional on the obtention of a residence or work permit, and despite the general movement towards the orientation of social protection towards a tool at the service of immigration policy, exceptions remained or were built in at later stages, through political intervention or upon intervention of (international) courts. And important arguments behind those extensions are related to the different generally admitted rationales behind the construction of communities of solidarity.

The idea of reciprocity lies at the heart of legal debates around the extension of contribution-based social insurance towards undocumented workers, as shown in Section 7.4. The discussion of the right to social assistance and right to healthcare in Sections 7.5 and 7.6 has shown the potential of the principle of dignity, or the concept of protection of fundamental rights essential for the dignity of the person, to promote inclusive solidarity and challenge legally national restrictive policies.

The principle of dignity is also linked to the special vulnerability of undocumented migrants, as the latter intensifies the positive obligation of states for the

47 Whether they are necessary or not for that purpose is another question.

48 This is also the rationale developed by the CJUE to grant access of economically inactive EU citizens in host Member States to social benefits, even if the initial concept of 'close links with the Member State of residence' has been turned into practice into a mere condition of length of residence.

49 Case C-184/99.

guarantee of the former. Adopting the point of view of vulnerability would also give us an additional justification for the inclusion of undocumented workers in insurance against industrial accidents. There is undoubtedly a higher susceptibility for migrant workers suffering industrial accidents, whatever the complex reasons behind that phenomenon. And vulnerability of employees as the weak party to the contract is also a justification behind maintenance of employment rights in case of employment of migrants without administrative authorisation.[50] It is also the vulnerability of Malian undocumented workers that led a French labour court to declare that those workers were victims of 'systemic discrimination' within which abusive acts of the employer were inscribed, the latter taking advantage of the lack of alternatives the workers had to provide for their basic needs. In the case at hand, the workers were not only discriminated against because of their race and/or nationality, but also because of their immigration status, which through its consequences reinforced the other forms of discrimination.[51]

This line of thought brings us also to the importance of intersectionality when speaking of the right to equal treatment of undocumented migrants in precarious administrative situations (Stasiulis et al. 2020). Recent studies show that the conditions for the delivery of authorisation to stay and/or work (and segmentation between categories of immigrants in general) create hierarchies among migrants based on gender, race/ethnicity, nationality, religion and class, rather than meritocratic factors in line with the objectives of immigration policy (Ellerman 2020).

Inscribing solidarity within the definition of the borders of organised solidarity systems highlights the vulnerability of undocumented immigrants, the contradictions between their exclusion from social protection systems and the logic of membership of those same systems, as well as the multiple discriminations to which undocumented migrants are subjected. All those elements would support the requirement of a higher level of scrutiny on the part of the Courts under the equality framework (Da Lomba 2014). As pointed out by some authors, when one considers the disputable character of the justifications put forward by the legislative power in the construction of exclusive solidarity systems, one cannot but wonder at the lightness with which Courts reviewing that legislation take those highly subjective reasonings for granted (Isidro 2016; Michelet 2007). In a context where there seems to be a gap between scientific findings and policy making (Carrera and Merlino 2009) the real extent of the contribution of social benefits or inclusion in social insurance to those situations is widely discussed and far from being obvious. It has been argued that social protection is a minor factor in the choice of country to

[50] Generally, in combination with the fact that legislation conceptualises the obligation of work authorisation for a valid employment contract as directed at the employer rather than the worker, see, for The Netherlands, Conclusions of the Advocate General to the judgment of 27 March 1981 of the Hoge Raad der Nederlanden, nr. 11698 (El Araichi/Roemo); for France, see Doroy (1996); for Germany, see Becker-Schaffner (1977).

[51] Conseil de Prud'hommes de Paris, 17 December 2019, no. RG F 17/10051.

which immigrate, while the level of employment and the presence of a diaspora capable of bringing an informal network of assistance are much more important (Giulietti and Kahanec 2013). Moreover, the supposed pressure of immigration on social expenses is far from being proved (Chojnicki and Ragot 2016) and the effects on the labour market are too complex to lead to a downward pressure on salaries or an increase in unemployment (Ortega and Peri 2009).

In this context, it is also important to consider that immigration seems not to be a strong determining factor explaining loss of support for a redistributive Welfare State (Brady and Finnigan 2014; Mau and Burkhardt 2009) and its potential to undermine the foundation of solidarity should be downplayed, weakening the case for exclusive solidarity.

Reciprocity, dignity and vulnerability are important elements explaining and legitimising solidarity. They are also connected to higher standards in terms of fundamental rights, in a context where symbolic and emotional aspects acquire great importance in the political debates on the subject. Alesino et al. (2019) for example find that 'when it comes to immigration, salience and narratives shape people's views more deeply than hard facts'. Inscribing solidarity within the equality framework and the positive obligations of the state to guarantee dignity for all would thus without doubt create possibilities for a reappraisal by courts and other legal actors of the liberal contradiction between universalism of rights and particularism in access to resources, shifting the balance towards universalism and inclusive solidarity.

REFERENCES

Alesino, Alberto, Armando Miano and Stefanie Stantcheva. 2019. 'Immigration and Redistribution', *NBER Working Paper Series* 24733.

Auspurg, Katrin, Josef Brüderl and Thomas Wöhler. 2019. 'Does Immigration Reduce the Support for Welfare Spending? A Cautionary Tale on Spatial Panel Data Analysis', *American Review of Sociology* 84, 4: 754–763.

Becker, Ulrich. 2007. 'Solidarity, Financing and Personal Coverage in German Statutory Health Insurance', *The Japanese Journal of Social Security Policy* 6, 1: 1–30.

Becker-Schaffner, Reinhard. 1977. 'Arbeitserlaubnis und Arbeitsvertrag', *Arbeit und Recht* 25, 3: 76–81.

Brady, David and Ryan Finnigan. 2014. 'Does Immigration Undermine Public Support for Social Policy?', *American Review of Sociology* 79, 1: 17–42.

Carrera, S and Merlino, M. 2009. Undocumented Immigrants and Rights in the EU Addressing the Gap between Social Science Research and Policymaking in the Stockholm Programme? CEPS Liberty and Security in Europe Policy Paper, December 2009.

Chojnicki, Xavier and Lionel Ragot. 2016. 'The Fiscal Impact of Immigration', *Informations sociales* 194, 3: 38–48.

Cinalli, Manlio and Carlo De Nuzzo. 2018. 'Disability, Unemployment, Immigration: Does Solidarity Matter in Times of Crisis in France?', in Veronica Federico and Christian

Lahusen, eds, *Solidarity as a Public Virtue? Law and Public Policies in the European Union*. Nomos, pp. 275–302.

Commissie Medische Zorg voor (Dreigend) Uitgeprocedeerde Asielzoekers en Illegale Vreemdelingen. 2007. *Arts en Vreemdeling*. Pharos.

Da Lomba, Sylvie. 2014. 'Vulnerability, Irregular Migrants' Health-Related Rights and the European Court of Human Rights', *European Journal of Health Law* 21: 339–364.

de le Court, Alexandre. 2016. *Desempleo y Derechos Fundamentales: El caso español en contexto*. Tirant lo Blanch.

Dembour, Marie-Bénédicte. 2012. '*Gaygusuz* Revisited: The Limits of the European Court of Human Rights' Equality Agenda', *Human Rights Law Review* 12, 4: 689–721.

Ellerman, Antje. 2020. 'Discrimination in Migration and Citizenship', *Journal for Ethnic and Migration Studies* 46, 12: 2463–2479.

Giulietti, Corrado and Martin Kahanec. 2013. 'Does Generous Welfare Attracts Immigrants? Towards Evidence-Based Policy Making', in Elspeth Guild, Sergio Carrera and Katharina Eisele, eds, *Social Benefits and Immigration*. Center for European Policy Studies, pp. 111–127.

González Ortega, Santiago, dir. 2008. *La Protección Social de los Trabajadores Extranjeros. Ministerio de Trabajo y Asuntos Sociales.*

Hendriks, Aart and Brigit Toebes. 2015. 'Recht op toegankelijke zorg: ook voor vreemdelingen', *Nederlands Juristenblad* 19: 1347–1352.

Hoop, Renaat. 2014. 'Political-Philosophical Perspectives on the Duty to Work in Activation Policies for the Unemployed', in Elise Dermine and Daniel Dumont, eds, *Activation Policies for the Unemployed, the Right to Work and the Duty to Work*. Peter Lang, pp. 33–57.

Isidro, Lola. 2016. 'La protection sociale des personnes étrangères. Pour un Nouveau critère d'accés aux prestations sociales', *Informations Sociales* 194: 106–116.

Jusot, Florence, Paul Dourgnon, Jerome Wittwer and Jawhar Sarhiri. 2019. 'Le recours à l'Aide médicale de l'État des personnes en situation irrégulière en France: premiers enseignements de l'enquête Premiers pas', *Questions d'économie de la santé* 245: 1–8.

Kanalan, Ibrahim. 2018. 'Sanktionen im Sozialleistungsrecht: Zur Verfassungswidrigkeit der Leistungseinschränkungen nach dem Asylbewerberleistungsgesetz', *ZFSH/SGB – Zeitschrift für die sozialrechtliche Praxis* 53: 247–256.

Kapuy, Claus. 2011. *The Social Security Position of Irregular Migrant Workers*. Intersentia.

Kolers, Avery H. 2012. 'Dynamics of Solidarity', *The Journal of Political Philosophy* 20: 365–383.

Krause Monika. 2008. 'Undocumented Migrants: An Arendtian Perspective', *European Journal of Political Theory* 7, 3: 331–348.

Mack, Annemie, Verbeek, Eline and Klaver, Jeanine. 2020. *Plan- en procesevaluatie Landelijke Vreemdelingenvoorzieningen. Eindrapport*. WODC.

Mau, Steffen and Christoph Burkhardt. 2009. 'Migration and Welfare State Solidarity in Western Europe', *Journal of European Social Policy* 19, 3: 213–229.

Michelet, Karine. 2007. 'Le droit des étrangers à la protection sociale: De l'affirmation du droit à sa mise en oeuvre', *Informations Sociales* 142: 80–91.

Mimentza Martin, Janire. 2011. *Die Sozialrechtliches stellung von Ausländern mit fehlendem Aufenthaltsrecht*. Herbert Utz Verlag.

Misic, Luka. 2018. 'Theories of Political philosophy as Guiding Principles in Social Security', *Studia z Zakresu Prawa Pracy i Polityki Społecznej* 25, 3: 271–291.

Montoya Medina, David. 2009. 'Reflexiones en torno al alcance de la protección de seguridad social del trabajador extranjero no autorizado', *Civitas. Revista Española de Derecho del Trabajo* 144: 863–882.

Nationale Ombudsman. 2013. Medische zorg vreemdelingen. Over toegang en continuïteit van medische zorg voor asielzoekers en uitgeprocedeerde asielzoekers. Report number 2013/125.

O'Cinneide, Colm. 2020. 'The Human Rights of Migrants with Irregular Status', in Sarah Spencer and Anna Tryandafyllidou, eds, *Migrants with Irregular Status in Europe*. Spinger Open, pp. 51–71.

Oosterlynck, Stijn, Maarten Loopmans, Nick Schuermans, Joke Vandenabeele and Sami Zemni. 2015. 'Putting Flesh to the Bone: Looking for Solidarity in Diversity, Here and Now', *Ethnic and Racial Studies* 39, 5: 1–19.

Ortega, Francesc and Giovanni Peri. 2009. 'The Causes and Effects of International Labor Mobility: Evidence from OECD Countries 1980–2005', *Human Development Research Paper* 2009/06.

Reshaur, Ken. 1992. 'Concepts of Solidarity in the Political Theory of Hannah Arendt', *Canadian Journal of Political Science* 25, 4: 723–736.

Schwiertz, Helge and Helen Schwenken. 2020. 'Introduction: Inclusive Solidarity and Citizenship along Migratory Routes in Europe and the Americas', *Citizenship Studies* 24, 4: 405–423.

Spiegel, Bernhard, ed. Katharina Daxkobler, Grega Strban and Anne Pieter van der Mei. 2015. *Analytical Report 2014: The Relationship between Social Security Coordination and Taxation Law*. European Commission.

Spitzlei, Thomas. 2017. 'Asylbewerberleistungsrecht und grundgesetzliches Existenzminimum', *Juristische Arbeitsblätter* 3: 165–171.

Supiot, Alain. 2015. 'Introduction', in Alain Supiot, ed., *La Solidarité. Enquête sur un principe juridique*. Odile Jacob Collège de France, pp. 7–32.

Stasiulis, Daiva, Jinnah Zaheera and Blair Rutherford. 2020. 'Migration, Intersectionality and Social Justice', *Studies in Social Justice* 14:1, 1–21.

Tangemann Julianne and Jan Grote. 2017. Illegal Beschäftigung von Drittstaatsangehörigen in Deutschland. Fokusstudie der deutschen nationalen Kontaktstelle für das Europäische Migrationsnetzwerk. Bundesamt für Migration und Flüchtlinge.

Thym, Daniel. 2015. 'The Elusive Limits of Solidarity: Residence Rights of and Social Benefits for Economically Inactive Union Citizens', *Common Market Law Review* 52, 1: 17–50.

van der Veen, Romke, Mara Yerkes and Peter Achterberg, eds. 2012. *The Transformation of Solidarity: Changing Risks and the Future of the Welfare State*. Amsterdam University Press.

van Oorschot, Wim and Femke Roosma. 2015. The Social Legitimacy of Differently Targeted Benefits. *ImPRovE Working Paper* No. 15/11. Herman Deleeck Centre for Social Policy – University of Antwerp.

8

Solidarity in Hard Times

The Politics of Labour Market and Social Protection Reform in Portugal (2010–2020)

Rui Branco and Daniel Cardoso

8.1 INTRODUCTION

This chapter deals with solidarity towards those made more vulnerable due to less security in employment and degraded social protection during hard times.[1] Stable, long-term employment paying a living wage shrunk over previous decades, as short-term, unstable, poorly paid jobs spread. Higher insecurity and instability affected standard and temporary employment, the latter rising everywhere. Particularly in segmentation-prone Birmarckian systems, such as the Portuguese, where social security is closely linked with enduring labour market participation, rising precarity in atypical employment (averaging 21 per cent from 2000 to 2018) is often compounded by weak or spotty social protection. The twin fragmentation of work and breakdown of the standard employment relation brought about a 'precarious periphery' and a 'destabilization of the stable' (Castel, 2003; 2007), accompanied by widespread 'privatization of risk' in the labour market and social protection due to increasing social and economic risk shifts from government and employers onto ordinary individuals and their families (Hacker, 2006).

These trends did not start with the Great Recession; they have prevailed for some time in advanced industrial economies, but found in crisis policymaking under conditionality an opportunity to evade constraints that hitherto had tamed or 'embedded' them. Looking at the Portuguese case, we study weather and how domestic politics and institutions mattered to counteract the dualisation, precarisation, and liberalising trends in employment relations and social protection during the Great Recession and beyond.

[1] We thank Julia López López and her leadership on the Project on Solidarity for supporting this research and convening several Seminars on 'Solidarity under the Perspective of Labour Law', concluding with 'Inscribing Solidarity: Labor Law and Beyond', held at Universitat Pompeu Fabra (Barcelona), and all participants for their warm support and pointed and insightful comments. Research was supported also by IPRI-NOVA FCT fund (UIDB/04627/2020).

In the Fall of 2008, eurozone countries responded to the financial crisis by enacting counter-cyclical measures: the €200Bi European Economic Recovery Plan, the nationalisation or capitalisation of financial institutions (e.g. Ireland, Spain, Portugal, UK) or adopted rescue plans (e.g. France, Germany) (Degryse, 2012). The initial response did not lift market pressure. Investors remained cautious, particularly towards the economic prospects of Southern European countries and Ireland, most of which ran current account deficits and were weakened by high private debt, bursting housing bubbles, and bank crises. Government bond yields remained high, increasing borrowing costs.

Early in 2010, trying to reassure debt and investment markets, the European Commission made a U-turn asking peripheral, indebted countries to enact fiscal consolidation measures and deregulatory structural reforms. However, economic and financial prospects worsened. Unable to finance itself in the markets, Greece asked for a bailout from the EU, implemented from May 2010. Ireland was next, in November 2010, followed by Portugal, Spain, and Cyprus. The funding depended on conditionality spelled out in adjustment programmes signed with a 'Troika' of creditors (the EC, the IMF, and the ECB).

Creditor and EU institutions demanded that southern eurozone countries liberalise their labour markets to facilitate internal devaluation and export-led recoveries in order to regain economic competitiveness, employment growth, and thus stable financial footing (Armingeon & Baccaro, 2012; Perez & Matsaganis, 2019). The opportunity presented by the crisis for market-making institutional reform through political regulation within the 'new European governance' would be wasted if resistance to (re)commodification put up by 'problematic' Southern European 'national political legacies' could not be overcome. As bluntly put by J. P. Morgan, initially

> it was thought that these national legacy problems were largely economic: overlevered sovereigns, banks and households, internal real exchange rate misalignments, and structural rigidities. But, overt time it has become clear that there are also national legacy problems of a political nature. The constitutions and political settlements in the southern periphery, put in place in the aftermath of the fall of fascism, have a number of features which appear to be unsuited to further integration in the region [such as] the constitutional protection of labor rights [and] the right to protest if unwelcome changes are made to the political status quo.
>
> (2013: 2, 12)

Across Southern Europe, reform outcomes varied against the backdrop of a general liberalising thrust (Thelen, 2014). The literature evinces how reforms were enacted and contested, detailing policymaking processes that brought together external and hierarchical pressures from European actors and market-based international institutions, national executives and parties, interest representatives, industrial and popular protest and social movements (Bermeo & Pontusson, 2012;

Petmesidou & Guillén, 2014; Guillén & Pavolini, 2015; Della Porta et al., 2016; Theodoropoulou, 2018; Fishman, 2019). While these factors combined to yield outcomes described as flexibilisation and retrenchment with instances of recalibration (Pavolini et al., 2016), domestic politics was one important driver of variation from country to country. If, for some, the centralisation of power in the executive and/or its ideological preferences determined the extent and direction of reforms (Cioffi & Dubin, 2016; Moury & Standring, 2017; Picot & Tassinari, 2017), others underline the effect of changing coalitional politics and blame allocation mechanisms (Asensio & Popic, 2019; Branco & Cardoso, 2022).

Here, we expand on the latter line of enquiry, exploring how political dynamics and institutions mattered in shaping employment and social protection statuses – crucial bases for the solidarity towards the vulnerable – in the decade between the Great Recession and the COVID-19 pandemic. Sections 8.2 and 8.3 detail how political actors and institutions, namely a broad, informal 'bailout coalition' of parties and social partners, and the Constitutional Court, helped to moderate or reverse liberalising and dualising labour market reforms from 2011 to the end of 2012, and the radicalisation of policy outputs following the 'bailout coalition's demise in early 2013, and attending increase in the Court's vetoes.

What happens when the conditions underlying the adoption of reforms change? From 2015, coming out of the crisis, did governments roll back unpopular reforms in 'response' to voters, or have they been 'responsible' vis-à-vis financial markets, creditors, and international institutions, thus preserving crisis-era reforms (Moury & Afonso, 2019)? Supply-siders expect reforms to remain because of functional reasons (economic efficiency) or for creating their own constituency of policy winners. Conversely, reversals can be expected to occur as soon as the conditions needed for the enactment of unpopular reforms are removed. Abated conditionality, under resumed growth and a larger fiscal space, creates the opening for the previous losing 'distributive coalitions' to act politically and bring about reversals (Branco et al., 2019).

What happened in Portugal? And – what role for politics? Section 8.4 explores how, from 2015 to 2019, amid waning conditionality economic recovery and improved labour market performance, the centre-left Socialist executive and supporting left partisan allies enacted a social policy agenda of reversals and recalibration – while keeping with the tenets of fiscal consolidation and European governance. With the backing of a renewed social concertation, policies favouring the labour market and social protection outsiders were enacted. Contrary to the crisis period, the gap between insiders and outsiders closed due to re-regulation of fixed-term, temporary, and self-employed work, improved work–family balance and gender equality in care and pay, revived social safety net, and bolstered disability protection.

Section 8.5 steps back from policy analysis to wrap the chapter around the theme of how political dynamics and institutions shape policy, and how policy kindled cleavages and solidarities during the crisis and beyond. We delineate how labour market and social protection policy responses during the crisis engendered social fault lines and cleavages, all the while promoting different kinds of class, group, and national solidarities, which then impacted the 2015 general elections, from which the Geringonça coalition arose. The Conclusion reiterates our main findings and briefly explores the theme of policy responses and solidarity during the COVID-19 pandemic.

8.2 COALITIONAL POLITICS AND LABOUR MARKET REFORM UNDER AUSTERITY AND CONDITIONALITY (2010 TO 2014)

8.2.1 *Before the MoU: Informal Political Cooperation Emerges under Austerity*

As the crisis worsened and fiscal and debt conditions deteriorated during 2010, the minority Socialist executive veered towards fiscal consolidation and flexibilisation.[2] Increasing austerity by the PS cabinet depended on the parliamentary cooperation of opposition centre-right parties (PSD and CDS). Three austerity packages (Stability and Growth Programmes, or SGPs) and the budget laws for 2010 and 2011 were passed with their assent. Negotiations towards a social concertation agreement, reliant on co-opting the moderate trade union UGT, bore fruit in March 2011, when a Tripartite Agreement (TA), combining cuts in severance pay, decentralisation of collective bargaining, and improved ALMP, was signed (CES, 2011).

This informal political cooperation between parties and social partners comprised an 'austerity coalition' cemented by a sense of duty and the need to avoid sharing the blame for a debt default. It was opposed in parliament by PCP and the Left Block (BE) – whose potentially lethal motions to censure the PS government were defeated by the abstention of PSD and CDS. In social concertation, the largest and PCP-aligned trade union, CGTP, rejected the 2011 TA.

As the crisis worsened with rising unemployment, popular protest, and strikes, the PSD's position became untenable. It could not go on losing political capital by supporting the PS cabinet, given very favourable opinion polls (De Giorgi et al., 2015). The situation came to a head with the SGP 4 (March 2011). On 23 March, a negative coalition of PCP, BE, PSD, and CDS defeated SGP 4 in parliament. PM Sócrates resigned; on 6 April, the PS caretaker government asked for international financial assistance; negotiations ensued.

2 Section 8.2 draws heavily on Branco & Cardoso (2022).

8.2.2 *Coalitional Politics Shapes Initial Labour Market Reforms under the MoU*

The MoU was signed on 17 May between the Troika and the caretaker government, but also by PSD and CDS, after consultation with social partners, in exchange for a €78bn bailout package. On 5 June, the centre-right coalition PSD-CDS won the general elections with an absolute majority, and took the executive.

Informal political cooperation continued despite PS and PSD trading places between government and opposition – now, a 'bailout coalition' – as it was held by international creditors as key for long-term fiscal adjustment and structural reforms, as noted by the incoming centre-right finance minister (Gaspar & Avillez, 2014: 256).

The MoU prescribed liberalisation and decentralisation to reform an 'overly rigid' labour market due to 'excessive' employment protection for permanent contracts, 'generous' unemployment benefits, and collective bargaining unable to keep wage growth aligned with productivity and external competitiveness. It also sought to combat dualism by focusing on segmentation, outsider and long-term unemployment protection, and ALMP (Directorate-General Economic and Financial Affairs, 2011: 24–25, 51–52, 77). This asymmetric blend of liberalisation and pro-outsider recalibration recalled the March 2011 social pact, as noted by Labour Secretary Pedro Martins, PSD, PS MPs in parliament (DAR, 1/9/2011), and UGT (2012: 2). January 2012, a TA was signed by the conservative government, UGT, and employers' confederations (CES, 2012), and then legislated by parliament.

Employment protection for insiders was hit. Dismissal compensation for new permanent contracts was cut from 30 to 20 days per year of tenure (and capped at 12 × the employee's monthly wage or 240 × the minimum wage), and then extended to all employees (Laws 53/2011 and 23/2012). Protection for fixed-term contracts was also hit. Severance pay for new hires went from thirty-six (shorter contracts) or twenty-four (those longer than six months) days per year of service to twenty. The renewal of fixed-term contracts was temporarily extended to eighteen months (Laws 53/2011 and 3/2012).

Unemployment protection reform lowered the cap on benefits from €1257 to €1048, cut 10 per cent in value after six months, and halved duration to eighteen months. On the other hand, the required contributory period was cut from fifteen to twelve months, coverage was extended to economically dependent self-employed workers, and benefits for unemployed couples and monoparental families were temporarily increased by 10 per cent (Decrees-law 64 and 65/2012; Law 23/2012).

Collective bargaining reform went a step further relative to the 2011 TA with the 'organised decentralisation of collective bargaining', allowing work councils in firms with at least 150 employees to negotiate agreements at plant level, under a mandate from trade unions (Law 23/2012).

How can policy outputs until the end of 2012 be said to be relatively more moderate? First, the unemployment protection reform, while cutting the amount and duration of benefits, shortened the required contributory period, widened access to economically dependent self-employed workers, allowed the partial accumulation of unemployment benefit with a new contract wage, and launched a host of 12 ALMP programmes to improve youth employability and correct segmentation.

Second, some measures fell 'short of the MoU'. Law 23/2012, following the 2012 social pact, broadened the criteria for just cause dismissal under 'inadaptation', but did not include as criteria 'the failure to meet "goals" set by the employer'. The cabinet minister acknowledged, 'the MoU went further than what was agreed in social concertation' (DAR 31/3/2012). The UGT claimed credit for 'preventing the single just cause dismissal criteria the Troika really wanted to introduce for the entire workforce' (2012: 8). The same is the case with the criteria for plant-level bargaining (at least 150 employees *instead of none*) and the *no change* in criteria for extending collective agreements, including a safeguard clause requiring the agreement of social partners for any future change (UGT, 2012: 10).

Third, the half-an-hour increase in daily working time for the private sector (not in the MoU) proposed by the government (14/12/2011) was defeated by a combination of industrial protest (general strike by UGT and CGTP, 24/11/2011) and social concertation. A deal-breaker for UGT, it was dropped by the executive on 16 January, two days before signing the 2012 TA.

This relatively moderate policy output reflects the bailout coalition's composition and policy process. Despite enjoying an absolute majority, the executive governed within a broad informal coalition and multilateral bargaining in parliament and social concertation. It followed the political calculus that a broader coalition disperses blame attribution and strengthens the legitimacy of reforms, easing compliance and consent.

In opposition, PS's preferences partially converged with the government. Recall that the PS had negotiated the 2011 TA and the MoU mostly comprises measures the Socialist government wanted to enact, and thus there would be room for agreement with the conservative executive as long as the enacted policy kept within its confines (Moury & Standring, 2017). A Socialist MP explained the party's stance on the 2012 Labour Code reform: 'There are some matters we agree with; others result from the Memorandum; some others come from the Tripartite Agreement' (DAR 31/3/2012). The Socialists abstained in three motions to censure the government presented by PCP and BE until March of 2013. Given that PS's censure would not have toppled the government, the abstention reads as tacit support. The PS cooperated with the government on major legislation during the first 15 months: voted in favour of Laws 3/2012 and 47/2012; abstained in the labour reform Law 23/2012 (which embodied the January 2012 TA); and the 2012 budget law.

The January 2012 TA was in line with, if not more generous than, the MoU. UGT leveraged its informal veto power in social concertation to shape policy outputs under increasingly constrained circumstances, from the social pact to the MoU in 2011, and again from the social pact to the labour reform in 2012. It influenced policy by pushing for recalibration, keeping measures within the MoU's confines ('there are no measures worse than the MoU') or even short of the MoU (blocking 'the single just cause dismissal criteria the Troika really wanted to introduce for the entire workforce'); and by preventing worse measures, not in the MoU, such as the half-an-hour increase in daily working time. UGT claimed credit for the outcome (2012: 8, 15–16). The social partners' moderating influence on policy via social concertation was recognised in parliament by government and the Socialist opposition alike (DAR 1/9/2011, 31/3 and 12/5/2012).

8.2.3 *The Bailout Coalition's Demise Ushers in the Second Phase of Reforms*

As the economy contracted throughout 2012 and unemployment soared to 16 per cent, bond yields stayed above 8 per cent. Worried that too much austerity would trigger a recessive spiral that would undermine general political support and fracture the governing coalition, the IMF urged the government to stimulate the economy.

In September, the executive announced a supply-side solution to jump-start economy: the revision of the TSU regime (mandatory social contribution on salary paid by workers and employers). Employer's share would drop from 23.75 per cent to 18 per cent to 'boost competitiveness and job creation', offset by a 7 p.p. increase (11 per cent to 18 per cent) paid by salaried workers.

A nerve snapped, and protests spread across the country with millions taking to the streets. Along both trade unions, employer confederations told the finance minister they would fight the measure (Gaspar & Avillez, 2014: 283). 'The pillar of social stability was attacked', one employer representative said (Távora & Gonzalez, 2016: 338). The proposal was dropped, and replaced in the 2013 budget law with a huge tax increase, raising the average rate of personal income tax by 3 p.p. to 13 per cent and the collected revenue by 28 per cent. This was a stopgap remedy. Going forward, the solution would be permanent public expenditure cuts of €4bn, particularly in the welfare state (IMF, 2013).

This sequence of events broke the 'bailout coalition' as PS and UGT moved to opposition. The Socialists first voted against the 2013 budget law (27/11/2012) and then presented a motion to censure the government (28/3/2013). Thereafter, PS voted with PCP and BE on all motions to censure presented until the end of the legislature in 2015. Despite the combined opposition of PS, PCP, and BE, the governing parties passed labour laws 69/2013, 76/2013, 27/2014, and 55/2014, and the budget laws for 2013, 2014, and 2015. Favourable opinion polls and the prospect of holding office eased the move from cooperation to conflict (De Giorgi et al., 2015). Moreover, acting responsibly was preventing the PS from being responsive to its electorate and popular protest. Further labour market liberalisation, welfare retrenchment, public sector cuts, and privatisations would destroy the party's power resources. In May 2014, the newly elected PS leader António Costa vowed to 'turn the page of austerity' and never enter into a coalition with either or both PSD and CDS after the upcoming 2015 elections.

UGT also moved to opposition, refusing to sign any TA until the end of the Programme in May 2014. It blasted the executive's newfound disrespect for the MoU's social dialogue process, the collective bargaining freeze, and the push to further flexibilisation and deregulation by revisiting policy that had already been settled via social pact. The huge demonstrations of 1/5/2013 resulted from UGT's collaboration with CGTP, as did the general strike in 27/6/2013.

Henceforth, the executive relied solely on PSD and CDS. Unconstrained by the informal coalition, its preferences aligned with the Troika: 'our interests are, in essence, fully aligned. There is no difference in goals', stated the finance minister (Gaspar & Avillez, 2014: 262).

As a result, from late 2012 LMP went 'beyond' the MoU and the 2012 TA in that it undermined collective bargaining, furthered liberalised employment relations, while dropping recalibration. First, in October 2012 the executive unilaterally ruled that collective agreements could only be extended to a whole sector if the negotiating employer organisation represented more than 50 per cent of employment in said sector (Council of Ministers Resolution 90/2012). This directly contradicted the MoU and 2012 TA. All trade unions and employers' associations opposed the measure as too restrictive, arguing it would undermine collective bargaining. Given the executive's unilateral stance, employer confederations wrote a joint letter to the IMF asking for the measure to be dropped, for compromising social peace and stability and distorting competition between firms (Bulfone & Afonso, 2020: 835). Also, the duration of collective agreements was cut from five to three years, their validity after expiry from eighteen to twelve months, and the favourability principle was inverted with priority given to company-level agreements over sectoral conventions (Laws 48-A/2014 and 55/2014; Afonso et al., 2021). Second, just cause dismissal compensation, which had been cut from thirty to twenty days, was, in 2013, further reduced to twelve days for all contracts – invoking the MoU's directive to align severance pay with the EU average (trade unions, notably UGT, insisted on eighteen days). Trade unions also argued that, according to both MoU and 2012 TA, it should apply only to new hires – not to all contracts. UGT threatened to reject the 2012 TA and cancel all further talks. The executive then finessed the proposal regarding new hires (employment contracts entered into force after 1/10/2013): compensation for collective dismissals was cut to twelve days per year; for individual permanent contracts, it was cut to eighteen days of base remuneration and seniority for the first three years of the contract plus twelve days for the following years (Law 69/2013).

Third, changes to the criteria for just cause dismissal (suitability and job extinction) also broke with the MoU and the 2012 TA, which stated the employer was responsible for their definition. Law 23/2014 featured a definition vetoed by the

Constitutional Court. In response, the executive unilaterally decided new criteria for employers when determining individual dismissals in the case of job extinction. These criteria were highly contested by trade unions and the largest employer confederation, CIP. Nevertheless, they were passed into Law 27/2014.In sum, LMP reforms under conditionality varied from a first phase where recalibration (e.g. unemployment protection) coexisted alongside hard liberalising measures (e.g. EPL for insiders) to a second phase where recalibration was dropped and liberalisation further deregulated employment protection and security and eroded collective bargaining. This is explained by the changing coalitional politics and blame allocation underpinning policymaking. Whereas initial reforms resulted from a broad informal political coalition through multilateral policymaking spanning the governing centre-right parties, the PS in opposition, the moderate trade union (UGT), and employer confederations in social concertation, its breakdown in late 2012 led to the conservative executive's increasing centralisation and the shutting down of social concertation, yielding more radical policy outputs against the opposition of the PS, both trade unions, and often employer organisations.

In the end, , the labour market regulation underwent a structural reform: (i) security in employment and in unemployment for standard workers (insiders) declined substantially; (ii) reform of collective bargaining shifted the balance of power towards employers, while a move from joint to statutory regulation stalled social concertation; (iii) despite initial inroads, neither trend was offset by a robust unemployment compensation strategy or activation effort targeted at outsiders, and no de-segmentation occurred in a historically dualised labour market. A worse situation for both insiders and outsiders points to wide flexibilisation and enduring segmentation, henceforth at a lower level of security, a pattern of 'liberalised dualisation' (Cardoso & Branco, 2018).

8.3 THE ROLE OF THE CONSTITUTIONAL COURT

The Portuguese Constitutional Court is composed of thirteen judges appointed for non-renewable terms of nine years, of which ten judges are appointed by parliament by a two-thirds majority, the remainder co-opted by sitting judges. Despite the super-majority requirement suggesting that legislative non-veto power actors would be included in the appointment of judges, in practice, the major centre-left (PS) and centre-right (PSD) parties jointly draw up a list of candidates. Usually, judges are evenly split between left- and right-wing parties, a political bargain that extends to two of the remaining judges, leaving one 'neutral' (Coroado et al., 2017). Comparatively, constitutional review is quite generous: the power to initiate proceedings is assigned to a wide array of legal and political actors and institutions (inter alia, President of the Republic, President of Parliament, MPs, the PM, the General Public Prosecutor, and the Ombudsman), with no time limits to request the review (Violante, 2019: 124).

The Portuguese Court is an important veto player in a political system with scant horizontal or vertical dispersion of power. Among the 'Programme Countries', the Portuguese was the first Court to deliver severe drawbacks to austerity policies. This is all the more significant given that historically the Court counter-majoritarianism has been comparatively low (Violante, 2019: 121). This pattern changed during the crisis, under conditionality.

Table 8.1 breaks down the eight vetoes over twelve rulings. From June 2011 to May 2014, the period of conservative government under conditionality, we find two vetoes in the aforementioned first phase v. six in the second. The constitutional challenges were presented by various litigants: opposition MPs (from the PS and other parliamentary minorities) and the President of the Republic, offering a check on absolute majority governance. Particularly in the second phase marked by executive

TABLE 8.1. *Constitutional Court rulings on austerity measures (2010–2014)*

Year	# Ruling	Subject	Litigants	Outcome
2010	399/2010	Surtax on personal income tax	President of the Republic	Court approves measures
2011	396/2011	Budget Law for 2011	Opposition MPs	Court approves measures, but: *imposes legal test to further cutbacks in public salaries and social benefits*: must be transitional in nature, due to compelling interest and follow the standard of 'proportional equality'
2012	353/2012	Budget Law for 2012	Opposition MPs	*Court vetoes measures*: annuls the suspension of 13th and 14th wage salaries for civil servants and pensioners from 2012 to 2014
2013	187/2013	Budget Law for 2013	President of the Republic	*Court vetoes measures*: struck down suspension of holiday allowance for civil servants, and pensioners; and surtax upon unemployment benefit recipients to pay social security contributions
2013	474/2013	Civil Service Law	President of the Republic	*Court vetoes measures*: struck down flexibilisation of the dismissal of civil servants for violating principle protection of legitimate expectations and of legal certainty
2013	602/2013	Labour Code reform	Opposition MPs	*Court vetoes measures*: struck down by violating constitutional ban of dismissal without just cause and provisions of collective labour regulation instruments
2013	794/2013	Civil Service Law	Opposition MPs (PS)	Court approves measures

2013	862/2013	Civil Service Law	President of the Republic	*Court vetoes measures*: struck down provisions to retrospectively cut by 10% pensions of retired civil servants (CGA fund) and less favourable formula for calculating pensions, for violation of the protection of legitimate expectations
2014	413/2014	Budget Law for 2014	Opposition MPs (PS)	*Court vetoes measures*: struck down additional contribution from unemployment benefit, the cut in survivors' pensions, and additional public wage cuts
2014	572/2014	Budget Law for 2014	Opposition MPs (PS)	Court approves measures
2014	574/2014	Public pay cuts	President of the Republic	*Court partially vetoes*: accepts pay cuts in 2014 and 2015, but vetoes future cuts
2014	575/2014	Pension and tax policy	President of the Republic	*Court vetoes measures*: struck down alignment rules of public sector pensions (CGA) with general social security system (RGSS) for violating the principle of equal protection and trust; struck down new 'sustainability contribution' as permanent levy on public sector pensions for violating the principle of trust

Source: own elaboration from Saurugger et al., 2020; Canotilho et al., 2015; Fasone, 2014.

centralisation of power and unilateral policymaking, the request for constitutional review provided the centre to left parliamentary opposition with an effective way to challenge reforms enacted by the conservative executive. Whereas in the first phase the check worked via bargain within the bailout coalition, in the second phase, the Court assumed more forcefully the role as veto player and ultimate check on the executive.

Looking at the Court's rhetoric, the vetoes do not spring from a principled refusal of any retrenchment of pensions or wages based on right to work or other constitutionally entrenched social rights. The reasoning turns on general principles of constitutional law, such as equal protection, the protection of legitimate expectations, and proportionality, elaborating early on the standard of 'proportional equality' (Ruling 396/2011). With such standards the Court envisions a fairer, more balanced enactment of austerity reforms. All workers and pensioners, either in the public or private sectors, ought to endure the burdens of austerity in roughly equal shares. The economic and financial emergency ought to be addressed by policies of a general nature and not by the continuous imposition of austerity measures upon public sector workers or pensioners. At the same time, however, the Court forcefully upheld the right to 'an essential core of an existential minimum', a 'constitutional parameter of a decent existence', so that 'there will always be a limit [to the reversibility of rights and expectations], even in a state of economic emergency' (Ruling 187/2013). Recalling that, from the social revolutionary inception, the democratic regime's legitimacy is closely linked to the provision of social rights, the Court's agency can be seen as an exercise in national sovereignty, a check on the demands from international creditors at a time when the remaining political institutions had their bargaining power constrained by strong financial needs (Cisotta & Gallo, 2014).

8.4 TURNING THE PAGE OF AUSTERITY: THE GERINGONÇA (2015–2019)

Following the general election in the Fall of 2015, the Socialist Party formed a minority government, taking office in November 2015, supported in parliament by the radical left parties PCP, BE (Left Bloc), and PEV (Greens). This novel coalition tore down the wall of political cooperation in government between PS, PCP, and BE, a legacy of the 1974–1976 revolutionary period – and came to be known in Portuguese political parlance as *geringonça*, or 'contraption'.

The Geringonça's political agenda was to end austerity and foster economic growth while keeping European fiscal commitments, and specifically to reverse the 'damaging effects of austerity on salaries and pensions' (Calado et al., 2019: 680). On the one hand, a substantial reversal of crisis-era austerity social policies occurred, albeit keeping some structural reforms (De Giorgi & Cancela, 2019; Moury, Cardoso & Gago, 2019). On the other, the executive, backed by a restored social concertation, enacted an expansive recalibration agenda in labour market and social protection. However, some key differences remained between the PS and the supporting left parties, which erupted in late 2019, showing the limits of the Geringonça as a progressive coalition.

8.4.1 *Policy Reversals and Income Recovery*

The Geringonça reversed most austerity policies enacted during the crisis: restored public sector wages and career progression, unfroze and hiked the mandatory minimum wage, increased public pensions and other social benefits, lowered taxes for the middle class, working families, and small and medium businesses, and stopped the privatisation of public transport companies in Lisbon and Porto. These measures boosted income recovery and internal demand, favouring economic growth with a sharp decline in unemployment.

The sustained raise in the minimum wage, covering ca. 22 per cent of salaried employees, is noteworthy. Enacted yearly, backed up by social concertation agreements in 2017 and 2018, it rose 26 per cent from €505 in 2015 to €635 in 2020, without harming labour market performance (2015 to 2019, the employed population grew 8 per cent while the unemployment rate dropped from 12.4 per cent to 6.5 per cent)

In addition to the reversal of cyclical measures, there were reversals of structural labour market and social protection reforms. All told, there were six structural policy reversals from the end of MoU in May 2014 to the end of 2019: two Constitutional Court vetoes to new permanent 'Sustainability Contribution' on all public pensions and new rules aligning CGA pensions with RGSS pensions (2014); a return to a 35-hour working week for the public sector (2016); eighteen months' suspension of any unilateral requests for cancellation of collective agreements (2017); end of representativeness criteria for extension of collective agreements (2017); and end of 10 per cent cut to unemployment benefit after six months (2017) (Branco et al., 2019: 213).

However, core structural LMP reforms remained despite the strong push to reverse them from radical left parties in parliament and CGTP in social concertation, to wit: severance pay cut; new criteria and definition of fair dismissal (unsuitability for the task and job extinction); and cut in unemployment benefit duration. Despite the overall political support coalition, the agreement between the PS, radical left parties, and trade unions, especially CGTP, was much harder on reversing crisis-era LMP structural reform than on reversing austerity cuts.

8.4.2 *An Expansive and Inclusive Recalibration Agenda*

The Geringonça enacted an inclusive recalibration agenda. Consequently, the gap between insiders and outsiders shrank because precarious short-term and self-employed workers, women, youth, long-term unemployed, those with disability and the elderly have been better protected, in the labour market and welfare. This agenda was enacted bringing back social concertation: the framework Tripartite Agreement in 2017 and the full-blown Agreement in 2018 led to a major Labour Code reform in September 2019. Next, we'll break down this agenda and focus on the coalition's inner strife around labour market reform.

8.4.2.1 Social Safety Net and Disability

The value and criteria for access to the Social Insertion Income and the supplemental income for the elderly were restored, expanding coverage and income security. A set of regulatory decisions and most importantly the reversal (in 25 per cent) of the previous cut in SII value stopped and reverted the downward trend in the number of beneficiaries (Pereirinha et al., 2020). In 2017, the protection of people with disability was expanded with the creation of a new social benefit.

8.4.2.2 Work–Family Balance and Gender Equality

Acknowledging the widening gender pay gap (from 8.5 per cent in 2007 to 17.5 per cent in 2017), legal action was taken, after consultation with social partners, to reduce occupational gender segregation and promote a more effective work life, stipulating actions from the labour inspectorate and sanctions against discriminatory treatment. The Social Dialogue for Reconciliation proposed adaptability of working hours and bank of hours to workers with children aged under 12 or with children with a disability or a chronic disease. It also pushed for provisions in collective agreements promoting reconciliation (Campos Lima & Carrilho, 2018).

Tackling gender inequality in care, Laws 90/2019 and 100/2019 reinforced the parental leave regime, particularly for fathers. Fathers are entitled to a mandatory initial parental leave of twenty working days, to be used within six weeks of the birth of a child, five of which must be used immediately after birth. Following this leave, fathers also have the right to an additional five working days of leave, as long as it takes place simultaneously with the mother's initial parental leave.

8.4.2.3 Collective Bargaining

Reversing crisis-era policy, the Council of Ministers (Resolution 82/2017) replaced the representativeness criteria for extension of collective agreements by a consideration of social policy goals, such as gender equality, thus promoting inclusiveness through collective bargaining while preventing the dualisation and inequality wrought by the steep reduction of extension ordinances during the crisis years.

The 2018 Tripartite Agreement (enacted in the 2019 Labour reform) fosters collective bargaining, preventing gaps in coverage from expiring agreements and promoting the collective dimension of labour regulation. Specifically, it creates arbitration mechanisms as a last instance before the expiring of agreements; broadens the scope of rights that workers keep after collective agreements expire, adding parental, health, and security rights; and sets company referendums organised by employers, under surveillance of trade unions and worker representatives, to decide on implementing 'working time accounts' to replace the previous regime of employer–employee individual agreements (Campos Lima & Carrilho, 2019).

Collective agreements recovered to near pre-crisis levels. The total number of new agreements (and extensions) rose from 138 (36) in 2015 to 208 (84) in 2017, as the number of employees covered rose from 490,377 to 820,083. However, the qualitative shift since 2012 towards company-level continues at the expense of branch and multi-employer agreements, suggesting a convergence towards 'a decentralised model of industrial relations' (Stoleroff, 2019: 184).

8.4.2.4 Self-Employed Workers

The executive improved the contributory careers and social rights of self-employed workers (17 per cent of employment in 2018). After improvements in 2012 and 2013 (unemployment benefit extended to economically dependent self-employed workers and self-employed employers), the Geringonça granted access to cash benefit assistance to children and grandchildren as well as for children with chronic disease or disability (major extant gaps relative to employees) (Decree-law 53/2018). Also, it set a more generous definition 'economically dependent', broadening access to unemployment benefits (Decree-law 2/2018). The record of contributions was aligned with salaried workers (360 days / previously 24 months) and contributions to social security dropped from 29.6 per cent to 21.4 per cent while employers' range from 7 per cent to 10 per cent (previously 5 per cent) (Decrees-law 2 and 53/2018). The waiting period for sickness benefits were cut from thirty to ten days. For the first time, regulation of UBER and electronic platform drivers (Law 45/2018), as regards employment contracts and working time.

8.4.2.5 Fixed-Term and Temporary Workers

The 2019 Labor Code reform re-regulates fixed-term and temporary contracts (22 per cent of the worforce in 2018), to reduce dualisation and steer companies to hire open-ended contracts: inter alia, cuts maximum duration; penalises companies for excessive use by additional social security contribution; restricts use when starting new businesses with less than 250 employees; and limits renewal by closely matching initial contract period with period necessary to satisfy company temporary needs. On the other hand, very short-term contracts increase from fifteen to thirty-five days, up to a maximum of seventy days per year with the same employer, and can now be held outside agricultural seasonal activities or touristic events. Also, seeking to boost open-ended contracts for first-time jobseekers and the long-term unemployed, it extends the trial period from 90 to 180 days.

8.4.3 *The Geringonça and the 2019 Labour Code: Compensation and Political Exchange*

The Labour Code reform generated mixed reactions among trade unions and radical left parties. While limits to the use and duration of fixed-term contracts were welcomed, measures extending very short contracts and the trial period for first-time jobseekers and long-term unemployed were decried as potential new sources of precarious work. CGTP, which had not signed the 2018 Social Pact, also opposed measures regarding collective bargaining, claiming the full restoration of the *favor laboratoris* principle (lost in the 2003 Labour Code reform) and the reversal of rules that allow agreements to expire on the basis of unilateral decision (Campos Lima & Carrilho, 2018).

BE, PCP, and The Greens voted against the new Labour Code (25/9/2019), then asked the Constitutional Court to review the extension of the trial period to 180 days when hiring first-time jobseekers and long-term unemployed and the increase in duration of very short-term contracts to thirty-five days. The Court later struck down the extension of the trial period for first-time jobseekers (Ruling 318/2021).

Despite the recalibration agenda and pressure from radical left parties and trade union allies (especially CGTP), the Geringonça did not touch Troika-era core labour market reforms: cuts in dismissal compensation, new definition of fair dismissal (case of unsuitability for the task), new criteria for dismissal (case of job extinction), and shorter duration of unemployment benefit – and the 2019 Labour Code reform did not reverse them. Why?

We argue the answer lies in a compensatory political exchange strategy involving the PS minority government with (i) trade unions, especially those allied with left parties BE and PCP and (ii) employers' confederations (Branco et al., 2019: 225). The continuity of crisis-era core labour market reform was made palatable to the Geringonça left allies by way of compensation in income policy and public sector regulation: large minimum wage hike, end of all cuts in salaries and pensions, and the redrawing of income tax brackets in the Budget Law for 2018. Employers have acquiesced to all 'income recovery' policies, but have forcefully signalled that no further reversals of core labour market reforms are acceptable. Until the Labour Code vote in September of 2019, with general elections in sight, there was ongoing tension (but no break) with the supporting left parties. The triangular compensation strategy both made the Geringonça possible and drew its limits, for the government did not wish to lose the ongoing support of employers in social concertation (in turn, needed for a successful income recovery policy). In fact. the Geringonça would finally break down in the Fall of 2021 over these same issues.

8.5 POLICY, CLEAVAGES, AND SOLIDARITIES IN PORTUGAL (2011–2019)

Above, we have detailed how social policy changed between 2010 and 2019. This section surveys the impacts of these changes upon societal cleavages and solidarities.[3]

European governments' policy responses during the Great Recession and beyond can be broadly classified as retreat of state interventionism or new forms of

[3] We employ Taylor-Gooby, Leruth, and Chung's definitions of 'cleavage' as division between variegated social categories, spawning different interests and norms and leading to social action, and 'solidarity', in this context, as the recognition of common interests or identities that support political action (2017: 2).

interventionism (Taylor-Gooby et al., 2017: 13). From 2011 to 2014, Portuguese policies retrenched the intervention of the state, with major focuses on austerity and individualisation, while new forms of interventionism prevailed from 2015 to 2019, with major responses in social investment and fightback policies.

Table 8.2 shows that from 2011 to 2014 policy orientation combined major retrenchment of the intervention and regulatory reach of the state, mainly through austerity cuts, enhancement of individual responsibility, and labour market deregulation, with minor responses in new forms of state intervention (e.g. the 2011 emergency social plan) and social investment policies (mainly a host of ALMP). Such policies kindle social cleavages, pitting advantaged and disadvantaged groups, old age (pensions) and youth (unemployed and unprotected), workers (say, civil servants) and non-workers (unemployed), middle class and vulnerable (less so secure v. precarious workers since liberalised dualisation impacted insiders without empowering outsiders). On the whole, such policies created extended 'losers' of the economic adjustment, without forging meaningful, inclusive solidarities, rather the potential for a broad and inclusive political fight-back coalition – which is generally the Geringonça's origin story.

On the other hand, recall that coalitional politics worked until the Fall of 2012 to moderate or blunt some of the dualising and inegalitarian effects of austerity reforms, and how the Constitutional Court vetoed legislation that would have entrenched some of said cleavages, therefore precluding even more inegalitarian, counter-solidaristic outcomes. Finally, note that these policy responses did not follow the path of welfare chauvinism with the emergence of a negative cleavage pitting denizens vs. immigrant and refugees, and the promotion of nationalism.

In the aftermath of the crisis, from 2015 to 2019, amid waning conditionality, economic recovery, and improved labour market performance, the Geringonça coalition enacted a social policy agenda of reversals and recalibration, closing the gap between insiders and outsiders, within the tenets of fiscal consolidation, new European governance, and market-based constraints. Nearly all social protection cuts ended and a handful of structural measures were reversed. Executive partisan and ideological turnover in 2015 was decisive to bring about reversals. Until that moment, absent such change, structural reversals were possible only through the Constitutional Court, as no other channels for change were available (Branco et al., 2019).

Policymaking from 2015 to 2019 yielded fewer cleavages while garnering broad-based support from middle classes while at the same time including precarious and outsider groups. There occurred three main policy responses within the broad category of 'new forms of interventionism': interventionism, social investment, and fight-back, variously embodied by the policy agenda of 'income recovery' with the reversal of prior austerity cuts, structural reversals in the labour market, and social protection, and an expansive recalibration agenda in the labour market and social protection. These promote an important set of solidarities: cross-alliance between

TABLE 8.2. *Policy responses in Portugal (2011–2019): Impact on cleavages and solidarities*

Conservative government 2011–2014	Geringonça coalition 2015–2019	Type of response	Policies	Cleavages	Solidarities
		Retreat from interventionist state			
MAJOR	NO	Cuts/austerity	Cutbacks; privatisations Prioritise pensions, healthcare not working-age benefits Prioritise wage supplements and low income tax; cut benefits Prioritise social insurance	Advantaged groups v. disadvantaged intergenerational Workers v. non-workers Secure v. precarious	None None None
MAJOR	NO	*Individual responsibility*	Privatisation; means testing; some forms of social investment	Middle class v. vulnerable	None
		New forms of interventionism			
MINOR	MINOR	Interventionism	State-led investment to create jobs; welfare spending to maintain demand from the poor		Class alliance between working-class and middle-class groups
MINOR	MAJOR	Social investment	Prioritise training and family support	Groups whose engagement in work skill level can be enhanced v. other	Groups marginal to the labour market
NO	NO	Pre-distribution	High minimum wage, rent and utility price control; better job opportunities	Low-waged v. high-waged	Across lower age groups
NO	MAJOR	Fightback	Anti-austerity measures; higher benefits; corporate tax		Solidarity of disadvantaged
NO	NO	Welfare chauvinism	Residence and citizenship tests; immigration control; national protectionism	Denizens v. immigrants	Nationalism

Source: own elaboration, adapted from Taylor-Gooby et al., 2017: 13.

working-class and middle-class groups, groups marginal to the labour market in need of inclusion, rights and protection, and solidarity of the disadvantaged.

Finally, we examine weather crisis-era *policies* generated a new *politics* down the line. In other words, how changes in solidarities and cleavages engendered by Troika-era policies influenced the electoral behaviour of social groups or strata that supported the Geringonça parties in the 2015 elections.

In the Fall 2015 elections, the conservative alliance fared badly with unemployed and low-income voters, those hardest hit by the economic crisis, while pensioners favoured the Socialists, and public sector and (especially) unionised voters were likelier to vote for either the PCP and the BE (Fernandes et al., 2018: 505–506). The higher-income strata (closely correlated with higher socio-economic class and status, and certain occupations such as big and small business owners, managers, and liberal professions) tended to vote for right-wing parties (Cancela & Magalhães, 2020: 117). It shows these strata did not punish PSD-CDS for adopting measures that impacted them during the crisis (such as levies on higher pensions or the steep progressive reform of taxes upon wage and pension income). The neoliberal, supply-side policy agenda (steep cut in the corporate tax, internal devaluation based on the flexibilisation of the labour market and downward adjustment in wage salaries) helped to keep electoral support despite some material loses. Conversely, this helped PS, CDU, and BE consolidate the support of groups with lower salaried income, paving the way to a parliamentary coalitional majority.

While from 2002 to 2011 the pensioner vote was apportioned equally between centre-right and centre-left parties, this electorate disproportionately voted for the centre-left Socialist Party in 2015. Pensioners were particularly hit during the crisis: freeze in pension updating; cuts in annual benefit value; one-off tax levies. The voting pattern of pensioners extended to the larger and very sizeable block of the elderly vote, always more prone to turn out. While up until 2011 this vote block favoured both PS and PSD, in 2015 (and also in 2019), the centre-right parties, especially PSD, fared much worse with the elderly (Cancela & Magalhães, 2020: 107). The making of an inter-class, intergenerational solidarity underpinned the Geringonça. Indeed, the other group particularly hit by the crisis, the young and unemployed (Rodrigues, Figueiras, & Junqueira, 2016), voted for left-wing parties in 2015.

The 2015 elections evince a cleavage between poor and rich and intergenerational solidarity between young and old, punishing centre-right incumbents. The Geringonça enacted a broad, inclusive, and solidaristic social policy agenda, both compensatory and expansive. Many reversals undid measures that had targeted the losers of the crisis, specifically pensioners, production workers, and low-salaried workers, such as the increase of the minimum wage, and the broadening in coverage and generosity of the minimum income and old-age support schemes. The PS-led government and radical left allies also enacted more inclusive policies, improving social protection for outsiders, such as those in atypical employment, a core base of the radical left, with measures such as the re-regulation of temporary employment (Bulfone & Tassinari, 2020). This set of policies were responsive to the intergenerational solidarity coalition that helped bring Geringonça to office in the first place.

8.6 CONCLUSIONS

In this chapter, we have probed how Portuguese domestic politics and institutions were able to counteract external pressures to liberalise the labour market and social protection regimes. The first conclusion is that *domestic political actors and institutions matter, even under formal external conditionality*. This was the case in the first years of the crisis (2010–2012) when an informal coalition of parties and social partners adopted, alongside significant liberalisation for insiders, a set of recalibration measures and moderated or blocked others in the MoU. It was again the case from late 2012 when the Constitutional Court vetoed further austerity and deregulatory measures. Finally, it was again the case from 2015 when, following the end of the Adjustment Programme, the centre-left government and supporting left partisan allies enacted a social policy agenda of reversals and recalibration – albeit keeping with the tenets of fiscal consolidation, European governance and market-based constraints.

On the other hand, there are *limits in the ability to moderate liberalisation, both under and without conditionality*. From 2012, no longer constrained by the informal bailout coalition, the PSD-CDS government fully aligned its preferences with the Troika. As a result, LMP 'went beyond' the MoU and the 2012 Social Pact in that it undermined collective bargaining and furthered liberalised employment relations, while dropping recalibration. From 2015, the progressive coalition could not agree on the reversal of core labour market structural reforms adopted during the crisis. Such reversals were strongly opposed by European institutions and international creditors and by employer confederations, which the Socialist government did not wish to antagonise, despite pressure from its left allies, which ultimately led to the fracture of the Geringonça over the 2019 Labour Code.

Ideological orientation also matters. The decade of labour market and social protection reforms can be demarcated between the Great Recession under conditionality with centre-right government and the post-crisis period with abated conditionality under a left-of-centre progressive coalition. Ultimately, reforms passed during the crisis worsened the security and protection of insiders and outsiders, while decentralising and weakening collective bargaining. The gap between outsiders and insiders narrowed not because the former fared better, but because the latter became less protected. Dualisation endured at a lower level of security – a pattern of 'liberalised dualisation'. In the post-crisis period, under the Socialist government and left partisan and trade union allies, the pattern of liberalised dualisation was partially reversed in that those in non-standard, atypical, and temporary contracts became better protected, both in the labour market and in social protection.

Lastly, we explored the impact of policy upon politics, looking at patterns of societal solidarities and cleavages issuing from labour market and social policy reforms. The analysis of the pivotal 2015 election showed that the 'losers' of the crisis (young workers, the unemployed, those in standard employment, civil servants, and pensioners) significantly punished the centre-right government and voted for opposition parties. The Geringonça was forged by an intergenerational solidarity among those made more vulnerable during the crisis, both insiders and outsiders, the young in atypical employment and pensioners. We argue that the broadly inclusive policies enacted by the Socialist government and supported by left partisan and trade union allies were responsive to these emerging bonds of solidarity, though not devoid of tensions and contradictions.

The COVID-19 pandemic hit in March 2020, with huge economic and social impacts. After a spell of healthy growth from 2016 to 2019, GDP dropped 8.5 per cent in 2020. Growth resumed in 2021 (+ 4.9 per cent), and will reach pre-pandemic levels only in 2022 (OE 2021: 47). After a budget surplus of 0.1 per cent in 2019, 2020 recorded a −7.3 per cent deficit, and then −4.3 per cent in 2021. The unemployment rate, after plunging to 6.5 per cent in 2019, has risen to 8.2 per cent in 2020, and is expected to level down during 2021. After the pandemic hit, 40 per cent of the employed saw their working hours decrease by July 2020. While feelings of job insecurity abated from the April peak, still 15 per cent of respondents fear losing their job by the end of year. The pandemic also hit hard work–life balance and gender equality. Women struggle with work–life balance more than men, particularly if they have young children, while poor work–life balance increases in proportion with teleworking parents, particularly for women, as they spend disproportionate time in caring activities or doing homework (Eurofound, 2020b).

During 2020 the Portuguese government enacted policy responses with an estimated cost of €5300M in direct public outlays (OE, 2021: 32), funded by a mix of national and European funds (SURE and REACT programmes). According to the Eurofound COVID-19 EU Policy Watch, the wide array of national-level responses (including Tripartite Agreements) focused on economic, labour market and social recovery, the protection of workers and the workplace, income protection beyond short-term work, and preventing social hardship (see also Eurofound 2020a). Concretely, in addition to the €504M supplement to the NHS, there were employment protection measures (e.g. simplified lay-off, active labour market policies, €800M), family support (extraordinary income support benefit and others, exceeding €250M), support to people in economic hardship (extraordinary income support benefit to non-standard workers) and to business companies (delaying of tax payments, €600M). In the Budget Law for 2021, and considering only direct expenditures (€3079M, 1.5 per cent of GDP), the major social protection and economic stimulus measures are: employment protection and activation (€965M), extraordinary income support benefit (€450M), PPE and other health (€300M), additional public sector employment in health and education (€210M), extraordinary pension raise (€99M), subsidy for medical staff (€60M), raise in the minimum value of unemployment benefit (€75M), and COVID-19 health income replacement benefit (€24M) (OE 2021: 65; see also Moreira et al., 2020).

These measures were adopted with broad political support, including the main centre-right apposition party, PSD, all social partners in social concertation, and the President of the Republic. For example, all twelve states of emergency declared until March 2021 met the approval of PSD in parliament. The supplementary COVID-response budget in mid-2020 and for 2021 were approved with the tacit assent of the centre-right PSD and the left Geringonça partners PCP and BE. This brings us to a final point regarding the behaviour adopted by the opposition towards the executive. Cooperation between government and opposition has been the pattern in Portugal during the pandemic, unlike in other Southern European countries (De Giorgi & Santana-Pereira, 2020). This chapter evinced how during hard times or national emergency the traditional governing parties PS and PSD, but also the social partners, have been able to cooperate in the legislative process, be it during the first phase of reforms under the Troika, or the ongoing pandemic, to bring about relatively more egalitarian and protective policies. But there is variation in the mode and intensity of said cooperation (Branco & Cardoso, 2020; De Giorgi et al., 2015): when there was none and conservative executive unilateralism prevailed, as during the latter stages of the Troika period, inverse outcomes obtained, and solidarity waned.

REFERENCES

Armingeon, K. & Baccaro, L. (2012). The Sorrows of Young Euro: Policy Responses to the Sovereign Debt Crisis, in N. Bermeo and J. Pontusson (eds), *Coping with Crisis: Government Reactions to the Great Recession*. New York: Russell Sage Foundation, 162–198.

Afonso, A., Dorigatti, L., Molina, O., & Tassinari, A. (2021). Labor Market (De)Regulation and Wage-Setting Institutions in Mediterranean Capitalism. In L. Burroni, E. Pavolini, & M. Regini (eds.), *Mediterranean Capitalism Revisited: One Model, Different Trajectories*. Ithaca: Cornell University Press, 115–148.

Asensio, M. & Popic, T. (2019). Portuguese healthcare reforms in the context of crisis: External pressure or domestic choice? *Social Policy & Administration*, 53(7), 1003–1017.

Bermeo, N. & Pontusson, J., eds. (2012). *Coping with Crisis: Government Reactions to the Great Recession*. New York: Russell Sage Foundation.

Branco, R. & Cardoso, D. (2022). The Politics of Change: Coalitional Politics and Labour Market Reforms during the Sovereign Debt Crisis in Portugal. *Journal of Social Policy*, 51 (1), 39–57.

Branco, R., Cardoso, D., Guillén, A. M., Sacchi, S. & Balbona, D. L. (2019). Here to Stay? Reversals of Structural Reforms in Southern Europe as the Crisis Wanes. *South European Society and Politics*, 24 (2), 205–232.

Bulfone, F., & Afonso, A. (2020). Business against Markets: Employer Resistance to Collective Bargaining Liberalization during the Eurozone Crisis. *Comparative Political Studies*, 53 (5), 809–846.
Bulfone, F. & Tassinari, A. (2020). Under Pressure: Economic Constraints, Electoral Politics and Labour Market Reforms in Southern Europe in the Decade of the Great Recession. *European Journal of Political Research*, doi: 10.1111/1475-6765.12414.
Calado, A., Capucha, L., & Estêvão, P. (2019). Welfare State Development in Portugal: From 'Stage Zero' to the Post-Crisis 'Leftist' Compromise against Austerity. *Comparative Sociology*, 18 (5–6), 658–686.
Campos Lima, M. P. & Carrilho, P. (2018). *Portugal: Developments in Working Life 2017*. Eurofound Report.
(2019). *Portugal: Developments in Working Life 2018*. Eurofound Report.
Cancela, J. & Magalhães, P. C (2020). As bases sociais dos partidos portugueses, in R Branco and T. Fernandes (eds), *45 anos de democracia em Portugal*. Lisbon: Assembleia da República, 99–128.
Canotilho, M., Violante, T., & Lanceiro, R. (2015). Austerity Measures under Judicial Scrutiny: The Portuguese Constitutional Case-Law: Portuguese Constitutional Court. *European Constitutional Law Review*, 11, 155–183.
Cardoso, D. & Branco, R. (2018). Liberalized Dualization: Labour Market Reforms and the Crisis in Portugal: A New Departure. *European Journal of Social Security*, 20 (1), 31–48.
Castel, R. (2003). *From Manual Workers, to Wage Labourers: The Transformation of the Social Question*. New Brunswick: Transaction.
(2007). Au-delà du salariat ou en deçà de l'emploi? L'institutionnalisation du précariat, in S. Paugam (ed.), *Repenser la solidarité. L'Apport des Sciences Sociales*. Paris: P.U.F., 415–433.
CES (2011). *Acordo Tripartido para a Competitividade e o Emprego*. Competitividade e o Emprego, Lisbon.
(2012). *Compromisso para o Crescimento*. Competitividade e o Emprego, Lisbon.
Cioffi, J. W., & Dubin, K. A. (2016). Commandeering Crisis: Partisan Labor Repression in Spain under the Guise of Economic Reform. *Politics & Society*, 44(3), 423–453.
Cisotta, R. & Gallo, D. (2014). *The Portuguese Constitutional Court Case Law on Austerity Measures: A Reappraisal*. Florence: EUI.
Coroado, S., Garoupa, N., & Magalhães, P. C. (2017). Judicial Behavior under Austerity: An Empirical Analysis of Behavioral Changes in the Portuguese Constitutional Court, 2002–2016. *Journal of Law and Courts*, 5(2), 289–311.
De Giorgi, E. & Cancela, J. (2019). The Portuguese Radical Left Parties Supporting Government: From Policy-Takers to Policymakers? *Government and Opposition*, 1–20. https://doi.org/10.1017/gov.2019.25.
De Giorgi, E., Moury, C. & Ruivo, J. P. (2015). Incumbents, Opposition and International Lenders: Governing Portugal in Times of Crisis. *The Journal of Legislative Studies*, 21 (1), 54–74.
De Giorgi, E. & Santana-Pereira, J. (2020). The Exceptional Case of Post-Bailout Portugal: A Comparative Outlook. *South European Society and Politics*, 25 (2), 127–150.
Degryse, C. (2012). *The New European Economic Governance*. Brussels: ETUI.
Della Porta, D., Andretta, M., Fernandes, T., O'Connor, F., Romanos, E. & Vogiatzoglou, M. (2016). *Late Neoliberalism and Its Discontents in the Economic Crisis: Comparing Social Movements in the European Periphery*. Cham: Palgrave Macmillan.
Directorate-General for Economic and Financial Affairs (2011). *The Economic Adjustment Programme for Portugal*, Occasional Papers 79.

Eurofound (2020a). COVID-19: Policy responses across Europe, Publications Office of the European Union, Luxembourg (September 2020).

(2020b). Living, working and COVID-19, Publications Office of the European Union, Luxembourg (October 2020).

(2020c). COVID-19 EU Policy Watch, www.eurofound.europa.eu/data/covid-19-eu-policy watch/database, accessed 16/10/2020.

European Commission (2016). *Employment and Social Developments in Europe 2015*. Luxembourg: Publications Office of the European Union.

Fasone, C. (2014). *Constitutional Courts Facing the Euro Crisis: Italy, Portugal and Spain in a Comparative Perspective*. Florence: IUE.

Fernandes, J. M., Magalhães, P. C., & Santana-Pereira, J. (2018). Portugal's Leftist Government: From Sick Man to Poster Boy? *South European Society and Politics*, 23(4), 503–524.

Fishman, R. (2019). *Democratic Practice: Origins of the Iberian Divide in Political Inclusion*. New York: Oxford University Press.

Gaspar, V. & Avillez, M. J. (2014). *Vitor Gaspar*, Lisbon: Dom Quixote.

Guillén, A. M. & Pavolini, E. (2015). Welfare States under Strain in Southern Europe: Overview of the Special Issue. *European Journal of Social Security*, 17, 2, 147–157.

Hacker, J. (2006). *The Great Risk Shift*. New York: Oxford University Press.

IMF (2013). *Portugal: Rethinking the State-Selected Expenditure Reform Options*. Washington, DC: International Monetary Fund – Fiscal Affairs Department.

Morgan, J. P. (2013). *The Euro Area Adjustment: About Halfway There. Europe Economic Research*, 28.

Moreira, A., Alonso Dominguez, Á., Antunes, C., Karamessini, M., Raitano, M., & Glatzer, M. (2015). Austerity-Driven Labour Market Reforms in Southern Europe: Eroding the Security of Labour Market Insiders. *European Journal of Social Security*, 17, 2, 202–225.

Moreira, A., Léon, M., Coda Moscarola, F., & Roumpakis, A. (2020). In the Eye of the Storm … Again! Social Policy Responses to COVID19 in Southern Europe. *Social Policy & Administration*. https://doi.org/10.1111/spol.12681.

Moury, C. & Afonso, A. (2019). Beyond Conditionality: Policy Reversals in Southern Europe in the Aftermath of the Eurozone Crisis. *South European Society and Politics*, 24(2), 155–176.

Moury, C., Cardoso, D., & Gago, A. (2019). When the Lenders Leave Town: Veto Players, Electoral Calculations and Vested Interests as Determinants of Policy Reversals in Spain and Portugal. *South European Society and Politics*, 24 (2), 177–204.

Moury, C. & Standring, A. (2017). Going beyond the Troika: Power and Discourse in Portuguese Austerity Politics. *European Journal of Political Research*, 56, 3, 1–20.

Orçamento, do E. (2021). Proposta de Lei e Relatório, Lisbon, Ministério das Finanças, https://oe2021.gov.pt/orcamento-do-estado-2021/, accessed 20/10/2020.

Pavolini, E., León, M., Guillén, A., & Ascoli, U. (2016). From Austerity to Permanent Strain? The EU and Welfare State Reform in Italy and Spain, in C. de la Porte & E. Heins (eds), *The Sovereign Debt Crisis, the EU and Welfare State Reform*. London: Palgrave Macmillan, 31–158.

Pereirinha, J. A., Branco, F., Pereira, E., & Amaro, M. I. (2020). The Guaranteed Minimum Income in Portugal: A Universal Safety Net under Political and Financial Pressure. *Social Policy & Administration*, 54(4), 574–586.

Perez, S. A. & Matsaganis, M. (2019). Export or Perish: Can Internal Devaluation Create Enough Good Jobs in Southern Europe? *South European Society and Politics*, 24(2), 259–285.

Petmesidou, M. & Guillén, A. M. (2014). Can the Welfare State as We Know It Survive? A View from the Crisis-Ridden South European Periphery. *South European Society and Politics*, 19(3), 295–307.

Picot, G. & Tassinari, A. (2017). All of One Kind? Labour Market Reforms under Austerity in Italy and Spain. *Socio-Economic Review*, 15, 2, 1–22.

Rodrigues, C. F.; Figueiras, R., & Junqueira, V. (2016). *Desigualdade do rendimento e pobreza em Portugal: as consequências sociais do programa de ajustamento*. Lisbon: FFMS.

Saurugger, S., Hofmann, A., & Warren, T. (2020). *National Constitutional Courts as Veto Players in the EMU Crisis*. SSRN: https://ssrn.com/abstract=3599037 or http://dx.doi.org/10.2139/ssrn.3599037.

Stoleroff, A. (2019). Trade Union Representation and Industrial Relations in Portugal before, during and Following the Economic and Financial Crises, in A. C. Pinto & C. P. Teixeira (eds), *Political Institutions and Democracy in Portugal*. Cham: Palgrave Macmillan, 167–193.

Távora, I. & González, P. (2016). Labour Market Regulation and Collective Bargaining in Portugal during the Crisis: Continuity and Change. *European Journal of Industrial Relations*, 22, 3, 251–265.

Taylor-Gooby, P., Leruth, B., & Chung, H. (2017). *After Austerity: Welfare State Transformation in Europe after the Great Recession*. Oxford: Oxford University Press.

Thelen, K. (2014). *Varieties of Liberalization and the New Politics of Social Solidarity*. New York: Cambridge University Press.

Theodoropoulou, S., ed. (2018). *Labour Market Policies in the Era of Pervasive Austerity: A European Perspective*. Bristol: Polity Press.

UGT (2012). *Parecer da UGT sobre a Proposta de Lei 46/XII que aprova a revisão do Código do Trabalho*. Lisbon: UGT.

Violante, T. (2019). The Portuguese Constitutional Court and Its Austerity Case Law, in Costa Pinto and C. Pequito Teixeira (eds), *Political Institutions and Democracy in Portugal*. Cham: Palgrave Macmillan, 121–143.

Index

For EU product safety concerns, contact us at Calle de José Abascal, 56–1°, 28003 Madrid, Spain or eugpsr@cambridge.org.

www.ingramcontent.com/pod-product-compliance
Lightning Source LLC
LaVergne TN
LVHW011815200926
848484LV00005B/1204

* 9 7 8 1 0 0 9 1 7 0 2 7 7 *